# The BEDDING PLANT EXPERT

### Dr. D.G. Hessayon

1st Impression            300,000

**Other books in the EXPERT Series:**

THE FLOWER EXPERT
THE TREE & SHRUB EXPERT
THE ROSE EXPERT
THE LAWN EXPERT
THE GARDEN EXPERT
THE VEGETABLE EXPERT
THE FRUIT EXPERT
THE HOUSE PLANT EXPERT
THE HOME EXPERT

**pbi** PUBLICATIONS

pbi PUBLICATIONS · BRITANNICA HOUSE · WALTHAM CROSS · HERTS · ENGLAND

# Contents

Printed and bound in Great Britain by Jarrold & Sons Ltd, Norwich

**ISBN 0 903505 34 7**

© D G HESSAYON 1991

# CHAPTER 1

# INTRODUCTION

Everybody thinks that they know what a bedding plant is, but nobody can provide a definition with which everyone will agree. "Annuals which are set out to provide a spring or summer display" is far too narrow a description — "Plants which have a life span in the garden of a year or less" is far too wide and vague a definition.

There are four basic features of a bedding plant. First of all, it is raised away from the final quarters in which it is placed — this may be in a greenhouse if the seedlings are frost-sensitive or in a nursery bed outdoors if the plant is hardy. Secondly, a bedding plant is grown for its decorative and not for its edible qualities, so ordinary vegetables are excluded. It is also planted out when it is actively growing, which means that dormant bulbs are excluded. Finally, the display period is limited — a matter of weeks or months rather than years.

Putting all these points together provides us with a workable definition of a bedding plant — **a plant which is moved at the leafy stage to its place in the garden or in a container where it provides a display for a limited period.** This definition describes a *use* for and not a *type* of plant. A Geranium kept indoors is a 'flowering house plant' — the same specimen planted outdoors in early summer is a 'bedding plant'. Winter Heather in the mixed border or shrub garden is a 'shrubby perennial' — growing in a container for a few months to provide a November-March display makes it a 'bedding plant'.

Bedding out has traditionally been the main use for these plants. The familiar pattern is to create a formal bed with annuals and a few biennials or perennials — the arrangement is geometric so that the groups of plants are in distinct lines, circles, squares etc. Two strongholds have remained faithful to this style from Victorian times to the present day — the small front garden and the public park.

The basic small garden approach has been to set out Tulips and other bulbs in autumn and then to plant around them with neat lines of Wallflowers, Double Daisies and Forget-me-nots. Out they come in late spring from the round beds or lawn surrounds and in go the hardy and half hardy annuals which were bought in trays — Salvias, Marigolds and Antirrhinums for bold colour and Alyssum, Lobelia and Ageratum as a frilly edging. At the same time the Geraniums and Fuchsias bought in pots are planted.

Parks departments took the basic plan much further, especially in the tourist towns. Lavish and intricate patterns have been created for generations, with subtropical dot plants such as Palms, Abutilons, Castor Oil Plants, Bananas or Cannas standing above the annuals below.

Elsewhere in the gardening world the creation of formal beds has largely been abandoned and it has long been fashionable to sneer at the idea. The criticism has sometimes been vicious, such as the Victorian writer who stated that "The common disposition of red, white and blue is better adapted to delight savages than represent the artistic status of civilised people". At other times the disapproval has been more restrained, as in the latest Dictionary of the Royal Horticultural Society — "We have therefore preserved with little alteration the recommendations contained in the old Dictionary, without ourselves suggesting the readoption of the practice on any considerable scale, for there are more interesting and more beautiful ways of using most gardens...."

Unfortunately the criticism of bedding out has spilled over on to bedding plants themselves, and this has never been fair. How else could the owner of a tiny garden provide an assortment of colours and flower shapes, and how could the owners of larger gardens fill gaps in the border or rockery with instant colour? And then why should the 'experts' sneer at an intricate floral carpet whilst rhapsodising over a woven one?

The criticism never made much sense — now it makes no sense at all. The recent boom in container growing and hanging baskets has made us all turn to bedding plants once again, and the $F_1$ hybrids of Impatiens and Begonia semperflorens have provided us with a splendid way to have summer-long sheets of colour under trees. Few areas of gardening have seen such dramatic changes as the bedding plant scene — there are now new and cheaper ways of buying seedlings and there are new varieties of traditional bedding plants. Examples include the Universal Pansy for winter display, the seed-raised Geranium and the knee-high Sweet Pea.

The public, as always, knows best. In the past 10 years the sales of bedding plants have more than doubled. If you belong to the group of people who believe that bedding plants are not for you, read the following pages and discover just how the picture has changed in recent years and how useful these plants can be in your garden.

# TYPES OF BEDDING PLANTS

### HALF HARDY ANNUALS

A half hardy annual (HHA) is raised from seed for a summer or autumn display — it lives, flowers and dies in a single season. The plant is sensitive to frost, so for a prolonged display it is necessary to raise such plants indoors and then transplant them outdoors when the danger of frost has passed. The time to sow depends on the speed of seedling development — some slow developers should be sown as early as January. Small seeds are sown thinly and the seedlings are separated by pricking out into fresh compost. Large seeds may be sown individually in small pots. Some half hardy annuals (e.g Antirrhinum, Zinnia) can be sown outdoors in May, but the flowering season is significantly reduced. Tender annuals such as Vinca and Portulaca need a warm season to produce their best display.

Most popular bedding plants belong here — examples include Impatiens, Lobelia, Petunia, Marigold, Nemesia, Salvia and Aster.

### HARDY BIENNIALS

A hardy biennial (HB) is raised from seed for a spring or occasionally a summer display — it produces stems and leaves in the first season and flowers in the following one. After flowering the plant dies, although a few plants treated as biennials such as Foxglove, Hollyhock, Sweet William and Wallflower are actually short-lived perennials. Seed is sown outdoors in May or June in a nursery bed and the seedlings are then moved in autumn to the place where they are to flower.

Most spring-flowering bedding plants belong here — examples are Daisy, Campanula, Forget-me-not and Wallflower. Summer-flowering ones include Hollyhock, Foxglove and Sweet William.

### HALF HARDY GARDEN PERENNIALS

A half hardy perennial (HHP) should live for years provided that it is protected from frost. The garden types are the ones commonly associated with outdoor cultivation and are usually planted out rather than being retained in their pots in the bed. They are raised from seed, cuttings or by division and are planted out in late May or early June. Some may be treated as annuals and are not retained (e.g Viola) — others are lifted and brought indoors before the frosts arrive (e.g Geranium and Fuchsia).

### HARDY PERENNIALS

A hardy perennial (HP) should continue to live in the garden for years. The usual place for the non-woody types is in the herbaceous border or rockery — the woody types either lose (deciduous) or keep (evergreen) their leaves in winter. Container growing and hanging baskets have brought evergreen hardy perennials into the bedding plant picture. Small conifers and other evergreen shrubs are occasionally used as centrepieces for containers planted for a winter display — Ivy is commonly used in hanging baskets and Winter Heather is one of a limited number of plants which can be bedded out to provide a floral display in the depths of winter.

### HALF HARDY EXOTIC PERENNIALS

A half hardy perennial (HHP) should live for years provided that it is protected from frost. The exotic types are the ones commonly associated with home or conservatory culture rather than the open garden. The usual practice for large specimens is to plunge the pots in the bed after the danger of frost has passed and then lift and return the pot to the greenhouse or conservatory before the onset of frost in the autumn. Examples include Palms, Tree Ferns, Canna, Grevillea, Datura, Abutilon, Castor Oil Plant, Agave and Banana. These are used as dot plants — smaller 'house plant' varieties such as Kalanchoe, Chlorophytum, Hypoestes etc are used for groundwork planting.

### HARDY ANNUALS

A hardy annual (HA) is raised from seed for a spring, summer or autumn display — when sown in spring it lives, flowers and dies in a single season. Seed is sown outdoors in late March or April — delay sowing if the soil is cold and wet. Seed can be put in where the plants are to flower or a nursery bed can be used, the seedlings being transferred to their permanent quarters in May. For earlier flowering some hardy annuals can be sown outdoors in September — see page 13 for examples. Another way to ensure earlier flowering is to treat them like half hardy annuals, raising the seedlings indoors and then planting out in May.

Many bedding plants belong here — examples include Alyssum, Cornflower, Clarkia, Godetia, Sunflower, Candytuft and Love-in-a-mist.

# HISTORY OF BEDDING PLANTS

Bearing in mind the hostile attitude of the gardening establishment to formal bedding, it is not surprising that the history of bedding and bedding plants has received little attention in the horticultural history books. But bedding *is* a vital part of our gardening heritage, and deserves better treatment.

Bedding out is often regarded as a product of the garishness and poor taste of the Victorians, but the bedding story began many years before the young Queen was crowned. In the 1820s a number of ingredients for the new style came together. The hatred of flowers by the landscape designers of the 18th century had declined and Repton had created many gardens with 'floral terraces'. A number of 'colour gardens' had been produced in Europe. The key fact, however, was that a steady flow of colourful half hardy plants had been arriving from America and South Africa since the 1750s. And so it was in the 1820s that the first beds with half hardy annuals appeared in Dublin, Windsor etc. Some of the plants used are no longer common in our gardens — Gilia, Platystemon etc, and the beds were not ornate. But bedding had started.

It was John Loudon who popularised the new concept of the 'Gardenesque' style. Gardens should no longer try to portray a natural scene — their purpose was to "display the individual beauty of trees, shrubs and plants." Massed planting was just one of the features in the Gardenesque garden, but in 1845 the Glass Tax was repealed and this provided the spark to ignite the Bedding Craze. Greenhouses were built in large gardens all over Britain and in the 1840–50 period our present-day basic plants became popular — Lobelia, Petunia, Geranium, Salvia and so on.

Writers and designers such as Barry, Paxton and Nesfield popularised the new style which symbolised the grandeur of the Victorian age. Beds became more complex, and variations appeared — Subtropical Bedding (decorative leaves rather than flowers) in the 1860s and Carpet Bedding (see page 88) in the 1870s.

At the same time, however, a protest movement started, rather quietly at first with pleas for pastel colours and a more natural approach from people like Hibberd and Watson. But the anti-brigade found its leader in the fiery Irishman William Robinson, whose writing in the 1870s and 1880s brought the fight against formalism to the attention of the public. "All such work is wrong and degrading to art and in its extreme expression is ridiculous," said Robinson — even more critical was his view that carpet bedding was "an aberration of the human mind."

*Victorian carpet bed reconstruction at Glasnevin, Dublin*

Robinson and Jekyll did bring in the herbaceous border and a more natural approach to gardening, and they did found the snobbishness towards bedding, but they certainly did not bring its practice to an end. Bedding out began to decline in the middle-class villas during the 1880s, but the case for the formal garden was put forward very forcibly by the architect Sir Reginald Blomfield in 1892. Blomfield and Robinson snarled at each other, and the horticulture world couldn't make up its mind. Bedding schemes actually became even more lavish in some grand gardens and public parks. In the bedding-out heyday at the turn of the century plants were sometimes changed for a weekend party at country houses. Vast coats of arms were bedded out in quite small public parks.

*Bedding display at Philips Park, Manchester 1913*

We shall never know whether it was the shortage of cheap labour or a change in horticultural taste which led to the decline of extensive bedding schemes in the grand houses of the 20th century, but their place in parks and the front gardens of suburbia remained. Things stayed fairly static until the 1980s, when the appearance of new varieties and the advent of the container and hanging basket boom stimulated interest once again in bedding plants throughout the land — an interest which is shared by gardeners of all types.

# BEDDING PLANT ORGANISATIONS

This Dutch-based organisation carries out impartial trials on new seed varieties. Nearly all important seed breeders and distributors are members, and each year new varieties are assessed at 22 trial sites throughout Europe, including 3 in the U.K. From Finland to Italy the plants and blooms are judged by a panel of experts. Their job is to make sure that any prize-winning variety is capable of flourishing under a wide range of climatic conditions and represents a definite step forward.

Until recently Gold, Silver and Bronze Medals were awarded. Now there are just 2 grades — the Gold Medal for "a really excellent and innovating novelty" and the Quality Mark for "a distinct, reliable and, in comparison to existing varieties, a real improvement". Seed catalogues distinguish each award winner with a small Fleuroselect symbol at the start of the descriptive paragraph.

This branch of the National Farmers Union represents the professional bedding plant growers of Britain. It sets out to promote and to carry out research on this group of plants and it also lays down the standards for the industry.

In 1990 the BBPA introduced a new set of standards — any member meeting all these quality points can put the Association symbol on his containers. This symbol on a pot, strip or tray indicates that the plants ● are true to the name on the label ● are free from pests, diseases, damage or signs of starvation ● have been treated with the minimum of chemicals ● have enough room to flourish whilst awaiting sale ● are able to acclimatise quickly after planting out ● are uniform in size ● have sufficient roots to ensure speedy establishment ● have been adequately fed. Hanging baskets and ready-planted pots should contain a slow-release fertilizer.

# BEDDING PLANT BEST-SELLERS

### The Top 15 Summer Bedding Plants

The change in fashion during the past 10 years in Britain has been dramatic. Impatiens, Bedding Begonia and Petunia have overtaken many age-old favourites such as Ageratum, Alyssum and Salvia. The U.K list of best-sellers is now quite similar to the U.S one, but there is one notable exception — Vinca (Madagascar Periwinkle) is very popular in the States but it is rarely grown in Britain.

| U.K | Best-sellers in alphabetical order | U.S.A |
|---|---|---|
| Ageratum | | |
| Alyssum | | Alyssum |
| Antirrhinum | | Antirrhinum |
| Bedding Begonia | | Bedding Begonia |
| Bedding Dahlia | | |
| | | Coleus |
| Fuchsia | | Fuchsia |
| Impatiens | | Impatiens |
| Lobelia | | Lobelia |
| Marigold | | Marigold |
| Nicotiana | | |
| Pansy | | Pansy |
| Pelargonium | | Pelargonium |
| Petunia | | Petunia |
| Salvia | | Salvia |
| Verbena | | Verbena |
| | | Vinca |
| | | Zinnia |

# BEDDING PLANT SALES

**Purchases in 1985: £3 per family**
**Purchases in 1990: £7 per family**

50–60 year olds are more likely to plant out bedding plants than 20–40 year olds

People in London are more likely to plant out bedding plants than people in Yorkshire

People without children are more likely to plant out bedding plants than people with children

**Where they are used:**

40% are used for planting out in beds and borders

35% are used for planting out in pots, tubs and window boxes

25% are used for planting out in hanging baskets

# BEDDING PLANT DISPLAYS

Bedding plants can be seen everywhere from spring to autumn, in tiny pots on patios to elaborate planting schemes in palace gardens. Browsing through new-season seed catalogues is an enjoyable winter pastime for millions of gardeners, and horticultural magazines often contain excellent illustrations. But there is no substitute for seeing growing plants and living displays if you are looking for new ideas.

### WALK DOWN THE STREET

Do not underrate this method of learning more about bedding plants. Any suburban street in summer will throw up a few new approaches ... and an equal number of poor combinations for you to avoid! Look especially at the hanging baskets and planted tubs on and around the front of the houses.

### STROLL IN THE PARK

Parks departments are the major creators of elaborate bedding displays. The finest and most lavish ones may be in the tourist towns, but the public parks in any urban area will contain colourful bedding schemes. Here you will find the classic arrangement of bold dot plants which are surrounded by groundwork plants and edged with low-growing specimens. Colours are bright and often garish and the plants are generally popular varieties rather than unusual ones, but novel combinations can occasionally be found.

### GO TO SPRINGFIELDS

Springfields Gardens in Spalding, Lincolnshire, is the showplace for bedding plants. From the end of March to late September the Gardens are open to the public, and here you will see a vast display of annual flowers in all their glory. Amongst the 25 acres of lawns, terraces and woodland are the beds which are filled with bulbs in spring and then annuals in summer. The highlight of the year is the Annual Exhibition in mid August — about 250,000 plants from a score of the world's largest seed houses are on display. Judging for the Scoop awards takes place during the Annual Exhibition — in order to qualify a variety must have performed outstandingly in the Gardens for the past 3 years.

### GO TO A GARDEN FESTIVAL

Bedding plants feature prominently at the National Garden Festivals which are held every 2 years. They are created on reclaimed sites and 3 to 4 million visitors pass through the turnstiles during the six month life span of the Festival. Sites used and proposed are Liverpool (1984), Stoke (1986), Glasgow (1988), Gateshead (1990) and Ebbw Vale (1992).

### WALK AROUND A GARDEN CENTRE

In May and June you will find bench after bench of pots, trays and strips of bedding plants. Many of the plants will be in flower and there will be lots of hanging baskets and other planted containers to study. Your visit should give you a good insight into the plants which are available, but it will not provide you with bedding scheme ideas.

### GO TO BRIGHTON

The 'Gardens of Greeting' Competition has been held annually in Preston Park since 1955. A series of bedding schemes are submitted by Local Authorities and Horticultural Societies — judging for the Rose Bowl takes place in August. Barnsley Parks Department leads the field having won the award 5 times, but other winners have been scattered around the country from Glasgow in the north to Slough in the south.

### GO TO A FLEUROSELECT DISPLAY GARDEN

Varieties which have won a Fleuroselect award (see page 6) during the past 5 years are grown in attractive displays in 33 gardens in Europe, India and the U.S. The Fleuroselect display gardens in the U.K are located in:

- Harlow Carr Gardens, Harrogate, North Yorks
- Sheffield Botanic Garden, Sheffield, South Yorks
- T.V. Garden, King's Heath Park, Birmingham
- R.H.S. Garden, Wisley, Surrey
- Wycliffe Hall Botanic Gardens, Barnard Castle
- West of Scotland College Garden, Auchincruive, Ayr
- Springfields Gardens, Spalding, Lincs
- The Guildhall, Swansea, West Glamorgan
- Capel Manor, Enfield, Gt. London
- Sir Thomas & Lady Dixon Garden, Belfast

### GO TO A 'BRITAIN IN BLOOM' TOWN

The 'Britain in Bloom' Competition began in 1964. Towns, cities and villages are judged and trophies are awarded to places having the most attractive and tidy floral displays. Streets, parks and buildings are carefully studied, and obviously attractive bedding plants are a fundamental feature of the winners. Towns and cities which have won a trophy more than once are Aberdeen (10 times), Bath (9), Harrogate (6), Douglas (4), Falmouth (4), Sidmouth (4), Cheltenham (3), Forres (3), Exeter (2), Kelso (2), City of London (2), Middlesbrough (2), Ryton (2), Shrewsbury (2) and Swansea (2).

## CHAPTER 2

# BUYING & RAISING BEDDING PLANTS

Plant a Rose bush and it will last for 20 years or more. Plant an Apple tree and it may well last a lifetime. But with bedding plants it is a different story — planting here is an annual event, so the subject of buying or raising your own stock is an important and constantly recurring task. To buy plants or raise your own — there is no simple or single answer to this question. It all depends on your needs and facilities.

### Advantages of buying plants

Much less trouble — there is no need for a greenhouse or propagator. Hardened-off seedlings can be bought in the spring when the weather is right for planting.

Some plants are difficult for the ordinary gardener to raise from seed — examples include Impatiens, Bedding Begonia and Petunia.

You can see what you are buying and what you will be planting out — no risk of losing tiny seedlings to disease or having to make do with substandard home-grown seedlings.

### Advantages of sowing seeds

Cheaper. The saving is considerable when compared with plants bought ready for putting out — the saving is less when compared with seedlings bought for potting on (see page 10).

Much greater variety. The usual pattern is for 4 or 5 varieties of popular bedding plants to be offered as hardened-off seedlings at the garden centre. A much larger selection is available in the seed catalogues. You can grow all sorts of novelties and choose single colours instead of the popular mixtures.

## Buying Plants

As a general rule you get what you pay for. It is not an absolute rule — there are times when you may be sold rubbish by a garden centre and many gardeners have obtained excellent plants from a market stall. But the general rule still applies — you get what you pay for.

Until quite recently buying plants instead of raising your own could be an expensive business, especially if you wanted pot-grown plants. Nowadays you can buy small seedlings from seed companies — they are potted on, hardened off and then planted out in the ordinary way. These seedlings are cheaper than ready-to-plant ones, and are worth considering if you need a large number of plants.

### Where to buy

#### GARDEN CENTRE
Generally agreed to be the best source of supply for bedding plants which are to be transplanted outdoors immediately after purchase. The range is usually large and varied, and if the garden centre is a reputable one you can be sure that half hardy annuals will have been properly hardened off. Advice is generally available and justifiable complaints will be taken seriously. Always keep your receipt.

#### HIGH ST. SHOP
You will find bedding plants offered in garden shops, florists, greengrocers, department stores and supermarkets once spring arrives. Convenience is the great advantage — you can pick up a few plants without having to make a special trip to the garden centre. Be wary if the plants are kept indoors in poor light and over-warm conditions — as a general rule it is wise to buy from the High St. shop at the start of the planting season.

#### MARKET STALL
Most experts warn against buying from a market stall. It is true that much inferior stock is sold — half hardy annuals offered before the danger of frost has passed and plants which are in full flower. The range is usually limited and there is no redress if the plants fail. There are, however, many good market stalls with knowledgeable owners and good-quality stock at an economical price. The rule is simple — only buy from someone with a good reputation or one who has satisfied you in the past.

#### MAIL ORDER
Plants for putting out are rarely purchased by mail order, although this is the only way to obtain the more unusual varieties. Mail order has come into its own during the past few years with the introduction of seedlings and young plants for growing on before the planting out stage. You will find these offered in the catalogues of the large seed houses — the range is unfortunately quite limited and the types of planting material on offer are described on page 10. Remember to order early.

### What to buy

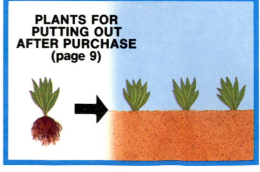

**PLANTS FOR PUTTING OUT AFTER PURCHASE** (page 9)

OR

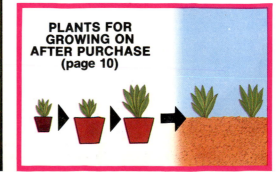

**PLANTS FOR GROWING ON AFTER PURCHASE** (page 10)

# PLANTS FOR PUTTING OUT AFTER PURCHASE

It used to be quite simple. Seedlings were raised in wooden trays and these were offered for sale in spring for bedding out. Rooted cuttings and choice plants raised from seed were offered in individual pots. Things are now more complex, but the changes which have been introduced make things better for the gardener. A word of warning — do not buy plants which are lifted out of the tray and then wrapped in newspaper.

## TRAYS

Wooden tray

Flimsy plastic tray

Half tray

The tray is the traditional method of buying bedding plants. It is the cheapest way, but roots are damaged when the plants are torn apart at planting time. Wooden trays holding 40–60 plants have been largely replaced by flimsy plastic ones — even more popular is the plastic half tray holding about 20 plants. Trays are recommended when you require a large number of tough grow-anywhere plants such as Alyssum and French Marigolds.

## STRIPS

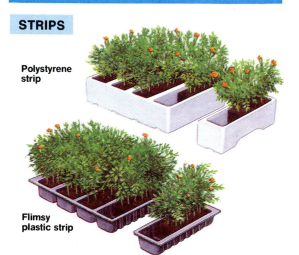

Polystyrene strip

Flimsy plastic strip

The strip has become the most popular way to buy bedding plants for transplanting into beds or containers. The plants are grown in a series of snap-off strips which are made of rigid white polystyrene or flimsy plastic. Each strip contains from 3 large plants such as Geraniums to 10–12 ordinary half hardy annuals such as Antirrhinums. Roots may be damaged as you prise the plants apart but this is less likely than with tray-grown ones.

## PACKS

4-pack container

15-pack container

The container is made of flimsy plastic and is made up of 4–24 individual pots. Each pot contains a single plant, and these pots are usually detached at the time of sale. It is more expensive to buy plants in this way than as strips, but there is no root disturbance at planting time. This type of unit is becoming increasingly popular, especially for the more expensive $F_1$ hybrids and for plants which hate root disturbance.

## CELLULAR TRAYS

6-cell container

The container is made of rigid polystyrene, and each cell contains a single plant. The number of cells may be as few as 4 or as many as 40, but the standard one is the 6-cell container. Root disturbance is avoided at planting out time — an advantage shared with packs and pots. Cellular trays are an excellent way of buying and also raising seedlings — containers bearing a large number of mini-cells are used by nurserymen to raise 'plugs' (see page 10) for sale.

## POTS

Clay pot

Plastic pot

Peat pot

2½–5 in. — usual size 3–3½ in.

Individual pots are the most expensive way to buy bedding plants, but this is the way to obtain dot plants and top-quality stock. Pots are usually plastic these days, but clay ones are still used and so are peat ones which can be planted directly into the soil. Plants are generally available over a long period and not just during the traditional bedding-out season. An excellent way to buy choice plants in full flower but too expensive for massed bedding.

# What to look for

## Good signs

Compact, sturdy stems with leaves near the base

Plants should be bushy and not packed too closely together. They should all be approximately the same size

The compost should be moist and there should be no sign of wilting leaves or drooping stems

## Bad signs

Plants in full flower. Abnormally early flowering is usually a sign of stress

Damaged or unlabelled container. Avoid trays, pots, strips etc which have been marked down for clearance

Lanky stems

Blemished, discoloured or diseased leaves

Roots growing through the base of the pot or tray

Pot plants are generally sold in flower. With strips and trays it is wise to buy plants in bud with just a few blooms open to show colour. Some bedding plants are nearly always in flower when bought — Mimulus, Impatiens, Bedding Begonia and French Marigolds are examples. Unless they are pot-grown avoid Geraniums and Petunias which are in flower.

## PLANTS FOR GROWING ON AFTER PURCHASE

These days you can leave the germination stage to someone else — seed houses and some garden centres offer Begonias, Geraniums, Pansies, Impatiens, Salvias and Polyanthus as seedlings or young plants for potting on. Order in good time in January or early February and open the package immediately on arrival. Keep at 55°–65°F for a day or two before pricking out or potting on.

## SEEDLINGS

This is the smallest stage at which you can buy plants for growing on, and they are the least expensive. The seedlings are despatched in a rigid polystyrene pack — 100 is the usual count but some seed houses offer 250 and 400 seedling packs. The tiny plants are at the expanded seed leaf stage and need to be pricked out shortly after arrival into trays or cellular trays (see page 12) filled with potting compost. Some growers offer seedlings at an even earlier stage ('Propaplants') — germinated seeds in jelly-filled test tubes. This method is used for vegetables and house plants rather than bedding plants.

## PLUGS

Trade names include 'Speedplugs', 'Easiplants', 'Starter Plants' and 'Plantlets'. Plugs are larger and more advanced than seedlings — they are small but well-rooted plants which are raised in cellular trays by the grower. A great advantage here is that there is no root disturbance when the plug is pricked out into compost or potted on individually into 3 in. pots. Plugs can be planted directly into hanging baskets but of course cannot be put outdoors until the danger of frost has passed. Plugs are sold in units of 35. Make sure that the compost does not dry out if potting on is delayed.

## YOUNG PLANTS

A 'Jiffy 7' is a block of compressed peat which expands when soaked in water — the plastic netting around it provides support. The Jiffy 7 is a popular method ('Jiffy Plants', 'Pot-ready Plants' etc) of selling Geranium and Fuchsia rooted cuttings by mail order. Young seed-raised plants of Impatiens and Begonia are also sold in this way. Jiffy Plants are sold in 5s or 10s in a polystyrene pack — transfer into compost-filled 3½–4 in. pots before moving the plants outdoors. Rooted cuttings of Geraniums and Fuchsias are sometimes offered in compressed soil blocks.

# Sowing Seeds

There are several reasons for raising bedding plants from seed rather than buying them ready for planting — saving money, having a much wider choice of varieties or just for the sense of achievement. Over 50 million packets of flower seeds are bought every year and most give great satisfaction. Some, however, are a source of disappointment because failure is almost certain if you try to grow plants under glass and you do not follow the basic rules set out below. Starter kits (plastic trays filled with pre-sown compost) make the job a little easier but the range of varieties is limited and the cost is understandably higher than starting from scratch.

## Seed types

**Open-pollinated seed** The traditional type of seed in the catalogues — no specialist hybridisation has been carried out and so it is generally less expensive than seed of $F_1$ or $F_2$ varieties. Remember, however, that a new open-pollinated variety may cost considerably more than an old favourite.

**$F_1$ hybrid seed** A variety produced by the careful crossing of two pure-bred parents. The plants are usually more vigorous and bushier and are often freer flowering. An important point is that they are outstandingly uniform, growing to the same height and blooming at the same time. Availability depends on the type of plant — almost all Bedding Begonias, Impatiens and Petunias are $F_1$ hybrids but there are no $F_1$ varieties of Alyssum and Lobelia. Seeds from $F_1$ hybrids do not come true to type.

**$F_2$ hybrid seed** The second generation bred from $F_1$ hybrid seed. Cheaper to buy and with the same vigour as the parent, but $F_2$ plants are less uniform and some colour reversion to the original parents usually takes place.

**Dressed seed** Seed which has been coated with a fungicide or fungicide/insecticide before packing by the nurseryman.

**Foil-packed seed** Seed which has been packed into vacuum-sealed foil sachets before being placed in paper envelopes. Such seeds maintain their viability much longer in an unopened packet than seeds packed in the ordinary way.

**Saved seed** Some seed is usually left over after sowing. Nearly all varieties can be saved for several years if stored in a screw-top jar or biscuit tin sealed with adhesive tape and then kept in a cool and dark place.

**Home-grown seed** It is tempting to save seed from flowers which have been left to form pods or seed heads. In most cases it is not advisable. $F_1$ hybrids will not breed true and the colours are unpredictable. It is a different story with vegetables — some champion growers insist on using their own seed.

**Tubed seed** At least one seed house offers very fine seed such as Begonia in small plastic tubes. At sowing time the end of the tube is cut off and the seed is gently poured out over the compost.

## Sowing seeds indoors

Most bedding plants are sensitive to frost. Waiting until the danger of frost has passed before sowing outdoors would seriously shorten the flowering season — for this reason seeds of half hardy annuals are sown in compost in spring and the trays or pots are kept in a greenhouse, propagator or on the windowsill. For most types mid March to early April is the best time to sow seed but there are variations — see the A–Z guide for the recommended timing for individual plants. The seedlings are set out in the garden in late May or early June. Indoor sowing is not restricted to half hardy subjects. It is also used for raising hardy annuals when early blooms are required or when the site is in a cold or wet area. Sow the seed in March and plant out in April or May when the soil condition is suitable.

To ensure success you need a greenhouse — this will provide the all-round light and warmth needed for young seedlings. Germination in March or April calls for additional warmth — you can heat part of the greenhouse or instal a heated propagator. If you do not have a greenhouse then windowsill cultivation is possible for many annuals, but it cannot be expected to produce first-class results.

## Germination facts

| Plant | Germination Temperature (°F) | Germination Time (days) | Plant | Germination Temperature (°F) | Germination Time (days) |
|---|---|---|---|---|---|
| Ageratum | 65–70 | 10–14 | Marigold & Tagetes | 65–70 | 7–14 |
| Alyssum | 60–65 | 14 | Mesembryanthemum | 65–70 | 14–21 |
| Antirrhinum | 60–65 | 10–21 | Mimulus | 65–70 | 14–21 |
| Aster | 65–70 | 10–14 | Nemesia | 65–70 | 14–21 |
| Begonia, Fibrous-rooted | 65–70 | 14–21 | Pelargonium | 70–75 | 7–21 |
| Carnation | 60–65 | 14–21 | Petunia | 70–75 | 7–14 |
| Cineraria | 70 | 14–21 | Phlox | 60 | 14–21 |
| Dahlia, Bedding | 65–70 | 14–21 | Salvia | 70–75 | 14–21 |
| Dianthus | 60–65 | 14–21 | Stock | 65 | 10–14 |
| Impatiens | 70–75 | 21 | Verbena | 65–70 | 21–28 |
| Lobelia | 65–70 | 21 | Zinnia | 65–70 | 7–14 |

## The 8 steps to success

**1** **SEED** You must start with good-quality seed. Buy from a reputable supplier and don't open the packet until you are ready to sow. Hard-coated seed should be shaken in a jar with coarse sand and then soaked overnight before sowing — chipping them is a risky business. Very fine seed should be mixed with dry silver sand before sowing.

**2** **CONTAINER** Many types of container are suitable provided they have holes or cracks at the base for drainage. Avoid old wooden trays — disease organisms are difficult to remove by washing. Choose plastic — full trays are usually too large and a better choice is a 3½–5 in. half pot or a half tray. Large seeds can be sown into the cells of cellular trays, peat pots filled with compost or into Jiffy 7s (see page 10).

**3** **COMPOST** A peat-based seed or multi-purpose compost is ideal — sterile, light and consistent. Fill the container with compost and firm gently with a piece of board — the surface should be about ½ in. below the top of the pot or tray. Sprinkle the surface with water the day before seed sowing — it should be moist but not wet when you scatter the seeds thinly over the surface. Larger seeds can be sown in rows.

**4** **COVER** Do not cover very fine seed with compost — examples include Begonia, Lobelia, Petunia and Mimulus. Other seeds should be covered with compost to a depth which is twice the diameter of the seed — this compost should be applied through a sieve to form a fine and even layer. Firm gently with a board after sowing. Most but not all seeds need darkness for successful germination — put brown paper over the tray or pot and place a sheet of glass on top. Condensation is absorbed by the paper and so does not drip on to the compost below. Change the paper if necessary. Do not use brown paper for seeds which need light in order to germinate — popular examples are Antirrhinum, Alyssum, Mimulus, Impatiens, Nicotiana and Begonia.

**5** **WARMTH** Most seeds require a fairly warm temperature (65°–70°F) for satisfactory germination. Heating a whole greenhouse in March or April can be wasteful — a thermostatically-controlled heated propagator is a better idea. Make sure you buy one which is large enough for your future needs. For windowsill propagation you will need a centrally-heated room where the temperature can be kept in the 60°–70°F range. Raise pots or trays from the sill so that they are level with the glass.

**6** **LIGHT & WATER** As soon as the seedlings break through the surface, remove the paper and prop up the sheet of glass. After a few days the glass should be removed and the container moved to a bright but sunless spot. Windowsill pots or trays should be turned every couple of days. Never let the compost dry out. The safest way to water is to use a fine sprayer such as a Bio Mister — watering with a fine-rosed watering can or soaking the container in a basin of water can dislodge tiny plants. Use dilute Cheshunt Compound rather than water if damping off has been a problem in the past.

**7** **PRICK OUT** As soon as the first set of true leaves has opened the seedlings should be pricked out into trays, small pots or 24-cell cellular trays (Propapacks) filled with Multicompost. Set the seedlings so that the seed leaves are just above the surface — handle the plants by the seed leaves and not the stems. The seedlings should be set 1–1½ in. apart in pots or trays. Large seedlings such as Dahlias and Pelargoniums should be pricked out into individual 3 in. pots. Keep containers in the shade for a day or two after pricking out. High temperatures are not required — 50°–55°F is satisfactory. Water as necessary — use Cheshunt Compound if damping off is a problem.

Correct stage for pricking out

**8** **HARDEN OFF** When the seedlings have recovered from the pricking out move, they must be hardened off to prepare them for the life outdoors. Increase the ventilation and move the containers to a cold frame. Keep the lights closed for a week or two and then open on dry and frost-free days. Later keep them open day and night — the plants should be left unprotected for 7 days before planting out. Windowsill seedlings should be moved into an unheated room and then to the porch before being stood out for a few days prior to planting in the open garden.

# Sowing seeds outdoors

Both hardy annuals and hardy biennials can be raised by sowing seeds outdoors. Germination takes place in a nursery bed, and when the seedlings are large enough they are transferred to the place where they are to flower.

By far the most important group here is the spring-flowering biennials — Daisy, Wallflower, Forget-me-not etc. Hardy annuals can be treated in this way, but for bedding it is more usual to raise them under glass and then bed out in April or May. Some hardy annuals hate root disturbance — these must be sown where they are to flower or raised under glass and then pricked out into individual pots or cells prior to planting.

## The 6 steps to success

**1** **PICK THE RIGHT TIME** Hardy biennials are sown between May and July — June is usually the best month. Hardy annuals are generally sown in March or April, but the weather is more important than the calendar — the soil should be warm enough to permit germination and dry enough to make a seed bed. Some hardy annuals (e.g Larkspur, Cornflower, Calendula, Iberis and Gypsophila) can be sown in September — these autumn-sown annuals bloom earlier than their spring-sown counterparts.

**2** **PREPARE THE NURSERY BED** Choose an open site away from trees — fork over, add peat but not fertilizer, tread over with your heels and then rake to produce an even and crumbly surface. Rotate the site of the nursery bed each year if possible — a spot in the vegetable garden is ideal.

**3** **PREPARE THE DRILLS** The drills should be 6–12 in. apart — they should be deep enough to allow the seeds to be covered with soil to about twice their size. Never water the bed after sowing — if the soil is dry it should be gently watered before sowing.

**4** **SOW SEED** Seed must be sown thinly. Do not sow directly from the packet — place some seed in the palm of your hand and gently sprinkle between thumb and forefinger. Aim to sow at ¼ in. intervals. Mix seed with silver sand before sowing. After sowing, carefully rake the soil back into the drill and then firm with the back of the rake or your fingers. Do not water — if the weather is dry then cover the surface with newspaper. Some seeds need protection from birds — cover the surface with wire guards or twigs.

**5** **THIN OUT** When the first true leaves have appeared, it is time to start thinning. At this first stage reduce the stand to one seedling every 2 in. — be careful not to disturb the seedlings you wish to retain. Repeat this thinning about 10 days later, leaving small varieties about 4 in. apart and larger ones at 6 in. intervals.

**6** **PLANT OUT** Lift biennials in autumn with a trowel and transfer to the bed, border or container where they are to flower. Spring-sown hardy annuals should be planted in May when the weather and soil are suitable — autumn-sown hardy annuals should be set out in their permanent site in April or May.

# Taking Cuttings

## The 3 steps to success

**1** The taking of cuttings is an important feature of the bedding plant story. Many varieties of Geranium and Fuchsia and several other plants (Conifers, Heather, Ivy etc) are raised in this way. The usual way to propagate half hardy annuals by this method is to dig up and pot plants in autumn and to take cuttings from the new growth in spring. Fuchsia and Geranium cuttings are usually taken in late summer.

Cut off leaves from lower half of the cutting

1–6 in. depending on the size of the parent plant

Leaf joint

Straight cut

Dip bottom ½ in. of the cutting into a rooting hormone such as Bio Roota

**2**

④ Insert cutting; firm around the base with the pencil. Label if necessary

② Trim foliage of large-leaved plants by half

⑤ Water in cutting very gently

③ Make a hole in the compost with a pencil

① Fill a 5 in. pot with seed & cutting compost or Multicompost

**3** **Polythene bag method**

① Place 4 canes in the pot and drape a polythene bag over them. Secure with a rubber band. Stand pot in a bright spot, away from direct sunlight

② Leave undisturbed until new growth appears. Lift out each rooted cutting after watering — transfer into a compost-filled 3 in. pot. Harden off in the usual way

**or**
**Propagator method**

① Place pots in the propagator. Keep at 65°–75°F. Shade and ventilate on hot days

② See above

# CHAPTER 3

# BEDDING PLANTS A~Z

On the following pages you will find illustrations and descriptions of all the popular and many unusual bedding plants. Naming, as always, poses a problem. To use latin names throughout would lead to confusion but to use only common names would be even less satisfactory. There is no perfect nor even a generally acceptable way of naming bedding plants, so a 'seed catalogue' approach has been used in this book. In most cases the latin name has been used as the title with the common name printed after it. In some cases (Godetia, Lobelia, Zinnia etc) the latin and common names are the same. With some plants the common name has been used as the title to avoid confusion — the Tagetes genus has been split into Marigold and Tagetes, the Dianthus genus has been divided into Carnation, Dianthus and Sweet William. Not perfect, but workable.

Even a quick glance through this A–Z will reveal a number of plants which are not usually regarded as bedding plants. There are Conifers, Grasses, Roses, Heathers, Ivy and so on. There are several reasons for this expansion to the bedding plant list. First of all, the boom in container growing has increased the interest in exotic plants which can serve as showpieces at the centre of the tub or trough. In addition the hanging basket boom has increased the call for trailers such as Ivies and Helichrysum petiolatum. Another reason for the enlarged bedding plant list is the growing realisation that many plants we regard as house plants will flourish perfectly happily outdoors during the summer months. Finally there is an increase in winter bedding, and so Heather and Conifers are included.

The A–Z may seem extensive but it is by no means complete. The low-growing foliage carpet bedders so loved by the Victorians have been omitted as they are now rarely used except by parks departments for their floral clocks. These include Alternanthera with its multitude of coloured varieties, Saxifraga, Sedum, Sagina, Sempervivum and Echeveria. Some well-known rockery perennials such as Arabis and Aubretia can be used as bedding plants for containers etc and then moved to more permanent quarters at the end of the season. The list in this chapter of flowering bedding plants which can be raised from seed may be extended to include the Daisy-like Osteospermum with bright orange flowers, the blue-flowering Nolana for hanging baskets, the low-growing Sanvitalia (Creeping Zinnia) for the

rockery and the feathery-leaved Gilia for the border. Plants grown for their silvery foliage are represented by the popular Cineraria and Pyrethrum in this A–Z but there are others, such as Centaurea ragusina, which can be raised from seed.

The traditional dot plant for the centre of a formal bedding scheme is a large greenhouse plant with eye-catching foliage or flowers which is brought out in the spring and then returned to the conservatory before the frosts arrive. You can read in this guide about Palms, Plumbago, Grevillea, standard Fuchsia, Eucalyptus, Datura and so on. But there are others which you will see in public gardens — Musa (Banana) which was a Victorian favourite and also the large Yucca and the Tree Ferns such as Dicksonia. Some dot plants such as Ricinus and Amaranthus are usually treated as half hardy annuals and disposed of at the end of the season — an attractive annual which can be included here is the purple-leaved Perilla.

A new trend is to use varieties which have long been sold as house plants but are not generally looked upon as bedding plants. Examples described in the following pages are Kalanchoe, Lantana, Hibiscus and Cuphea. There are others — the well-known Chlorophytum is being increasingly used in public gardens and so is the pink-spotted Hypoestes. The blood red Iresine was popular with Victorian gardeners and so was the Asparagus Fern (Asparagus plumosus).

Only one vegetable is included in the A–Z guide — the Ornamental Brassica which is grown for its display and not for its culinary use. Vegetables grown for the kitchen are not regarded as bedding plants according to the definition on page 3, but there are a few vegetables which deserve a place in the ornamental garden. Top of the list are the silver-veined Swiss Chard and the red-veined Ruby Chard. In addition there are the red-leaved version of the Salad Bowl Lettuce and the Tumbler Tomato for hanging baskets (see page 98).

The plants from Abutilon to Zinnia on the following pages and the additional ones noted on this page clearly show that there is a vast choice nowadays of varieties for display in bed, border or container. It really is time that the bedding plant critics looked above and beyond the Alyssum, Lobelia and Salvia schemes if they wish to understand the range and versatility of this aspect of gardening.

# ABUTILON Flowering Maple

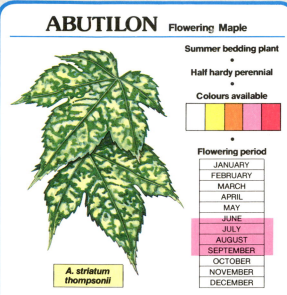

**Summer bedding plant**

•

**Half hardy perennial**

•

**Colours available**

•

**Flowering period**

| JANUARY |
|---|
| FEBRUARY |
| MARCH |
| APRIL |
| MAY |
| JUNE |
| JULY |
| AUGUST |
| SEPTEMBER |
| OCTOBER |
| NOVEMBER |
| DECEMBER |

**A. striatum thompsonii**

Abutilons are listed in the textbooks as subjects for the conservatory or as tender shrubs to be grown in sheltered, frost-free sites. You can, however, grow a couple of types as striking and distinctly unusual bedding plants. The first type is the Variegated Leaf Abutilon grown as a dot plant for its brightly coloured foliage rather than its flowers. The Flowering Abutilons are quite different — the leaves are plain, but large, bell-like flowers are borne. These flowering ones can be used as dot plants in beds, but a better plan is to grow them in pots or containers which are stood in a sheltered part of the garden.

**VARIETIES:** Just one *Variegated Leaf* type is grown — **A. striatum thompsonii**. The 4 in. long Sycamore-like leaves are dark green with bright yellow splashes and spots. This shrub will reach 5 ft or more under glass but will only grow 2–3 ft outdoors. The *Flowering* types can be raised from seed — you will find **A. 'Large-flowered Mixed'** listed in some catalogues. In specialist catalogues you may find several named varieties of **A. hybridum**, such as **'Boule de Neige'** (white), **'Fireball'** (red) and **'Golden Fleece'** (yellow). These plants grow about 2 ft tall.

**SITE & SOIL:** Well-drained soil and full sun are required. Flowering Abutilons are best grown in large containers.

**PLANT DETAILS:** Height 2–3 ft. Spacing — use as a dot plant.

**PROPAGATION:** Abutilons are generally bought in pots. A. striatum thompsonii can be raised from cuttings, but the Flowering Abutilons can be propagated from seed. Sow in February at 65°–75°F — prick out into 3 in. pots and plant out in early June.

Abutilon striatum thompsonii

Abutilon 'Fireball'

# AGERATUM Floss Flower

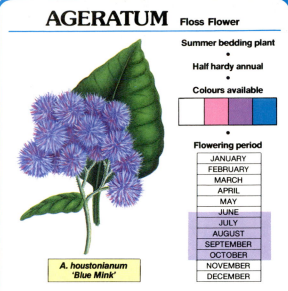

**Summer bedding plant**

•

**Half hardy annual**

•

**Colours available**

•

**Flowering period**

| JANUARY |
|---|
| FEBRUARY |
| MARCH |
| APRIL |
| MAY |
| JUNE |
| JULY |
| AUGUST |
| SEPTEMBER |
| OCTOBER |
| NOVEMBER |
| DECEMBER |

**A. houstonianum 'Blue Mink'**

The popular varieties of Ageratum are neat mounds about 6–10 in. high, with hairy leaves covered with clusters of powder-puff flowers all season long. The usual colours are blue and mauve — white varieties turn an unpleasant brown colour with age and the pink ones have never caught the public fancy. Use Ageratum to edge formal beds or to fill bare patches at the front of the border. Dead-head regularly and water copiously in dry weather.

**VARIETIES:** Despite the introduction of many fine F$_1$ hybrids, the old favourite **'Blue Mink'** remains the best-selling variety of **A. houstonianum**. The mid blue flowers are large and the plants are rather tall (8–10 in.). **'Adriatic'** is paler, the plants are smaller and it is just one of the many recent blue varieties — these range from the pale blue **'Ocean'** to the deep blue **'Blue Cap'**. Mauves and lilacs are well represented — look for **'Blue Angel'** and **'Bengali'**. Most Ageratums are rather pale — for strong colours choose **'North Sea'** (deep violet-blue) or **'Pacific'** (purplish-violet). According to some experts the best of the blue-mauves are **'Blue Danube'** (powder blue, 6 in., very free flowering) and **'Blue Blazer'** (mid blue, 5 in., very early). For white choose **'Summer Snow'** — the best pink one is **'Pink Powderpuffs'** (6 in.). **'Swing'** offers something different — a mixture of blues, mauves and pinks. For cutting choose one of the tall (18 in.) Ageratums — **'Tall Blue'** or **'Wonder'**.

**SITE & SOIL:** Any reasonable garden soil in sun or light shade.

**PLANT DETAILS:** Height 6 in.–1½ ft. Spacing 6–9 in.

**PROPAGATION:** Sow in February-March in gentle heat. Plant out in late May.

Ageratum 'Blue Danube'

Ageratum 'Summer Snow'

# ALTHAEA Hollyhock

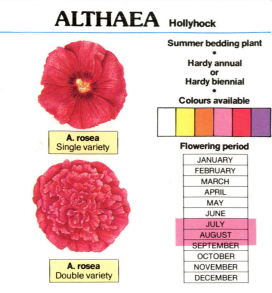

**A. rosea**
Single variety

**A. rosea**
Double variety

Summer bedding plant
•
Hardy annual
or
Hardy biennial
•
Colours available

**Flowering period**

| |
|---|
| JANUARY |
| FEBRUARY |
| MARCH |
| APRIL |
| MAY |
| JUNE |
| JULY |
| AUGUST |
| SEPTEMBER |
| OCTOBER |
| NOVEMBER |
| DECEMBER |

Hollyhocks are sometimes grown as perennials in the border, but rust disease generally weakens the plant and it soon becomes a sorry sight. It is better to treat Hollyhock as a biennial or to grow one of the annual varieties. The old-fashioned types have long been part of the cottage garden scene and are the giants of the bedding plant world, although traditionally they have been sown where they are to flower. The tall spires of funnel-shaped papery blooms should be staked firmly — water freely in dry weather.

**VARIETIES:** Once there were many single-flowered varieties of **A. rosea** but all you are likely to find now is a **'Single Mixture'** of various pastel colours. The doubles have taken over, and the most popular one is **'Chater's Double'** (6 ft, with 4 in. wide Paeony-like blooms). **'Powder Puffs'** (4 ft) is rather smaller and the blooms are fluffy and ruffled. If you want to grow Althaea as an annual then choose **'Summer Carnival'** for a tall double variety which will bloom early. For many gardens one of the modern annual dwarfs is a better idea. There is **'Majorette'** (2½ ft) with 4 in. wide flowers and the semi-double **'Pinafore'** (3 ft).

**SITE & SOIL:** Any reasonable garden soil will do — thrives in a sunny sheltered spot.

**PLANT DETAILS:** Height 2½–6 ft. Spacing 1½–2 ft.

**PROPAGATION:** Sow biennials in May — plant out in September. With annuals sow seed in February in gentle heat. Plant out in May.

*Althaea rosea*

# ALYSSUM Sweet Alyssum

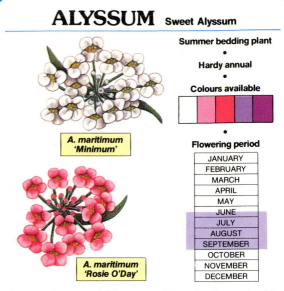

**A. maritimum**
**'Minimum'**

**A. maritimum**
**'Rosie O'Day'**

Summer bedding plant
•
Hardy annual
•
Colours available

**Flowering period**

| |
|---|
| JANUARY |
| FEBRUARY |
| MARCH |
| APRIL |
| MAY |
| JUNE |
| JULY |
| AUGUST |
| SEPTEMBER |
| OCTOBER |
| NOVEMBER |
| DECEMBER |

The single row of Alyssum edging the flower bed is obviously overdone, but the experts who are critical should realise that millions of gardeners don't want to be adventurous. So the dwarf cushions covered with tiny, honey-scented flowers will remain in the bestseller lists for years to come. These plants can be used in many ways — in hanging baskets, containers, rockeries, filling cracks between paving stones etc. Avoid over-rich soil which results in lush foliage and few flowers — trim off dead blooms with scissors to encourage continuous flowering. Prolonged hot and dry weather can be a problem — plants tend to turn brown and stop flowering.

**VARIETIES:** The white varieties of **A. maritimum** (now renamed **Lobularia maritima**) are the most popular. The old favourite **'Little Dorrit'** (6 in.) is rather tall and upright — more compact varieties include **'Snow Drift'**, **'Carpet of Snow'** and **'Minimum'**. For larger flowers grow **'Snow Carpet'** or **'Snow Crystals'**. **'Rosie O'Day'** is the popular pink one and the purple Alyssums are **'Royal Carpet'** and **'Oriental Night'**. A new colour which appeared recently is rich rosy-red — **'Wonderland'** (3 in.) is the variety to look for.

**SITE & SOIL:** The soil should be well-drained and not too fertile — thrives best in full sun.

**PLANT DETAILS:** Height 3–6 in. Spacing 9 in.

**PROPAGATION:** Sow seed in February under glass. Plant out in mid May. Alternatively sow outdoors in April where they are to flower.

*Alyssum*
*'Snow Drift'*

*Alyssum*
*'Royal Carpet'*

# AMARANTHUS  Love-lies-bleeding

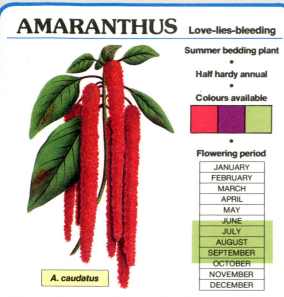

Summer bedding plant

•

Half hardy annual

•

Colours available

Flowering period

| JANUARY |
|---------|
| FEBRUARY |
| MARCH |
| APRIL |
| MAY |
| JUNE |
| **JULY** |
| **AUGUST** |
| **SEPTEMBER** |
| OCTOBER |
| NOVEMBER |
| DECEMBER |

*A. caudatus*

The usual way to use Love-lies-bleeding is to plant one or more as a centrepiece in a formal bedding scheme, but it also makes an excellent container plant. During the summer the 18 in. long tassels of tiny blooms are a spectacular feature which can be used fresh or dried in flower arrangements. Keep the plants watered during dry spells to prolong the flowering period and to ensure an attractive autumn display of red stems and bronzy leaves. Support the stems with twigs if the site is exposed.

**VARIETIES:** **A. caudatus** is the most popular type — a tropical plant with large green leaves and crimson tassels. It can be treated as a hardy annual in southern counties. For a change from the basic species try the deep red variety **atropurpureus** or the bright green **viridis** — all grow 2–3 ft tall. For something quite different choose a dwarf (1–1½ ft) variety with erect flower heads — **'Pygmy Torch'** (red) or **'Green Thumb'** (green). More spectacular but also more difficult to find is **A. paniculatus 'Red Cathedral'** (4 ft, red foliage, erect purple tassels). You can try a different sort of Amaranthus if you have a warm and sheltered site — **A. tricolor** is grown for its multicoloured foliage and not for its insignificant flowers. Look for the varieties **'Illumination'** and **'Joseph's Coat'**.

**SITE & SOIL:** Any well-drained and non-acid soil will do — thrives best in full sun.

**PLANT DETAILS:** Height 1–4 ft. Spacing 9 in.–2½ ft.

**PROPAGATION:** Sow seed in March in gentle heat — transplant A. tricolor into individual pots. Plant out in late May — with A. tricolor wait until early June.

*Amaranthus caudatus viridis*

*Amaranthus caudatus atropurpureus*

# ANCHUSA  Bugloss, Summer Forget-me-not

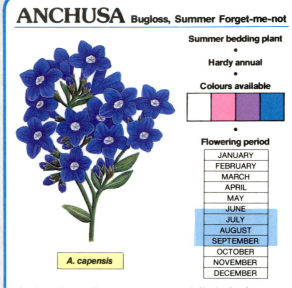

Summer bedding plant

•

Hardy annual

•

Colours available

Flowering period

| JANUARY |
|---------|
| FEBRUARY |
| MARCH |
| APRIL |
| MAY |
| JUNE |
| **JULY** |
| **AUGUST** |
| **SEPTEMBER** |
| OCTOBER |
| NOVEMBER |
| DECEMBER |

*A. capensis*

Anchusa is usually grown as a perennial in the herbaceous border, but there is a compact annual species which bears neat clumps of branching stems. The starry flowers are small, but they are borne in large numbers throughout the summer months. When in bloom the plant looks like a large-flowered version of the much better known Myosotis or Forget-me-not (see page 57). Use Anchusa for bedding, growing in containers or in the rockery. The secrets of success include cutting off the flower heads when the first flush has faded, watering in dry weather and spraying against mildew if white spots appear on the leaves.

**VARIETIES:** The variety of **A. capensis** you will find in nearly all the catalogues is **'Blue Angel'**. Each erect plant grows about 9 in. high — the leaves are narrow and hairy, the flowers are ultramarine blue. You won't find an Anchusa with a better or stronger blue than 'Blue Angel', but there are taller types. **'Blue Bird'** (1½ ft, indigo blue) is listed in some catalogues — **'Bedding Blue'** (1½ ft, sky blue) is more difficult to find. A new one has entered the scene in recent years — **'Dawn'** (9 in.). This is a mixture of white, pink, blue and mauve flowers with a reputation for being especially attractive to bees.

**SITE & SOIL:** Any well-drained soil will do — it should not be too fertile. Thrives best in a sunny, open situation.

**PLANT DETAILS:** Height 9 in. or 1½ ft. Spacing 9 in.

**PROPAGATION:** Sow seed in March in gentle heat. Plant out in May.

*Anchusa 'Dawn'*

# ANTIRRHINUM Snapdragon

**Summer bedding plant**

**Half hardy annual**

**Colours available**

**Flowering period**

| |
|---|
| JANUARY |
| FEBRUARY |
| MARCH |
| APRIL |
| MAY |
| JUNE |
| JULY |
| AUGUST |
| SEPTEMBER |
| OCTOBER |
| NOVEMBER |
| DECEMBER |

**A. majus**

**A. 'Rembrandt'**
Snap type

**A. 'Trumpet Serenade'**
Open-faced type

Antirrhinum has long been a favourite bedding plant, but the arrival of rust disease about 60 years ago threatened to remove this much-loved plant from our gardens. The effect of rust is devastating, and none of the pre-War varieties had any resistance to its ravages. Now there are a number of varieties which show reasonably good resistance — always choose one of these if your plants have developed brown leaves quite early in previous seasons. The traditional type is known to every child — upright spikes which are about 1½ ft high and clothed with lipped tubular flowers which open when squeezed. Nowadays there are all sorts of variations on this theme. Apart from these *Snap* varieties there are the *Open-faced* ones — snapless flowers which may be single, semi-double or double. Antirrhinums are really perennials which can withstand short periods of frost, but they are usually grown as half hardy annuals. When the plants are about 3 in. high, pinch out the growing points to encourage bushiness. Stake tall varieties if the site is exposed and remove faded spikes to prolong the flowering season.

**VARIETIES:** There are several ways of classifying the scores of varieties of **A. majus** — perhaps the best approach is to divide them into 4 groups. The *Tall* group is grand for bold displays and cutting, but is not very popular. You can grow the trumpet-shaped **'Bright Butterflies'** or the ruffled **'Supreme Double'**. The *Intermediate* group is the most popular — here you will find the much-praised $F_1$ hybrid **'Coronette'** renowned for its bushiness and resistance to wet weather. **'Vanity Fair'** and **'Cheerio'** are other popular mixtures — for single colours or bicolours there are **'Black Prince'**, **'White Wonder'**, **'Purple King'**, **'Rembrandt'** etc. Where rust is a problem you should choose one of the **'Monarch'** varieties — if you want something different then choose the open-faced **'Madame Butterfly'** with double Azalea-like flowers. The *Short* group is useful for small beds and edging — **'Tom Thumb'** and **'Floral Carpet'** are the basic ones — for open-faced flowers choose **'Pixie'** or **'Trumpet Serenade'**. The *Dwarf* group are bushy plants for edging or containers — look for **'Little Gem'** (4–6 in.) and **'Magic Carpet'** (6 in.).

**SITE & SOIL:** Any well-drained garden soil, but light or medium land is preferred. Choose a sunny spot.

**PLANT DETAILS:** Tall: Height 2–3 ft. Spacing 1½ ft.
Intermediate: Height 1–2 ft. Spacing 1 ft.
Short: Height 9 in.–1 ft. Spacing 1 ft.
Dwarf: Height 4–9 in. Spacing 6–9 in.

**PROPAGATION:** Sow seed in February-March in gentle heat. Plant out in late May. Not easy to propagate — damping-off can be a problem.

Antirrhinum
'Monarch Mixed'

Antirrhinum
'Madame Butterfly Mixed'

Antirrhinum
'Magic Carpet Mixed'

# ASTER  China Aster, Annual Aster

**Summer bedding plant**

•

**Half hardy annual**

•

**Colours available**

**Flowering period**

| JANUARY |
|---|
| FEBRUARY |
| MARCH |
| APRIL |
| MAY |
| JUNE |
| JULY |
| AUGUST |
| SEPTEMBER |
| OCTOBER |
| NOVEMBER |
| DECEMBER |

*C. chinensis*
Single group

*C. chinensis*
Plume group

*C. chinensis*
Pompon group

*C. chinensis*
Ball group

*C. chinensis*
Chrysanthemum group

Callistephus is generally listed as Aster in seed catalogues and by bedding plant suppliers. There is a single species (Callistephus chinensis), and from the original purple single flowered plants introduced from China a bewildering array of varieties has been developed. Colours range from white to near black, heights from 6 in. mounds to 3 ft high widely-branching leafy plants and there are flowers which range from small singles to large, tightly-packed doubles. But despite these variances there are a number of features common to all Asters. Blooming is at its peak from August to late September, making this plant the queen of late bedders according to some experts. The blooms are Chrysanthemum-like, and they make excellent and long-lasting cut flowers. Shared virtues, but nearly all Asters also share a problem. Aster wilt is a serious soil disease which cannot be cured. Never grow these plants in the same spot year after year and grow a resistant variety ('Ostrich Plume' or 'Milady') if you know the disease has affected your garden. For really good results with Asters you should always water carefully, dead-head regularly, spread a mulch around them after planting and stake tall varieties.

**VARIETIES:** The *Single* group includes the old-fashioned sorts and are not often grown, but here you will find tall varieties (2–3 ft) which can be used as dot plants in a small bedding scheme. Recommended ones include **'Super Sinensis'**, **'Andrella'** and **'Madeleine'**. The double varieties exhibit a number of flower forms. The large *Chrysanthemum* group ranges from the tall **'Duchess'** strain bearing incurved blooms which are 4–5 in. across to the 1 ft high **'Milady'** and the even smaller **'Pinocchio'** and **'Dwarf Queen'**. The *Ball* group is a limited one — **'Miss Europe'** and **'Milady Rose'** have flowers of this type. Long feathery petals are the feature of the *Plume* group — examples include the old favourite **'Ostrich Plume'** and the large-flowered **'Totem Pole'**. Finally there is the *Pompon* group with button-like flowers — included here are **'Lilliput'** (15 in.) and **'Pompon Mixed'** (20 in.). The list above illustrates the wide range available and is by no means complete. In the catalogues you will find a selection of dwarfs such as the 8 in. **'Colour Carpet'**, intermediates such as the 1½ ft **'Powderpuffs'** and the stately 3 ft **'Compliment'**.

**SITE & SOIL:** Well-drained garden soil in a sunny, sheltered spot is the ideal situation. Add lime if the soil is acid.

**PLANT DETAILS:** Height 6 in.–3 ft. Spacing 9 in.–1½ ft.

**PROPAGATION:** Sow seed in March in gentle heat. Plant out in May — late spring frosts are rarely a problem as Callistephus is almost hardy.

*Callistephus chinensis*
'Madeleine Mixed'

*Callistephus chinensis*
'Ostrich Plume Mixed'

*Callistephus chinensis*
'Duchess Mixed'

# ARCTOTIS African Daisy

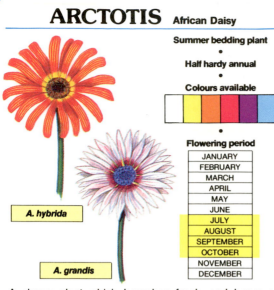

Summer bedding plant
•
Half hardy annual
•
Colours available
•
Flowering period

| JANUARY |
| FEBRUARY |
| MARCH |
| APRIL |
| MAY |
| JUNE |
| **JULY** |
| **AUGUST** |
| **SEPTEMBER** |
| **OCTOBER** |
| NOVEMBER |
| DECEMBER |

A. hybrida

A. grandis

A showy plant which branches freely and bears an abundance of large Daisy-like flowers on the long stems. Well-grown hybrids offer an eye-catching sight on a warm and sunny day — a brilliant mix of reds, oranges, yellows and purples. The feature which has kept this plant out of the popular lists is the way the flowers close in the afternoon and do not open at all on dull and rainy days. Still, if you grow Arctotis well and the summer is kind then you should have a fine display. Pinch out the growing points of the plants when they are about 5 in. high and support the stems with twigs.

**VARIETIES:** In the catalogues you will find two basic types which differ quite markedly in both height and flower colour. **A. grandis** is the tall one, reaching a height of 2–3½ ft. The blooms appear in large numbers, 2–3 in. across with white, purple-backed petals and a central blue disc. Much more popular are the varieties of **A. hybrida**. The plants are smaller (1–1½ ft) and the blooms are larger (3–3½ in. across). These are usually sold as **'Harlequin Mixed'** or **'Large-Flowered Hybrids'** — a medley of brightly coloured flowers which are frequently zoned.

**SITE & SOIL:** Thrives best in light and well-drained soil but most soils apart from clays will do. Choose a sunny situation.

**PLANT DETAILS:** Height 1–3½ ft. Spacing 9 in.–1½ ft.

**PROPAGATION:** Sow seed in March in gentle heat. Plant out in late May.

Arctotis grandis

Arctotis hybrida

# BALSAM Touch-me-not

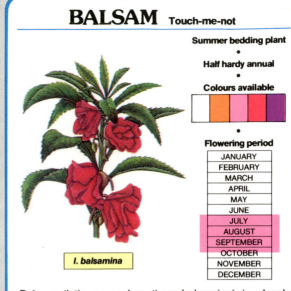

Summer bedding plant
•
Half hardy annual
•
Colours available
•
Flowering period

| JANUARY |
| FEBRUARY |
| MARCH |
| APRIL |
| MAY |
| JUNE |
| **JULY** |
| **AUGUST** |
| **SEPTEMBER** |
| OCTOBER |
| NOVEMBER |
| DECEMBER |

I. balsamina

Balsam (latin name Impatiens balsamina) is closely related to the much more popular Busy Lizzie, but it differs in two important respects — Balsam needs full sun in order to thrive and it does not do well in cool and wet summers. It was a great favourite in Victorian gardens but is no longer in the bestseller lists. Flower form is not the problem — the large double blooms are Camellia- or Azalea-like and are available in a variety of colours. The main drawback is that the blooms are borne on the stems between the leaves, and on older varieties they were sometimes half-hidden by the foliage. Secrets of success include pinching back taller types to induce bushiness, watering in dry weather and thinning leaves if flowers are hidden.

**VARIETIES: 'Camellia Flowering'** is the usual type of **I. balsamina** listed in the catalogues — 3 in. double flowers in white, salmon, pink, red and purple. The plants in the mixture grow about 1½ ft tall — where smaller plants are needed choose **'Tom Thumb'** — a 9 in. Balsam with Camellia-like flowers. For the novelty-minded there is **'Peppermint Stick'** (2 ft) with white-spotted red blooms. There is also **'Carambole'** (9 in.) which bears its Azalea-like flowers well above the foliage.

**SITE & SOIL:** Thrives best in fertile soil and a warm, sunny situation.

**PLANT DETAILS:** Height 9 in.–2 ft. Spacing 6 in.–1 ft.

**PROPAGATION:** Sow seed in February–March in gentle heat. Plant out in late May.

Impatiens balsamina
'Camellia Flowering'

# BEGONIA, FIBROUS-ROOTED Bedding Begonia

**Summer bedding plant**

•

**Half hardy annual**

•

**Colours available**

•

**Flowering period**

| |
|---|
| JANUARY |
| FEBRUARY |
| MARCH |
| APRIL |
| MAY |
| JUNE |
| JULY |
| AUGUST |
| SEPTEMBER |
| OCTOBER |
| NOVEMBER |
| DECEMBER |

*B. semperflorens*

*B. 'Thousand Wonders'*

*B. 'Cocktail'*

It now seems strange that not many years ago Begonia semperflorens was regarded as a compact house plant rather than a summer bedding plant. There has been a dramatic change — the Fibrous-rooted Begonia has joined the top ten favourites and is now seen everywhere. There are two basic reasons for this increase in popularity — a range of free-flowering F$_1$ hybrids has appeared with an even and compact growth habit, and more and more people have learned that only this plant can rival Impatiens as a source of bright colour in shade and under trees from June until October. The usual height is 6–8 in. and the colour range is limited. There are red, pink and white plus one or two new varieties which are salmon. Foliage is usually green or bronze, but red and brown are also available. One of the easiest plants to grow, but do follow the rules for really good results. Buy seedlings or plugs — seed propagation is for the skilled. Do not plant out too early — wait until early June when the plants are in flower. Enrich the soil with some organic matter before planting out and water when the weather is dry. Do these things and you will have a fine display in beds, borders, tubs, window boxes and hanging baskets.

**VARIETIES:** You can save money and buy ordinary **B. semperflorens 'Mixed'**, but it is much better to buy one of the F$_1$ hybrids. There are 4–6 in. dwarfs such as **'Rusher Red'** and the **'Coco'** series — for 12 in. high plants choose **'Party Fun'** (a mixture with green- and bronze-leaved plants) or **'Danica'** (a bronze-leaved variety with red flowers). A tall-growing, upright novelty is **'Frilly Pink'** or **'Frilly Red'** — the edges of the large flowers are ruffled. **'Organdy'** (8 in., green or bronze foliage) is one of the old favourites — a new colour breakthrough is **'Olympia Salmon Orange'**. Most varieties are compact bushes with a spread which is equal to their height. For a hanging basket you should choose a pendant variety — look for **'Pink Avalanche'** or the new **'Illumination'** which bears pink, double blossoms. Most people prefer green-leaved varieties, but there is a wide span of foliage colour. It ranges from pale green (**'Thousand Wonders'** 8 in. with white, pink or red flowers) to chocolate brown (**'Cocktail'** 6 in. with a non-stop display of flowers until the frosts arrive).

**SITE & SOIL:** Thrives best in humus-rich soil and partial shade.

**PLANT DETAILS:** Height 4 in.–1 ft. Spacing 6 in.–1 ft.

**PROPAGATION:** Sow seed in January in gentle heat. Plant out in early June. Do not cover seed with compost — propagation is not easy.

*Begonia semperflorens*

*Begonia 'Illumination'*

*Begonia 'Cocktail Mixed'*

# BEGONIA, TUBEROUS-ROOTED   Tuberous Begonia

**Summer bedding plant**

•

**Half hardy perennial**

•

**Colours available**

•

**Flowering period**

| |
|---|
| JANUARY |
| FEBRUARY |
| MARCH |
| APRIL |
| MAY |
| JUNE |
| JULY |
| AUGUST |
| SEPTEMBER |
| OCTOBER |
| NOVEMBER |
| DECEMBER |

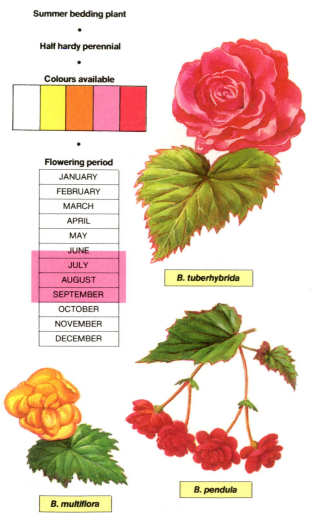

*B. tuberhybrida*

*B. pendula*

*B. multiflora*

Just think of it — 6 in. wide double blooms. Several varieties of B. tuberhybrida can provide this display for you, and few other plants can match it in providing such a dazzling range of colours to grace beds, borders, hanging baskets, tubs and rockeries until the first frosts arrive. They will flourish in sun or light shade provided that the soil is enriched with organic matter before planting and if they are watered regularly during dry weather. Tubers are planted in peat indoors in early spring or plants are purchased in pots for planting out in June. Nowadays you can buy seed of reliable varieties, but seed raising is not easy — careful control of both temperature and watering are essential. With B. tuberhybrida the small female flowers under each showy male one should be pinched out. Lift tubers in mid October — remove stems after the foliage has died down and store tubers in dry peat in a frost-free place.

**VARIETIES:** The large-flowered **B. tuberhybrida** is the best-known group, its Rose-like blooms measuring 2–6 in. across. There is a wide range of shapes and colours — flowers may be single or double, plain-edged or ruffled and self- or bi-coloured. You will find a large range of plants in pots on offer at garden centres — do be careful not to plant out before the danger of frost is past. Named varieties include **'Harlequin'** (white, edged pink), **'Midas'** (yellow), **'Diana Wynyard'** (white), **'Double Picotee'** (cream, edged red), **'Guardsman'** (red) and **'Sugar Candy'** (pink). The problem with buying plants in pots is the cost if you have a large area to cover — seed would seem to be the answer. You will find the $F_1$ hybrid **'Non-Stop'** in most catalogues and it is thought to be the best choice. The fully double 2–3 in. wide flowers are borne on 1 ft plants and blooming continues until the frosts arrive. **'Pavilion'** bears much larger flowers — **'Clips'** and **'Musical'** bear smaller blooms. Raising plants from seed is not easy — it is usually better to buy plugs. **B. multiflora** produces masses of small double flowers on low-growing plants. **B. pendula** bears slender, drooping stems and 1–2 in. flowers — a good choice for hanging baskets. Choose the semi-double **'Chanson'** or the double **'Picotee Cascade'**.

**SITE & SOIL:** Needs soil which is rich in organic matter with little or no lime present. Thrives best in light shade.

**PLANT DETAILS:** B. tuberhybrida: Height 9 in.–1½ ft. Spacing 1 ft.
B. multiflora: Height 9 in. Spacing 9 in.
B. pendula: Length 1–2 ft. Spacing 9 in.

**PROPAGATION:** Sow seed in January under glass. With tubers press into boxes of damp peat in March — place hollow side uppermost. Keep at 60°–70°F and transplant into pots when leafy shoots appear. Plant out in early June.

Begonia tuberhybrida
'Diana Wynyard'

Begonia tuberhybrida
'Non-Stop Rose'

Begonia pendula
'Picotee Cascade'

# BELLIS Daisy

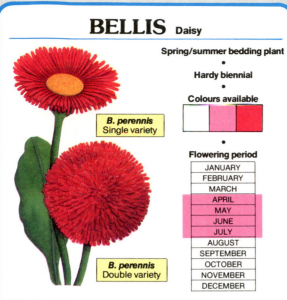

**B. perennis**
Single variety

**B. perennis**
Double variety

Spring/summer bedding plant
•
Hardy biennial
•
Colours available

•
Flowering period

| Month | |
|---|---|
| JANUARY | |
| FEBRUARY | |
| MARCH | |
| APRIL | ■ |
| MAY | ■ |
| JUNE | ■ |
| JULY | ■ |
| AUGUST | |
| SEPTEMBER | |
| OCTOBER | |
| NOVEMBER | |
| DECEMBER | |

The double Daisy was once a very popular spring bedding plant, but it lost its place to the brighter Pansy and Viola. Now it is making a come-back as gardeners begin to realise its many uses — ground cover, edging and planting in window boxes, tubs and in gaps in the rockery. The Daisy is a perennial plant which can be kept from year to year, but it is usually grown as a biennial. There are red and pink varieties as well as the white colour of the native species, and the central yellow disc has been obliterated in the double varieties. Dead-head regularly to prevent seeding.

**VARIETIES:** The common or garden Daisy has given rise to a large number of ornamental varieties over the years, and almost all are fully double. The giant-flowered ones bear blooms which are 2 in. across — look for the **'Monstrosa'**, **'Goliath'** and **'Super Enorma'** strains. Miniatures bearing masses of ½–1 in. flowers are often preferred — included here are a number of named varieties such as **'Lilliput'** (red), **'Rob Roy'** (red), **'The Pearl'** (white) and the attractive **'Dresden China'** (pink). Popular miniature strains include **'Pomponette'** with quill-petalled, button-like flowers and the neat **'Carpet'** types noted for their regular growth habit.

**SITE & SOIL:** Any reasonable garden soil in sun or partial shade.

**PLANT DETAILS:** Height 3–6 in. Spacing 6 in.

**PROPAGATION:** Sow seed in May or June — plant out in autumn. Some varieties such as 'Dresden China' and 'Rob Roy' do not set seed — divide plants after flowering.

*Bellis perennis 'Monstrosa'*

*Bellis perennis 'Pomponette'*

# BRACHYCOME Swan River Daisy

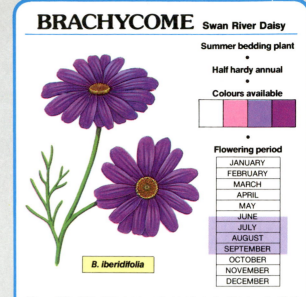

**B. iberidifolia**

Summer bedding plant
•
Half hardy annual
•
Colours available

•
Flowering period

| Month | |
|---|---|
| JANUARY | |
| FEBRUARY | |
| MARCH | |
| APRIL | |
| MAY | |
| JUNE | |
| JULY | ■ |
| AUGUST | ■ |
| SEPTEMBER | ■ |
| OCTOBER | |
| NOVEMBER | |
| DECEMBER | |

You will find this little-known Australian plant in nearly all of the popular seed catalogues but not on display at the garden centre in spring. Surprising at first, because the compact plants bear masses of Daisy- or Cineraria-like flowers which are sweetly fragrant. The stems branch freely and the leaves are feathery — despite the delicate appearance the Swan River Daisy is almost hardy and can be safely planted out in May. But there are problems — it does not do well in heavy and infertile soils, and in warm summers the flowering period can be quite short.

**VARIETIES:** Once there were numerous named varieties of **B. iberidifolia** on offer, but nowadays it is generally sold as a mixture — white, lilac, pink and purple flowers measuring 1–1½ in. across. Grow in containers, rockeries or as an edging plant — the dark-centred blooms are sometimes used in flower arrangements. The wiry stems need staking and dead-heading is necessary in August in order to prolong the flowering season. Some suppliers offer **'Purple Splendour'**, a richly-coloured variety which grows 9–12 in. high.

**SITE & SOIL:** Rather fussy — rich, free-draining soil or compost is necessary and there must be some shelter from the prevailing wind.

**PLANT DETAILS:** Height 9–15 in. Spacing 9 in.–1 ft.

**PROPAGATION:** Sow seed in March under glass. Plant out in May. Late spring frosts are rarely a problem. Pinch out tips of young plants to induce bushiness.

*Brachycome iberidifolia 'Mixed'*

*Brachycome iberidifolia 'Purple Splendour'*

# BRASSICA Ornamental Cabbage

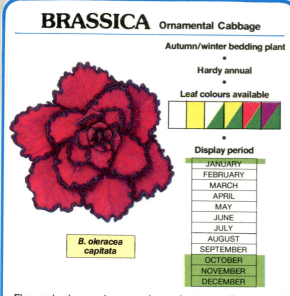

**B. oleracea capitata**

Autumn/winter bedding plant
•
Hardy annual
•
Leaf colours available

Display period

| JANUARY |
|---------|
| FEBRUARY |
| MARCH |
| APRIL |
| MAY |
| JUNE |
| JULY |
| AUGUST |
| SEPTEMBER |
| OCTOBER |
| NOVEMBER |
| DECEMBER |

Flower beds are barren places between the end of October and January, and yet interest in autumn and winter bedding plants is quite small. Ornamental Cabbages and Kales are very popular in Japan and are used in park displays in many countries, yet they are a rare sight in Britain. The Cabbages have flat open heads and are planted in groups as a form of modern-day carpet bedding — the Kales are rather taller with the foliage more loosely arranged. The ornamental interest is that the colour of the inner leaves changes dramatically when the temperature stays below 50°F. The plants are edible and useful as a garnish, but the taste is insipid or bitter.

**VARIETIES:** Some but not all catalogues list one or more varieties of Ornamental Cabbage (**B. oleracea capitata**) or Ornamental Kale (**B. oleracea acephala**). The leaves may be smooth-edged but are more usually intricately curled and fringed. The standard pattern is an outer ring of dark green leaves with a tightly-packed centre in a different colour — white (**'White Xmas'**, **'White Osaka'** and **'White Peacock'**) or red (**'Prima Donna'** and **'Red Osaka'**). There are variations on this theme — purple-edged green leaves, cream-veined leaves, green-edged white leaves etc. Pests can be a problem — slugs, of course, but also wood pigeons.

**SITE & SOIL:** Any well-drained garden soil will do — thrives best in full sun.

**PLANT DETAILS:** Height 9 in.–1½ ft. Spacing 1–1½ ft.

**PROPAGATION:** Sow seed in July in gentle heat — prick out into 3 in. pots. Plant out in September.

*Brassica oleracea 'White Peacock'*

# CALANDRINIA Rock Purslane

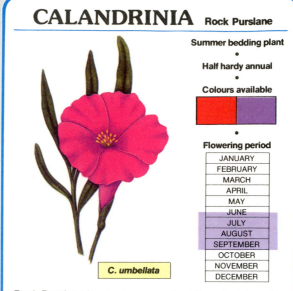

**C. umbellata**

Summer bedding plant
•
Half hardy annual
•
Colours available

Flowering period

| JANUARY |
|---------|
| FEBRUARY |
| MARCH |
| APRIL |
| MAY |
| JUNE |
| JULY |
| AUGUST |
| SEPTEMBER |
| OCTOBER |
| NOVEMBER |
| DECEMBER |

Rock Purslane is an uncommon bedding plant, found in some seed catalogues but not set out for sale with other bedders in the spring. There is basically one species, low-growing and mat-forming, with red flowers in summer. This is a plant for the rockery, between paving stones or as an edging for beds and borders provided that the strong colour of the bowl-shaped flowers does not clash with other blooms. Pot up a few plants and place on a windowsill indoors. A good choice if you want a bright splash in a sandy warm spot, but definitely to be avoided if the site is heavy and wet.

**VARIETIES:** The only species you are likely to find is **C. umbellata**. The hairy leaves are greyish-green and the magenta flowers are about ¾ in. across. The standard variety is **'Amaranth'** which grows about 6 in. high. Be careful not to overwater — this plant thrives best in hot and dry soils. In specialist catalogues you may find taller Calandrinias. **C. speciosa** grows about 1½ ft high and produces fragrant bright red blooms. Even taller is **C. discolor** (2 ft) which bears 2 in. pale purple blooms.

**SITE & SOIL:** Requires dry, sandy soil and a sunny, sheltered situation.

**PLANT DETAILS:** Height 6 in.–2 ft. Spacing 9 in.–1 ft.

**PROPAGATION:** Sow seed in March in gentle heat. Plant out in late May. Not an easy plant to raise — the seed is very fine and the compost must be kept rather dry.

*Calandrinia umbellata 'Amaranth'*

# CALCEOLARIA Slipper Flower

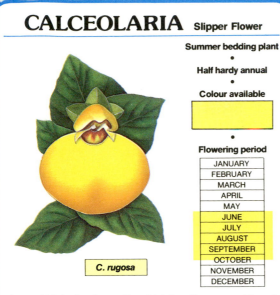

Summer bedding plant
•
Half hardy annual
•
Colour available

•
Flowering period

| | |
|---|---|
| JANUARY | |
| FEBRUARY | |
| MARCH | |
| APRIL | |
| MAY | |
| JUNE | ■ |
| JULY | ■ |
| AUGUST | ■ |
| SEPTEMBER | ■ |
| OCTOBER | |
| NOVEMBER | |
| DECEMBER | |

**C. rugosa**

A great Victorian favourite which lost its way and is only now coming back into favour. There were two reasons for this decline in popularity — French Marigolds took over as the standard golden bedding plants in post War gardens and Calceolaria was notoriously difficult to raise from seed. The Victorian plants were grown from overwintered cuttings which had been kept in the greenhouse. The appearance of the F$_1$ hybrids has changed all this — now you can have masses of pouched flowers on neat seed-raised plants all summer long. These modern varieties can be raised at quite low temperatures, but for most gardeners it is better to buy pot-grown specimens for bedding out or planting in containers.

**VARIETIES:** Outdoor Calceolarias are all-yellow varieties of **C. rugosa** (**C. integrifolia**) — do not confuse them with the multicoloured hybrids sold as house plants. The most widely grown outdoor variety is '**Sunshine**', sometimes listed as '**Gold Bouquet**'. The golden flowers are about ½ in. long. Another fine seed-raised variety is '**Midas**' — earlier than 'Sunshine' and with pure yellow flowers. '**Golden Bunch**' is a smaller variety, growing about 8 in. high with paler blooms than the popular 'Sunshine' and 'Midas'.

**SITE & SOIL:** Any reasonable garden soil in sun or light shade.

**PLANT DETAILS:** Height 8–15 in. Spacing 9 in.

**PROPAGATION:** The best plan is to buy potted seedlings for transplanting in late May. Plants can be raised from seed, but this is not easy as the seed is so fine — more than 1 million per ounce! Sow in January–March in gentle heat. Plant out in late May.

*Calceolaria rugosa* 'Sunshine'

# CALENDULA Pot Marigold, English Marigold

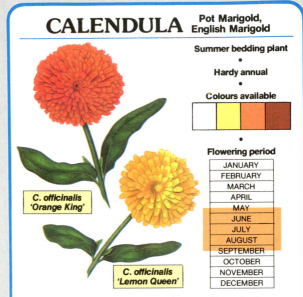

Summer bedding plant
•
Hardy annual
•
Colours available

•
Flowering period

**C. officinalis 'Orange King'**

**C. officinalis 'Lemon Queen'**

| | |
|---|---|
| JANUARY | |
| FEBRUARY | |
| MARCH | |
| APRIL | |
| MAY | |
| JUNE | ■ |
| JULY | ■ |
| AUGUST | ■ |
| SEPTEMBER | |
| OCTOBER | |
| NOVEMBER | |
| DECEMBER | |

The Pot Marigold was first used as a culinary herb many hundreds of years ago, but today it belongs in the flower bed or cottage garden. It is an easy-to-grow plant which will thrive in sun and partial shade, in poor soil and salt-laden air. But it is not quite as trouble-free as the seed packet suggests — failure to dead-head and the onset of greenfly and mildew sometimes result in flowering coming to an end before autumn arrives. Use dwarf varieties for edging and massed planting — all types make excellent cut flowers. Pinch out growing points on young stems to induce bushiness and stake tall varieties.

**VARIETIES:** Numerous varieties of **C. officinalis** are available — colours include yellow, cream, orange and mahogany. The most popular dwarf is '**Fiesta Gitana**' (9–12 in.) which is noted for its dense growth. The selling points of the F$_1$ hybrid '**Mandarin**' include its large bright orange blooms and early flowering habit. In the 18 in. range are the old favourites '**Radio**', '**Lemon Queen**' and the widely grown '**Orange King**'. The most popular tall ones (24 in.) are the '**Art Shades**' mixture and the multicoloured '**Pacific Beauty**'. Look out for '**Kablouna**' (20 in.) with its central disc of quilled petals and the Japanese varieties such as the deep orange '**Muraji**' which are highly recommended for cutting.

**SITE & SOIL:** Any reasonable garden soil will do in sun or partial shade.

**PLANT DETAILS:** Height 9 in.–2 ft. Spacing 9 in.–1 ft.

**PROPAGATION:** Sow seed in January–March under glass. Plant out in April or May.

*Calendula officinalis* 'Fiesta Gitana'

*Calendula officinalis* 'Mandarin'

# CAMPANULA Canterbury Bell

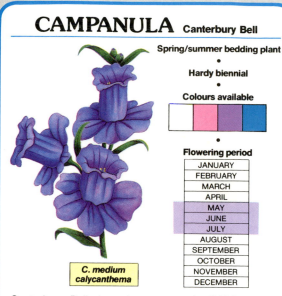

Spring/summer bedding plant

•

Hardy biennial

•

Colours available

•

Flowering period

| JANUARY |
| FEBRUARY |
| MARCH |
| APRIL |
| MAY |
| JUNE |
| JULY |
| AUGUST |
| SEPTEMBER |
| OCTOBER |
| NOVEMBER |
| DECEMBER |

*C. medium calycanthema*

Canterbury Bells have been grown in British cottage gardens for hundreds of years and they continue to be used widely in beds and borders. The newer dwarf varieties are suitable for the rockery and all are excellent for cutting. Above the wavy-edged, hairy leaves numerous spikes of bell-shaped flowers appear. The blooms may be single, semi-double or double and colours include pink as well as the more familiar white and blue. Support will be needed for the tall varieties — plant them close together or stake the stems. Protect the plants from slugs in winter.

**VARIETIES:** The Canterbury Bell is **C. medium** and the most popular variety is **C. medium calycanthema**. This is listed as **'Cup and Saucer'** in the catalogues because of the shape of the semi-double flowers borne on the 2½ ft stems. Compact Campanulas are available — look for **'Dwarf Bedding Mixture'** (15–18 in.). **'Bells of Holland'** (18 in.) is a single variety which does not bear a saucer below the bell-shaped flower. The giant is the 4 ft **C. pyramidalis**. In the catalogues you may find a quite different Campanula — **C. isophylla 'Stella'**. This half hardy annual produces trailing stems and starry blue or white flowers — a good choice for hanging baskets.

**SITE & SOIL:** Any well-drained garden soil will do — thrives in a sunny or lightly shaded spot.

**PLANT DETAILS:** Canterbury Bell: Height 1½–2½ ft. Spacing 6 in.–1 ft.

**PROPAGATION:** Canterbury Bell: Sow seed in May or June — plant out in autumn. Alternatively sow in February under glass and plant out in April.

*Campanula medium calycanthema*

*Campanula pyramidalis*

# CANNA Indian Shot

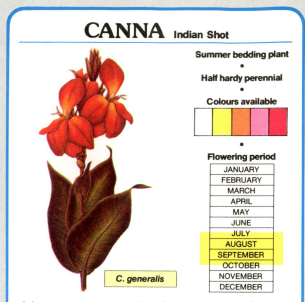

Summer bedding plant

•

Half hardy perennial

•

Colours available

•

Flowering period

| JANUARY |
| FEBRUARY |
| MARCH |
| APRIL |
| MAY |
| JUNE |
| JULY |
| AUGUST |
| SEPTEMBER |
| OCTOBER |
| NOVEMBER |
| DECEMBER |

*C. generalis*

A beauty to serve as a dot plant in a large bed or as a container specimen in a sheltered spot. The decorative leaves are over 1 ft long and often bronze or purple — the bright Gladiolus-like flowers are up to 5 in. across. There are no serious problems, but you will need to protect the shoots from slugs and remember this plant needs shelter from the wind and is not suitable for cool northern climes. Rooted rhizomes are planted out after the danger of frost has passed, and they are lifted before the onset of winter.

**VARIETIES:** Many named varieties of **C. generalis** (**C. hybrida**) are available. They are divided into 2 groups — the *Green-leaved* varieties and the *Coloured-leaved* ones. Varieties in the latter group are highly decorative even when the flowers are absent — choose one of them for maximum effect. Examples of the Coloured group include **'Dazzler'** (4 ft, red flowers, bronze foliage), **'Tyrol'** (4 ft, pink flowers, purple foliage), **'Assault'** (4 ft, red flowers, purple foliage) and the eye-catching **'Lucifer'** (3 ft, yellow-edged red flowers, purple foliage). The Green-leaved group includes **'Orange Perfection'** (2½ ft, orange flowers), **'President'** (3 ft, red flowers) and **'J.B. van der Schoot'** (3 ft, red-spotted yellow flowers).

**SITE & SOIL:** Humus-rich soil and full sun are essential.

**PLANT DETAILS:** Height 2–4 ft. Spacing — use as a dot plant.

**PROPAGATION:** Start rhizomes in peat indoors in March — keep at minimum 60°F. Plant out in early June. Lift the plants in autumn, allow the rhizomes to dry and then store in slightly damp sand or peat. Canna can be raised with difficulty from seed. Sow singly in pots in February — keep at 65°–75°F.

*Canna 'J.B. van der Schoot'*

*Canna 'Lucifer'*

# CARNATION Annual Carnation

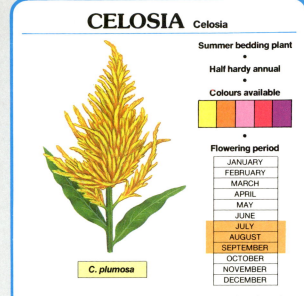

Summer bedding plant
•
Half hardy annual
•
Colours available
•
Flowering period

| | |
|---|---|
| JANUARY | |
| FEBRUARY | |
| MARCH | |
| APRIL | |
| MAY | |
| JUNE | |
| **JULY** | |
| **AUGUST** | |
| **SEPTEMBER** | |
| OCTOBER | |
| NOVEMBER | |
| DECEMBER | |

**D. caryophyllus**

We usually think of Carnations as herbaceous border plants which are propagated by means of layering or taking cuttings. But the annual varieties make excellent bedding plants now that there are dwarf types and tall ones which do not require staking. They have a pleasant fragrance and the colour range is extensive — plain and picoteed, pure white to deepest red. Choose one of the dwarfs for containers or window boxes, a taller-growing variety for bedding or cutting, and a trailing variety for hanging baskets. An excellent choice for alkaline soil — take care not to overwater.

**VARIETIES:** These hybrids of **Dianthus caryophyllus** bear double blooms which are 1½–2 in. across. You will find the reliable old favourite **'Giant Chabaud'** (1½ ft) in many catalogues, but you are more likely to find the F₁ hybrid **'Knight Mixed'** these days. This 1 ft dwarf is bushy with strong stems which do not require support — there are a wide range of colours and patterns in the blooms which appear all summer long. **'Lilliput Mixed'** (9 in.) is even smaller. At the other end of the scale look for **'Scarlet Luminette'** (1½–2 ft) — a strong-stemmed tall variety with bright scarlet flowers. **'Trailing Mixed'** is the one for hanging baskets.

**SITE & SOIL:** Any well-drained garden soil which is not acid will do — choose a sunny spot.

**PLANT DETAILS:** Height 9 in.–2 ft. Spacing 9 in.–1 ft.

**PROPAGATION:** Sow seed in January-March in gentle heat. Plant out in May.

Dianthus 'Knight Mixed'

Dianthus 'Lilliput Rose'

# CELOSIA Celosia

Summer bedding plant
•
Half hardy annual
•
Colours available
•
Flowering period

| | |
|---|---|
| JANUARY | |
| FEBRUARY | |
| MARCH | |
| APRIL | |
| MAY | |
| JUNE | |
| **JULY** | |
| **AUGUST** | |
| **SEPTEMBER** | |
| OCTOBER | |
| NOVEMBER | |
| DECEMBER | |

**C. plumosa**

Celosia is best known as a showy house plant bearing large and brightly coloured flower heads. It will also serve as a bold bedding plant if you pick the right type and if the chosen spot is sheltered and sunny. There are two basic sorts — the crested ones with tightly-clustered flowers forming a 3–5 in. wide cockscomb and the plumed ones with feathery flower spikes which are 3–6 in. long. These blooms make excellent cut flowers, either fresh or dried. Celosias are tender plants — harden them off properly before planting out when all danger of frost is past.

**VARIETIES:** The crested ones are varieties of **C. cristata** (common name Cockscomb). The only one you are likely to find is the 9 in. high **'Jewel Box'** — it belongs in the house, greenhouse or conservatory. The plumed ones are **C. plumosa** varieties (common name Prince of Wales' Feathers) — these are the types which can be grown outdoors in the more favoured parts of the country. Choose a tall one such as **'Century'** (2 ft) or **'Pampas Plume'** (2½ ft) for the centre of the bed or an average-sized one such as **'Fairy Fountains'** (1½ ft). There are a number of 9 in.–1 ft dwarfs such as **'Lilliput'** and **'Red Glitters'** — the best is **'Dwarf Geisha'**. The most popular single-colour variety is **'Apricot Brandy'** (1½ ft).

**SITE & SOIL:** The soil must not be heavy and the site should be warm and sunny.

**PLANT DETAILS:** Height 9 in.–2½ ft. Spacing 9 in.–1½ ft.

**PROPAGATION:** Sow seed in February-March in gentle heat. Plant out in early June.

Celosia 'Dwarf Geisha'

# CENTAUREA Cornflower

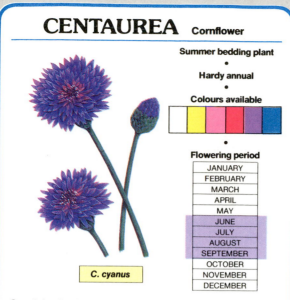

Summer bedding plant
•
Hardy annual

**Colours available**

**Flowering period**

| JANUARY |
| FEBRUARY |
| MARCH |
| APRIL |
| MAY |
| JUNE |
| JULY |
| AUGUST |
| SEPTEMBER |
| OCTOBER |
| NOVEMBER |
| DECEMBER |

*C. cyanus*

Careful selection and breeding have turned one of our common farmland weeds into a colourful bedding plant. The blue of the native Cornflower remains the most popular colour but a wide range of shades is now available, from white to maroon. Wiry stems bear Thistle-like heads above greyish-green leaves — the plants will need support on exposed sites. Cornflower is an easy plant for nearly all gardens and is often sown where it is to grow and flower. Sometimes the flowering season is disappointingly short — dead-head regularly to keep the plants blooming until September. Cornflowers have long been popular as cut flowers.

**VARIETIES:** The *Tall* group of **C. cyanus** grows 2–3 ft high. The most popular and perhaps best true blue is **'Blue Diadem'** — others include **'Blue Ball'** and **'Blue Boy'**. **'Red Ball'** (deep pink) is a good choice and for something different choose **'Frosty'** with its white-flecked flowers. Different, but not particularly attractive. The *Dwarf* group (12–15 in.) are ideal for the smaller, exposed plot — you can choose the deep blue **'Jubilee Gem'** or **'Polka Dot'** mixture. Sweet Sultan (**C. moschata**) is an old favourite which is quite different to the ordinary Cornflower — there are powder-puff fragrant flowers in a variety of colours on bushy (1½–2 ft) plants.

**SITE & SOIL:** Any well-drained, non-acid soil will do — thrives best in full sun.

**PLANT DETAILS:** Height 1–3 ft. Spacing 9 in.–1 ft.

**PROPAGATION:** Sow seed in March under glass. Plant out in May.

Centaurea cyanus
'Blue Diadem'

Centaurea
moschata

# CERASTIUM Snow-in-summer

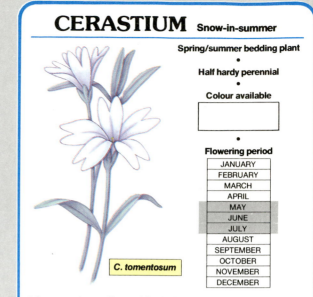

Spring/summer bedding plant
•
Half hardy perennial

**Colour available**

**Flowering period**

| JANUARY |
| FEBRUARY |
| MARCH |
| APRIL |
| MAY |
| JUNE |
| JULY |
| AUGUST |
| SEPTEMBER |
| OCTOBER |
| NOVEMBER |
| DECEMBER |

*C. tomentosum*

Many readers will consider it distinctly odd that this over-popular rockery perennial should be included in a book on bedding plants. The immense popularity during the past few years for hanging baskets, containers and window boxes is the reason — Cerastium is an attractive silvery trailer for such locations. It is also useful as a low-growing ground cover underneath taller plants in a flower bed — the pale leaves and white flowers provide an excellent contrast to dark-leaved varieties. It is an invasive plant, but this should not be a problem when grown as a bedding plant. At the end of the season the clumps can be transferred to the border or rockery, although it is far too rampant to be grown amongst choice alpines.

**VARIETIES:** **C. tomentosum** is the basic species and is to be seen in rockeries everywhere. Look for the variety **'Silver Carpet'** if you plan to grow from seed. The starry flowers are about ½ in. across and cover the slightly woolly foliage in early summer. You will find **C. biebersteinii** in specialist catalogues — the leaves are larger and woollier and the flowers are distinctly larger, reaching 1 in. in diameter.

**SITE & SOIL:** Any well-drained soil will do — thrives best in full sun.

**PLANT DETAILS:** Height 6 in. Spacing 1 ft.

**PROPAGATION:** The easiest method is to remove small rooted pieces from the rockery and pot up in seed compost in autumn. Plant out in April or May. Alternatively sow seed in February–March under glass and plant out in April or May.

Cerastium tomentosum

# CHRYSANTHEMUM  Annual Chrysanthemum

Summer bedding plant

•

Half hardy annual
or
Hardy annual
or
Hardy perennial

•

Colours available

•

Flowering period

| JANUARY |
| FEBRUARY |
| MARCH |
| APRIL |
| MAY |
| JUNE |
| JULY |
| AUGUST |
| SEPTEMBER |
| OCTOBER |
| NOVEMBER |
| DECEMBER |

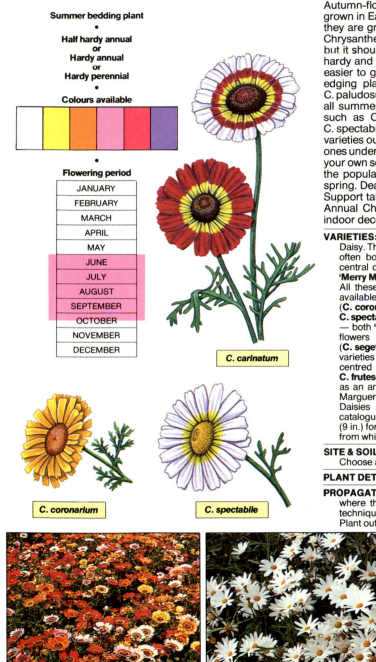

C. carinatum

C. coronarium

C. spectabile

Autumn-flowering or Florist Chrysanthemums have been grown in Eastern gardens for over 2000 years and today they are great favourites all over the world. The Annual Chrysanthemum raised from seed may be a lowly cousin, but it should certainly be more popular. There are both hardy and half hardy types — few plants are showier or easier to grow than the colourful C. carinatum and few edging plants are more reliable and floriferous than C. paludosum with its masses of simple Daisy-like flowers all summer long. There are neat, low-growing species such as C. multicaule and 3 ft high bold ones like C. spectabile. All are easy to raise — sow seeds of hardy varieties outdoors in early spring and start the half hardy ones under glass in late winter. It will be necessary to grow your own seedlings for some of the species below — only the popular types are available as young plants in the spring. Dead-head regularly and spray against greenfly. Support tall-growing varieties and water in dry weather. Annual Chrysanthemums are excellent cut flowers for indoor decoration.

**VARIETIES:** C. carinatum (C. tricolor) is the spectacular Painted Daisy. The flowers on the branched stems of this 2 ft plant are often boldly zoned in bright colours surrounding a dark central disc. Choose **'Court Jesters'**, **'Rainbow Mixture'** or **'Merry Mixture'**. Reds and yellows dominate **'Flame Shades'**. All these varieties are single — double varieties are also available. Another hardy annual is the Crown Daisy (**C. coronarium**) — 1½ ft high with 2 in. wide yellow Daisies. **C. spectabile** is the giant amongst Annual Chrysanthemums — both **'Lemon Sorbet'** and **'Cecilia'** bear yellow and white flowers on 3 ft stems. The wild flower Corn Marigold (**C. segetum**) has produced a number of interesting garden varieties — look for **'Prado'** (1½ ft) with its golden, black-centred blooms. The perennial Marguerite (1–2 ft high) **C. frutescens (Argyranthemum frutescens)** is usually grown as an annual. More useful as an edging plant is the Mini-Marguerite **C. paludosum** — masses of yellow-eyed white Daisies on 9 in. bushy plants with ferny foliage. Some catalogues include the bright yellow **C. multicaule 'Gold Plate'** (9 in.) for edging — there is certainly no shortage of species from which to choose!

**SITE & SOIL:** Thrives best in light soil containing adequate lime. Choose a sunny spot.

**PLANT DETAILS:** Height 9 in.–3 ft. Spacing 9 in.–2 ft.

**PROPAGATION:** Sow seed of hardy varieties in March or April where they are to flower. Alternatively use the half hardy technique — sow seed in February or March in gentle heat. Plant out in late May.

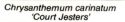

Chrysanthemum carinatum
'Court Jesters'

Chrysanthemum frutescens

Chrysanthemum multicaule
'Gold Plate'

# CINERARIA Dusty Miller

Spring/summer bedding plant
•
Half hardy annual
•
Leaf colours available

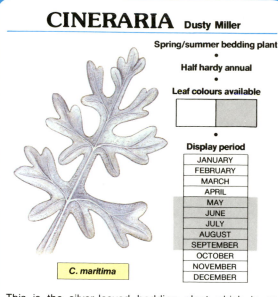

Display period

| JANUARY |
| FEBRUARY |
| MARCH |
| APRIL |
| MAY |
| JUNE |
| JULY |
| AUGUST |
| SEPTEMBER |
| OCTOBER |
| NOVEMBER |
| DECEMBER |

*C. maritima*

This is the silver-leaved bedding plant which is an indispensible part of many planting schemes. Use it as a neat edging or in clumps or lines to enrich the colours of Salvias, Petunias, Begonias and Pelargoniums. Cinerarias do produce small yellow flowers, but these should be removed at the flower bud stage. This plant is really a shrubby perennial which will survive most winters in the Midlands and South, but it is usually treated as a half hardy annual. An easy plant which will withstand salt-laden air, but it may rot in cold, sodden ground.

**VARIETIES:** There is a collection of latin names for Dusty Miller — **Cineraria maritima**, **Senecio maritima**, **S. cineraria** and **S. bicolor**. However, there is not a wide assortment of varieties on offer. Many catalogues just list the basic one —**'Silverdust'**. The silvery-white leaves are deeply and intricately cut to give a ferny or lace-like appearance. It is quite compact, reaching 6–9 in. **'White Diamond'** is taller (12–15 in.) but less silvery. The only variety you are likely to find apart from 'Silverdust' is **'Cirrhus'**. The leaf form is quite different — the oval leaves are notched and not deeply cut and the colour changes from silvery-green to silvery-white with age.

**SITE & SOIL:** Any well-drained soil will do — thrives in full sun.

**PLANT DETAILS:** Height 6–15 in. Spacing 1 ft.

**PROPAGATION:** Cuttings can be taken in spring or autumn, but it is usually propagated from seed. Sow in February-March in gentle heat. Plant out in mid May.

Cineraria maritima
'Silverdust'

Cineraria maritima
'Cirrhus'

# CLARKIA Clarkia

Summer bedding plant
•
Hardy annual
•
Colours available

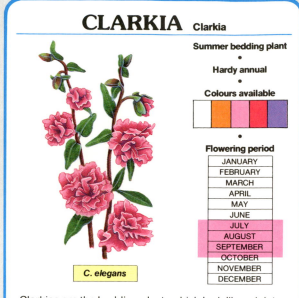

Flowering period

| JANUARY |
| FEBRUARY |
| MARCH |
| APRIL |
| MAY |
| JUNE |
| JULY |
| AUGUST |
| SEPTEMBER |
| OCTOBER |
| NOVEMBER |
| DECEMBER |

*C. elegans*

Clarkias are the bedding plants which look like miniature Hollyhocks — double frilly flowers in pinks, reds and mauves on upright spikes. An easy plant but it does not like transplanting — sowing where it is to grow and flower is preferred to bedding out. Pinch out the growing points of seedlings to induce bushiness and avoid overwatering. Plant Clarkias in groups rather than in lines or singly — support the stems of the taller (2 ft) types with twigs. An excellent cut flower — remove the leaves from stems before placing in water.

**VARIETIES:** The usual species is **C. elegans** — a popular cottage garden plant which is not as old-established as it looks. It was discovered by Douglas in N. America in the 19th century. Single-colour varieties are available but you won't see them listed. In the catalogues you will find **'Bouquet Mixed'** or **'Royal Bouquet Mixture'** — 1½–2 ft plants with blooms 1½–2 in. across in a variety of colours. In a few catalogues you will see the dwarf Clarkia **C. pulchella 'Filigree'** — a smaller (1 ft) and daintier plant with semi-double white, rose and lilac flowers.

**SITE & SOIL:** Thrives best in light or medium soil which is slightly acid. Choose a sunny spot, although it will succeed in light shade.

**PLANT DETAILS:** Height 1–2 ft. Spacing 9 in.

**PROPAGATION:** Sow seed in March under glass . Prick out into individual pots and plant out in mid May.

Clarkia elegans
'Royal Bouquet Mixture'

# CLEOME Spider Flower

Summer bedding plant

Half hardy annual

Colours available

Flowering period

| JANUARY |
| FEBRUARY |
| MARCH |
| APRIL |
| MAY |
| JUNE |
| JULY |
| AUGUST |
| SEPTEMBER |
| OCTOBER |
| NOVEMBER |
| DECEMBER |

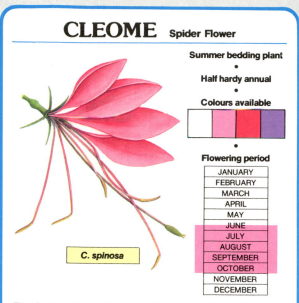

C. spinosa

The Spider Flower is an excellent choice if you like to see the unusual and the exotic in your garden. Large and bushy with 7-lobed leaves, it can be used as a dot plant in the centre of a flower bed or as a gap filler in a mixed border. Cleome can also be used as a short-lived hedge and the blooms are recommended for cutting. These scented flowers are 3 in. or more in length and the long stamens give a spidery appearance. When the seed pods form the appearance is even more spider like — the common name is most appropriate. No problems, but keep watch for greenfly on young plants and water copiously in dry weather.

**VARIETIES:** All the garden types are varieties of **C. spinosa** — the latin name refers to the thorns at the base of the leaves. It is much more widely used in public plantings than in home gardens, but nowhere can it be considered a popular plant. The usual choice is the **'Colour Fountain'** mixture — pink, carmine, and deep mauve. A white variety (**'Helen Campbell'**) is available, but the usual flower colour is pale purple or rose. It is generally easy to tell the colour from the name on the seed packet — **'Rose Queen'**, **'Pink Queen'**, **'Cherry Queen'** and **'Violet Queen'**.

**SITE & SOIL:** Most soils will do — a fertile, well-drained site is ideal. A sunny spot is necessary.

**PLANT DETAILS:** Height 2–4 ft. Spacing 1½–2½ ft.

**PROPAGATION:** Sow seed in February–March in gentle heat. Plant out in late May.

*Cleome spinosa*

# COBAEA Cup & Saucer Plant

Summer bedding plant

Half hardy annual

Colours available

Flowering period

| JANUARY |
| FEBRUARY |
| MARCH |
| APRIL |
| MAY |
| JUNE |
| JULY |
| AUGUST |
| SEPTEMBER |
| OCTOBER |
| NOVEMBER |
| DECEMBER |

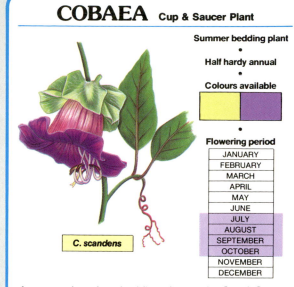

C. scandens

An unusual use for a bedding plant — the Cup & Saucer Plant or Cathedral Bells provides a quick-growing but temporary screen. They may survive the winter in mild districts but the usual practice is to discard the plants in late autumn. The stems attach themselves to trelliswork, pergolas, fences etc by means of tendrils which arise from the leaf stalks. The large bell-like blooms appear throughout the summer — colourful, eye-catching and popular with flower arrangers, but this is not a plant for every garden. Cobaea will not flourish if the soil is heavy and wet or if the site is cool and exposed.

**VARIETIES:** There is a single species — **C. scandens**. The violet flowers which appear above the bright green foliage are about 3 in. long and bear prominent curving stamens. The floral display is sometimes disappointing — flower-shyness is usually due to poor drainage, underwatering, overfeeding or failure to harden off the plants properly before planting out. A few catalogues offer **C. scandens alba**. This variety grows to the same height as its better-known parent, but the flowers are a yellowish-green — not white as its name would suggest.

**SITE & SOIL:** A well-drained site is necessary — thrives best in full sun.

**PLANT DETAILS:** Height 10 ft. Spacing 2 ft.

**PROPAGATION:** Sow seed in February under glass — set the seed sideways in individual pots. Plant out when the danger of frost has passed.

*Cobaea scandens alba*

# COLEUS Flame Nettle

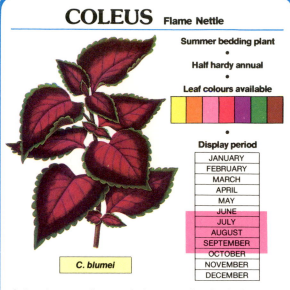

- Summer bedding plant
- Half hardy annual

**Leaf colours available**

**Display period**

| |
|---|
| JANUARY |
| FEBRUARY |
| MARCH |
| APRIL |
| MAY |
| JUNE |
| JULY |
| AUGUST |
| SEPTEMBER |
| OCTOBER |
| NOVEMBER |
| DECEMBER |

*C. blumei*

Coleus is generally regarded as a pot plant for the home or conservatory, but it also makes a fine bedding plant for containers, window boxes, beds and borders outdoors. It is grown for its decorative foliage and not for the insignificant blue flowers which should be removed when they appear. The Nettle-like leaves provide a kaleidoscope of colour from setting-out time until the frosts arrive, and the plants are useful in semi-shady situations where many flowering annuals would give disappointing results. Rooted cuttings flourish better than seed-sown plants — pinch out stem tips occasionally to induce bushiness.

**VARIETIES:** There are numerous varieties of **C. blumei**, but the usual plan is to buy a mixture when starting from seed. **'Rainbow Mix'** (12–15 in.) is the popular one — medium-sized leaves in a wide variety of colours which are blended, lined or spotted in all sorts of ways. **'Fashion Parade'** is shorter (8–12 in.) and leaf shape as well as colour are varied. The shortest varieties are the **'Milky Way'** (6 in.) and **'Wizard'** series. For long and narrow leaves choose **'Sabre'**. You can sometimes find single-colour varieties — the most popular ones are the bright red **'Volcano'** and **'Red Monarch'**. A must for hanging baskets — the pendant variety **'Scarlet Poncho'** with gold-edged red leaves.

**SITE & SOIL:** Any well-drained soil in sun or partial shade.

**PLANT DETAILS:** Height 6 in.–1½ ft. Spacing 6 in.–1 ft.

**PROPAGATION:** Take stem cuttings in spring or sow seed in February–March in gentle heat. Plant out in late May.

*Coleus blumei* 'Wizard Mixed'

# CONIFER

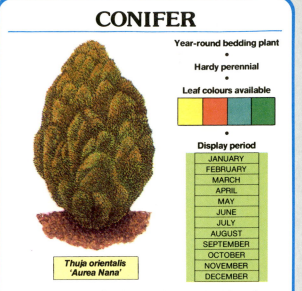

- Year-round bedding plant
- Hardy perennial

**Leaf colours available**

**Display period**

| |
|---|
| JANUARY |
| FEBRUARY |
| MARCH |
| APRIL |
| MAY |
| JUNE |
| JULY |
| AUGUST |
| SEPTEMBER |
| OCTOBER |
| NOVEMBER |
| DECEMBER |

*Thuja orientalis 'Aurea Nana'*

It is strange to find Conifers in a book on bedding plants, but the increased interest in both container growing and winter bedding has created a demand for Conifers to provide a temporary display. The usual procedure is to leave the tree in its pot so that the specimen can be easily lifted and moved to another part of the garden when the bed or container is needed for another scheme. The role of the Conifer is generally to serve as a dot plant — spreading, bushy or upright depending on the variety chosen. Pick a slow-growing type and water in dry weather as the root area is restricted. Replace the surface compost with fresh material each spring.

**VARIETIES:** Dwarf varieties are used — these are types which would grow to 5 ft or less after 10 years in open soil. Pick one of the following. **Abies balsamea 'Hudsonia'** (green, bushy), **Chamaecyparis lawsoniana 'Ellwoodii'** (grey-green or blue, upright), **C. lawsoniana 'Ellwood's Gold'** (yellow-tipped, upright), **C. lawsoniana 'Minima Aurea'** (yellow, oval), **C. pisifera 'Boulevard'** (silvery-blue, conical), **Juniperus communis 'Compressa'** (grey-green, columnar), **Picea pungens 'Koster'** (blue, conical), **Pinus mugo 'Gnom'** (dark green, globular), **Thuja occidentalis 'Rheingold'** (coppery, conical), **Thuja orientalis 'Aurea Nana'** or **Taxus baccata 'Elegantissima'** (yellow, bushy).

**SITE & SOIL:** Any reasonable soil in sun or partial shade.

**PLANT DETAILS:** Height 6 in.–4 ft. Spacing — use as a dot plant.

**PROPAGATION:** Can be raised from seed or cuttings, but it is usually much better to buy a pot-grown plant.

*Chamaecyparis lawsoniana* 'Ellwoodii'

# CONVOLVULUS Dwarf Morning Glory

**Summer bedding plant**
•
**Hardy annual**
•
**Colours available**

**Flowering period**

| |
|---|
| JANUARY |
| FEBRUARY |
| MARCH |
| APRIL |
| MAY |
| JUNE |
| JULY |
| AUGUST |
| SEPTEMBER |
| OCTOBER |
| NOVEMBER |
| DECEMBER |

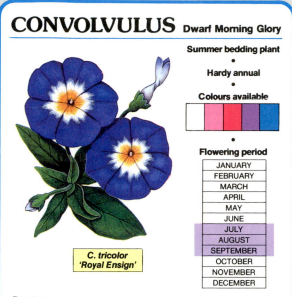

*C. tricolor 'Royal Ensign'*

Don't be put off by the name — this Convolvulus is not an invasive climber which gets everywhere. It is a bushy plant which forms a mound of freely-branching reddish stems, 9–12 in. in height and width. Throughout the summer months the showy flowers appear. Each one is a wide-mouthed trumpet, brightly coloured with a yellow or golden heart. Unfortunately the glory is short-lived — the flowers open in the morning and their life-span ends in the evening. A good choice for the rockery and front of the border, especially if the soil is sandy. Dead-head regularly.

**VARIETIES:** Several varieties of **C. tricolor** (**C. minor**) are available. The dark blues are the showiest — the one you are most likely to find is **'Royal Ensign'** which grows about 1 ft tall and is particularly eye-catching. Most suppliers, however, prefer to offer a mixture of colours and that means you will obtain pastel pinks and mauves as well as brilliant blues. For a window box or a tiny bed choose **'Dwarf Rainbow Flash'**. The plants reach about 6 in. but the flowers are full-sized. Convolvulus tricolor deserves to be more widely grown — the 'Convolvulus major' of the catalogues is Ipomoea purpurea (page 49).

**SITE & SOIL:** Any well-drained soil will do — it should not be too fertile. Thrives best in full sun.

**PLANT DETAILS:** Height 6 in.–1 ft. Spacing 9 in.

**PROPAGATION:** Sow seed in March in gentle heat. Soak the seeds for 24 hours before sowing in individual pots. Plant out in May whilst plants are still small.

*Convolvulus tricolor 'Dwarf Rainbow Flash'*

# COREOPSIS Tickweed

**Summer bedding plant**
•
**Hardy annual**
•
**Colours available**

**Flowering period**

| |
|---|
| JANUARY |
| FEBRUARY |
| MARCH |
| APRIL |
| MAY |
| JUNE |
| JULY |
| AUGUST |
| SEPTEMBER |
| OCTOBER |
| NOVEMBER |
| DECEMBER |

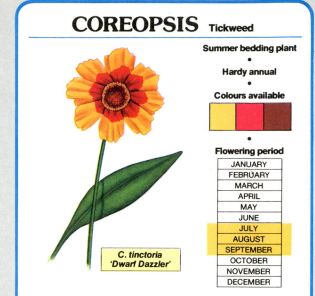

*C. tinctoria 'Dwarf Dazzler'*

A free-flowering plant bearing a profusion of large Marigold-like flowers on stiff stems. Tall (2–3 ft) varieties are available but the favourite ones are the dwarfs which grow no higher than 1 ft. These are useful selections for the front of the border or for growing in containers. They are good for cutting and will succeed in most situations, but Coreopsis does not like heavy clay and will produce few flowers in shady situations. Tall-growing types should be staked and faded blooms should be regularly removed. The colour range is limited — the flowers are yellow with red and brown in various combinations.

**VARIETIES:** The annual forms of Coreopsis are sometimes listed as Calliopsis in the catalogues. **C. tinctoria** (1–3 ft) has given rise to a number of garden varieties. In specialist catalogues you will find named types such as **'Dwarf Dazzler'** (1 ft, crimson flowers with broad golden edges). In most cases, however, catalogues list mixtures such as **'Dwarf Delight'** and **'Dwarf Mixed'**. **C. drummondii** has a popular variety **'Golden Crown'** (2 ft, golden flowers with deep red centres). For something different grow a dwarf variety of the perennial **C. grandiflora**. The best choice is **'Sunray'** — 1 ft plants bearing double golden flowers.

**SITE & SOIL:** Thrives best in sandy or medium soil. Choose a sunny spot.

**PLANT DETAILS:** Height 1–3 ft. Spacing 1 ft.

**PROPAGATION:** Sow seed in February-March in gentle heat. Plant out in May.

*Coreopsis tinctoria 'Dwarf Mixed'*

*Coreopsis grandiflora 'Sunray'*

# COSMOS Cosmea

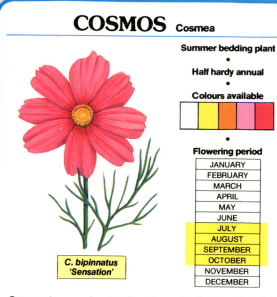

- Summer bedding plant
- Half hardy annual
- Colours available

| | | | | |
|---|---|---|---|---|

- Flowering period

| |
|---|
| JANUARY |
| FEBRUARY |
| MARCH |
| APRIL |
| MAY |
| JUNE |
| **JULY** |
| **AUGUST** |
| **SEPTEMBER** |
| **OCTOBER** |
| NOVEMBER |
| DECEMBER |

**C. bipinnatus 'Sensation'**

Cosmos is grown in mixed borders or beds where height is required — the slender stems of the most popular varieties reach 3 ft or more. The large blooms and delicate ferny foliage make it an excellent cut flower. Many people think of Cosmos as long-stemmed white and pink flowers which look like single Dahlias, but recent introductions offer interesting variations. All thrive in poor, light soils and will bloom until the frosts arrive if you occasionally dead-head faded blooms. Stake tall-growing varieties.

**VARIETIES:** Most garden Cosmeas are varieties or hybrids of **C. bipinnatus**. The usual choice is **'Sensation'** — 3 ft tall with 3 in. single flowers in white, pink and red. **'Purity'** is a white-flowered variety and **'Candy Stripe'** bears white flowers which are striped, spotted or blotched with red — different, but not really attractive. Worthwhile novelties include **'Daydream'** (3 ft) with pale pink petals around a deep pink centre and **'Sea Shells'** (3 ft) with petals which are rolled into tubes. The varieties of **C. sulphureus** have wider leaves and flowers in yellow, orange or red. **'Bright Lights'** (2 ft) is the popular mixture — others include **'Sunny Gold'** (1–1½ ft) and **'Sunny Red'**.

**SITE & SOIL:** Any well-drained garden soil, but sandy or medium land is preferred. Choose a sunny spot.

**PLANT DETAILS:** Height 1–3 ft. Spacing 1–1½ ft.

**PROPAGATION:** Sow seed in March–April in gentle heat. Plant out in late May.

Cosmos 'Sensation Mixed'

Cosmos 'Bright Lights'

# CUPHEA Cuphea, Cigar Plant

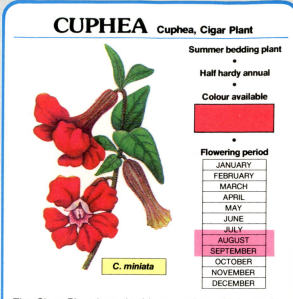

- Summer bedding plant
- Half hardy annual
- Colour available

| |
|---|

- Flowering period

| |
|---|
| JANUARY |
| FEBRUARY |
| MARCH |
| APRIL |
| MAY |
| JUNE |
| JULY |
| **AUGUST** |
| **SEPTEMBER** |
| OCTOBER |
| NOVEMBER |
| DECEMBER |

**C. miniata**

The Cigar Plant is a shrubby pot plant which can be planted outdoors during the summer months. It is a perennial which is treated as a half hardy annual for use in the garden. The flowers are narrow red tubes, colourful and interesting when seen close to, but rather insignificant when viewed from a distance. The place for this unusual bedder is in a window box, hanging basket, rockery or a small raised bed. Dead-head when the first flush of flowers has died down, and the plants can be lifted and taken indoors before the frosts arrive.

**VARIETIES:** There are two types. **C. miniata** (sometimes listed as **C. lanceolata**) **'Firefly'** is the favourite one for bedding. The 1½ in. long flowers are bright red — the bushy plants with their white-haired leaves are about 1 ft high. **C. ignea** (**C. platycentra**) is more often grown as a house plant than a garden one. It needs more protection from cold winds than C. miniata and the flowers are more unusual. The tip of each red tube bears white and dark purple 'ash' — with imagination, a tiny cigar and hence the common name Mexican Cigar Plant.

**SITE & SOIL:** Any well-drained and non-acid soil will do — thrives best in full sun but will grow in partial shade.

**PLANT DETAILS:** Height 1 ft. Spacing 1 ft.

**PROPAGATION:** Take cuttings in early spring. Alternatively sow seed in March–April — do not cover with compost. Plant out in late May or early June.

Cuphea miniata 'Firefly'

Cuphea ignea

# DAHLIA  Bedding Dahlia

**Summer bedding plant**

**Half hardy annual**

**Colours available**

**Flowering period**

| JANUARY |
| FEBRUARY |
| MARCH |
| APRIL |
| MAY |
| JUNE |
| JULY |
| AUGUST |
| SEPTEMBER |
| OCTOBER |
| NOVEMBER |
| DECEMBER |

**D. 'Dandy'**
Collarette group

**D. 'Piccolo'**
Single group

**D. 'Redskin'**
Semi-double group

The Border Dahlia is known to everyone — tall, half hardy perennials raised each year from tubers or cuttings. Blooms can be the size of plates and a wide range of flower types is available. The Bedding Dahlia is less imposing, reaching only 1–2 ft with flowers which rarely exceed 3 in. across. But it is also less trouble to grow as new plants are easily raised from seed and it requires little attention after planting out. Still, there are a few cultural requirements — dig in organic matter before planting out, put down Slug Pellets if holes appear in the leaves and dead-head regularly to prolong the flowering season. Bedding Dahlias, like their loftier cousins, are thirsty and hungry plants — water in dry weather and occasionally feed with a liquid fertilizer. Few bedding plants provide such a bright and long-lasting display. The autumn show is especially welcome at a time when many bedders have reached the end of their flowering life. Once the 1½–2 ft single varieties dominated the scene, but these days you are more likely to find one of the dwarf semi-double or double types. All make excellent cut flowers for indoor decoration.

**VARIETIES:** The old favourite is **'Coltness Mixture'**. The 1½ ft plants produce large single flowers in a wide variety of colours — some will be streaked or ringed with a second colour. **'Sunburst'** is a larger single variety (2 ft with 4 in. wide flowers) — **'Piccolo'** is a smaller one (1 ft with 2–3 in. wide flowers). The most popular dwarf is **'Rigoletto'** — a 1–1½ ft bushy plant which bears semi-double and double blooms. **'Figaro'** is more compact (1 ft) and is regarded as an improvement, but perhaps best of all is the only F$_1$ hybrid — **'Sunny'** (1 ft) with red, rose or yellow semi-double blooms. For something different you can grow a bronzy-leaved semi-double variety (**'Redskin'** — 1½ ft) or a quill-petalled type such as **'Quilled Satellite'** or **'Disco'**. Most eye-catching is **'Dandy'**, a 2 ft plant bearing 3 in. collarette flowers — large petals with an inner ring of small and narrow petals. This list does not cover the full range of Bedding Dahlias — there are old favourites such as **'Unwin's Dwarf Hybrids'** (1½ ft, semi-double and double flowers) and new ones such as the dwarf **'Amore'**. Apart from these 1–2 ft Bedding Dahlias you can grow 3–5 ft Dahlias from seed which will bloom in the first year. There are Pompom, Cactus and Decorative varieties, but they do not come true from seed.

**SITE & SOIL:** A well-drained fertile soil is needed — choose a sunny spot.

**PLANT DETAILS:** Height 1–2 ft. Spacing 1 ft.

**PROPAGATION:** Sow seed in February–March in gentle heat — prick out into individual pots. Plant out in late May. Tubers may be lifted and stored for planting out next year.

Dahlia 'Coltness Mixture'

Dahlia 'Rigoletto'

Dahlia 'Dandy'

# DATURA Datura

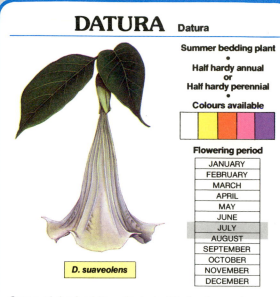

- Summer bedding plant
- Half hardy annual
  or
  Half hardy perennial
- Colours available

Flowering period

| |
|---|
| JANUARY |
| FEBRUARY |
| MARCH |
| APRIL |
| MAY |
| JUNE |
| JULY |
| AUGUST |
| SEPTEMBER |
| OCTOBER |
| NOVEMBER |
| DECEMBER |

**D. suaveolens**

Some of the bedding plants in this book can be seen during the summer months in every suburban street in the country, but you would have to search hard and long for this one. Still, it would be worth the search — pendulous, sweet-smelling trumpets which are 6 in. or more in length. There are problems — plants for bedding out are hard to locate and all parts are poisonous. There are two ways to grow the varieties listed below — raise from seed and bed out as a half hardy annual, or buy a plant in a pot and bring inside during the winter months for bedding out again next year.

**VARIETIES: D. suaveolens** (Angel's Trumpet) is the old favourite. Buy seed or a young plant and keep in a pot for bedding out each year. Flaring trumpets 6–8 in. long on shrubby plants reaching 5 ft or more — white is the usual colour, but nurseries now offer pink, orange and yellow. Seeds of **D. meteloides** and **D. metel** are available — plants grow about 3 ft high. **D. candida** (3–4 ft) can be bought as seed or as a potted shrub and when well-grown will produce white pendant flowers which can be 9 in. long. Much smaller is the new **D. hybrida 'La Fleur Lilac'** (1–1½ ft) which bears sweet-smelling 4 in. lilac trumpets in midsummer.

**SITE & SOIL:** Any well-drained garden soil will do. Choose a sheltered sunny spot.

**PLANT DETAILS:** Height 1–6 ft. Spacing — use as a dot plant.

**PROPAGATION:** Taking cuttings is difficult — buy as a pot-grown plant. Alternatively sow seed in February–March in gentle heat. Plant out when all danger of frost has passed.

Datura metel

# DIANTHUS Annual Pink, Indian Pink

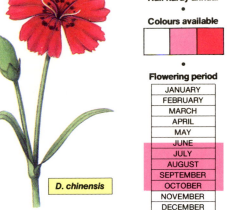

- Summer bedding plant
- Half hardy annual
- Colours available

Flowering period

| |
|---|
| JANUARY |
| FEBRUARY |
| MARCH |
| APRIL |
| MAY |
| JUNE |
| JULY |
| AUGUST |
| SEPTEMBER |
| OCTOBER |
| NOVEMBER |
| DECEMBER |

**D. chinensis**

Here we deal with Annual or Indian Pinks, grown each year from seed. Don't confuse them with Garden or Rockery Pinks (which are perennials) or Annual Carnations (which are taller plants with double flowers — see page 27). Annual Pinks are compact tufts of grassy leaves bearing upright stems with flowers which are usually single. These blooms have notched or 'pinked' petals and measure about 1½ in. across. The fragrance is slight and the colours are often bright and intricate. They need non-acid soil, regular watering in dry weather and dead-heading to prolong the flowering season.

**VARIETIES:** All Annual Pinks are varieties of **D. chinensis.** Flowering starts early and goes on until the first frosts arrive but some types bloom in distinct flushes. A number of older varieties such as **'Snowflake'** (white) and **'Double Mixed'** (various colours) are still offered. **'Baby Doll'** is a popular assortment of white, pink and crimson large-flowered Pinks. The F₁ hybrids have become firm favourites in recent years. **'Telstar'** (8 in.) is a free-flowering mixture noted for its bright colours. **'Magic Charms'** (6 in.) is more compact — the **'Princess'** strain (12 in.) is a tall-growing modern variety. **'Snowfire'** (8 in.) bears flowers which are white with a distinct red eye — **'Merry Go Round'** is a non F₁ hybrid version of this colour scheme.

**SITE & SOIL:** Any well-drained garden soil which is non-acid will do — choose a sunny spot.

**PLANT DETAILS:** Height 6 in.–1 ft. Spacing 6–9 in.

**PROPAGATION:** Sow seed in March in gentle heat. Plant out in late May.

Dianthus 'Magic Charms'

Dianthus 'Merry Go Round'

# DIGITALIS  Foxglove

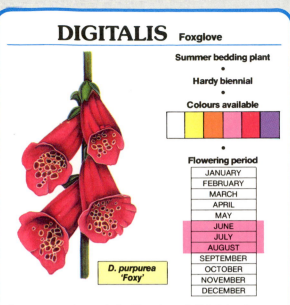

Summer bedding plant
•
Hardy biennial
•
Colours available
•
Flowering period

| | |
|---|---|
| JANUARY | |
| FEBRUARY | |
| MARCH | |
| APRIL | |
| MAY | |
| **JUNE** | |
| **JULY** | |
| **AUGUST** | |
| SEPTEMBER | |
| OCTOBER | |
| NOVEMBER | |
| DECEMBER | |

**D. purpurea 'Foxy'**

It may seem strange to find Foxgloves in this list — they are generally associated with the herbaceous or woodland garden and you will certainly not find them in the bedding plant trays on display at your garden centre in spring. But they do have a bedding plant role because there are very few plants which can add height to a damp and shady bed. Usually grown as biennials, there is one diminutive type ('Foxy') which can be treated as an annual. An easy plant to grow, but you must water copiously in dry weather. Remember that the plant and seeds are poisonous.

**VARIETIES:** The wild species **D. purpurea** is sometimes grown in gardens but it is more usual to choose a showy hybrid. The standard one is **'Excelsior'** — 5 ft plants with bell-like flowers densely packed all round the spikes. Colours are white, yellow, pink, red and purple — maroon mottling is clearly seen inside each bell. 'Excelsior' is a biennial for sowing outdoors in summer and transplanting in autumn for a June–August display. The bedding plant Foxglove is **'Foxy'** — 3 ft high with spotted white, cream, pink or red flowers. Follow the half hardy annual technique (see below) for July–August flowers.

**SITE & SOIL:** The soil should be lime-free and reasonably rich in humus. Thrives best in partial shade.

**PLANT DETAILS:** Height 3–5 ft. Spacing 1½–2 ft.

**PROPAGATION:** Sow 'Foxy' seed in February in gentle heat. Plant out in May.

*Digitalis 'Foxy'*

# DIMORPHOTHECA  Star of the Veldt

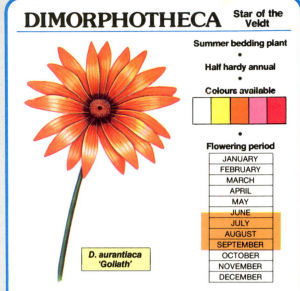

Summer bedding plant
•
Half hardy annual
•
Colours available
•
Flowering period

| | |
|---|---|
| JANUARY | |
| FEBRUARY | |
| MARCH | |
| APRIL | |
| MAY | |
| JUNE | |
| **JULY** | |
| **AUGUST** | |
| **SEPTEMBER** | |
| OCTOBER | |
| NOVEMBER | |
| DECEMBER | |

**D. aurantiaca 'Goliath'**

Hardly any bedding plant is more different to the Foxglove described in the adjoining column. Dimorphotheca forms flat sheets of bright open flowers, not tall spires of tubular bells. Furthermore it positively detests shade — the Daisy-like blooms refuse to open in a shady spot and will even close up on a dull day in summer. A fussy plant, then, but give it the right conditions in a rockery, window box or bed and there are few better ground covers — 2 in. scented flowers in bright colours which sparkle in the sunshine. If possible plant in large groups for maximum effect and be careful not to overfeed nor overwater. Dead-head to extend the flowering season.

**VARIETIES:** The garden varieties of Dimorphotheca are hybrids of **D. aurantiaca**. Around the dark central disc the petals may be white, cream, yellow, salmon, orange or pink. In most cases a multicoloured mixture such as **'Aurantiaca Hybrids'** is bought, but you can get single colours. The most popular one is undoubtedly **'Glistening White'** — glistening, silvery-white petals with a pale violet tinge. **'Tetra Polestar'** (15 in.) is taller and the white flowers have a prominent purple eye. **'Dwarf Salmon'** is a compact variety — for the largest flowers choose **'Goliath'** or **'Orange Glory'**.

**SITE & SOIL:** A well-drained sandy soil is necessary. A sunny location is essential.

**PLANT DETAILS:** Height 6–15 in. Spacing 1 ft.

**PROPAGATION:** Sow seed in March in gentle heat. Plant out in late May.

*Dimorphotheca 'Glistening White'*
*& Dimorphotheca 'Dwarf Salmon'*

# ECHIUM Annual Borage, Viper's Bugloss

**Summer bedding plant**

•

**Hardy annual**

•

**Colours available**

•

**Flowering period**

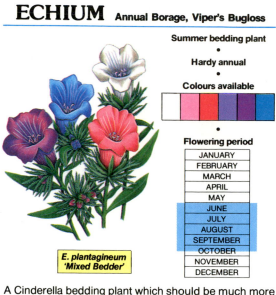

*E. plantagineum 'Mixed Bedder'*

| | |
|---|---|
| JANUARY | |
| FEBRUARY | |
| MARCH | |
| APRIL | |
| MAY | |
| JUNE | ■ |
| JULY | ■ |
| AUGUST | ■ |
| SEPTEMBER | ■ |
| OCTOBER | ■ |
| NOVEMBER | |
| DECEMBER | |

A Cinderella bedding plant which should be much more popular, especially in sandy areas. If your flower bed is in an open sunny situation and the soil drains freely then this unusual variety is well worth considering. It makes a welcome change from the usual range of low-growing annuals and the fragrant upturned bells are attractive to bees. The freely-branching stems bear hairy narrow leaves and throughout the summer the long-lasting blooms appear in large numbers. Staking is not needed — do not water unless the weather is very dry.

**VARIETIES:** Echium is a native plant found in coastal areas — tall (3 ft) with blue flowers. The garden varieties of **E. plantagineum** have been much improved in recent years. No longer are you restricted to the original blue — white, rose, red, mauve and purple are available. But the blue ones are perhaps the best, and **'Blue Bedder'** (9 in.–1 ft) is the one you will find in the catalogues — deep-coloured flowers from early summer to autumn. The only other seed you are likely to be offered is **'Mixed Bedder'** (9 in.–1 ft) — an assortment of white-, pink- and blue-flowered hybrids.

**SITE & SOIL:** Any well-drained garden soil will do, but light or medium land is preferred. Choose a sunny spot.

**PLANT DETAILS:** Height 9 in.–1 ft. Spacing 9 in.

**PROPAGATION:** The usual plan is to sow seed in August or April where they are to flower. For bedding, sow seed in March and prick out into individual pots. Plant out in May.

*Echium 'Blue Bedder'*

# ERICA Winter Heather

**Winter bedding plant**

•

**Hardy perennial**

•

**Colours available**

•

**Flowering period**

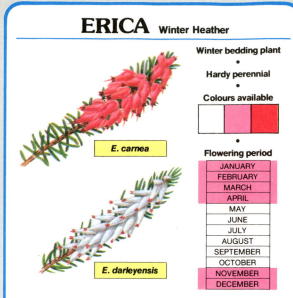

*E. carnea*

*E. darleyensis*

| | |
|---|---|
| JANUARY | ■ |
| FEBRUARY | ■ |
| MARCH | ■ |
| APRIL | ■ |
| MAY | |
| JUNE | |
| JULY | |
| AUGUST | |
| SEPTEMBER | |
| OCTOBER | |
| NOVEMBER | ■ |
| DECEMBER | ■ |

There are many more attractive plants than Heather for spring or summer bedding, but the Winter Heathers are extremely useful for providing colour between Christmas and Easter. Some bloom as early as November and others as late as April, but most varieties flower between January and March. Unlike many other Heathers and Heaths these winter ones do not demand lime-free soil or compost — any ordinary growing medium is suitable and hard water will not harm them when watering. Use varieties of E. carnea for ground cover or small containers — the larger E. darleyensis is usually used as a dot plant.

**VARIETIES:** E. carnea (6–10 in.) is by far the most popular Winter Heather and many varieties are available — buy as seedlings or plants in pots. Look for **'Aurea'** (gold foliage, pink flowers), **'Eileen Porter'** (dwarf, red flowers, long blooming period), **'James Backhouse'** (large pink flowers, late), **'Winter Beauty'** (pink flowers, early), **'Springwood White'** (bright green foliage, white flowers) and **'December Red'** (red flowers, early). The urn-shaped flowers hang in large numbers from the upright needle-clothed stems. **E. darleyensis** has the same growth habit but it is a much larger plant, reaching 2 ft. The most popular variety is **'Darley Dale'** (pink flowers).

**SITE & SOIL:** Well-drained soil is necessary — full sun is preferred. Add peat at planting time.

**PLANT DETAILS:** Height 6–10 in. or 1½–2 ft. Spacing 9 in. or 1 ft.

**PROPAGATION:** Layer shoots or plant 1–2 in. stem cuttings in a cold frame in summer.

*Erica carnea 'Springwood White'*

*Erica darleyensis 'Darley Dale'*

# ESCHSCHOLZIA Californian Poppy

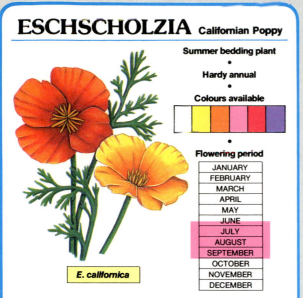

- Summer bedding plant
- Hardy annual
- Colours available
- Flowering period

| | |
|---|---|
| JANUARY | |
| FEBRUARY | |
| MARCH | |
| APRIL | |
| MAY | |
| JUNE | |
| **JULY** | |
| **AUGUST** | |
| **SEPTEMBER** | |
| OCTOBER | |
| NOVEMBER | |
| DECEMBER | |

*E. californica*

Few garden plants are easier to raise than Californian Poppies — a sprinkling of seed over bare ground in autumn or spring produces a drift of silky-petalled flowers from June to September. The much-branched stems bear blue-grey deeply-cut leaves and the flowers flutter in the breeze. For bedding out, the seeds are sown in spring and transplanted whilst the seedlings are still small. The quality of the display depends on the soil and situation — flowers will be sparse and disappointing if the soil is heavy and rich and the site is shaded. Dead-head regularly. After flowering the plants produce self-sown seedlings.

**VARIETIES:** The deep yellow flowers of **E. californica** cover large areas of the 'Golden West' (hence the name) of America. There are now garden hybrids in many colours and a rainbow mixture is the usual selection. Look for **'Single Mixed'**, **'Monarch Art Shades'** (frilled petals, semi-double) and **'Ballerina'** (frilled or fluted petals, semi-double or double). All are about 1 ft high — so are the single-colour varieties **'Cherry Ripe'** (cerise), **'Orange King'** (orange) and **'Milky White'** (white). Much less commonly seen is the dwarf **E. caespitosa 'Sundew'** (6 in.). Above the small mounds of ferny foliage are scented yellow flowers. **'Miniature Primrose'** is similar with a tufted growth habit and 2 in. wide blooms.

**SITE & SOIL:** A well-drained soil in full sun is necessary.

**PLANT DETAILS:** Height 6 in.–1 ft. Spacing 6 in.

**PROPAGATION:** Dislikes transplanting. For bedding, sow seed in March-April under glass and prick out into individual pots. Plant out in May.

Eschscholzia 'Monarch Art Shades'

Eschscholzia 'Cherry Ripe'

# EUCALYPTUS Blue Gum

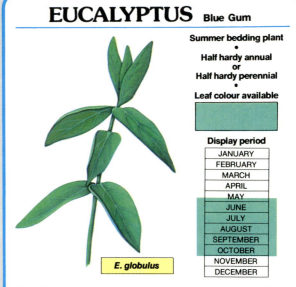

- Summer bedding plant
- Half hardy annual or Half hardy perennial
- Leaf colour available
- Display period

| | |
|---|---|
| JANUARY | |
| FEBRUARY | |
| MARCH | |
| APRIL | |
| MAY | |
| **JUNE** | |
| **JULY** | |
| **AUGUST** | |
| **SEPTEMBER** | |
| **OCTOBER** | |
| NOVEMBER | |
| DECEMBER | |

*E. globulus*

The Eucalyptus trees of Australasia grow into imposing specimens in their native habitat, but few are hardy in our climate. The common features include leaves which are aromatic when crushed and which change shape as the plant ages — the silvery juvenile foliage is the reason for growing Eucalyptus, so young specimens are the plants chosen for display. The hardy species grown as a garden tree is E. glaucescens — the one used as a pot plant is E. globulus. This Eucalyptus is rather too vigorous for growing in the living room but it does make an unusual dot plant in a summer bedding scheme.

**VARIETIES:** You will find seeds of **E. globulus** listed in some catalogues and you may also find pot-grown specimens in your local garden centre. The pale blue leaves are attractive, and the plants grow rapidly to produce a robust shrub which will survive until the first frosts arrive. It is hardy in favoured southern localities, but the usual procedure is to discard the plants in autumn. However, you can keep the specimen in its 5 in. pot when bedding out and then move the pot indoors during the winter months.

**SITE & SOIL:** Any reasonable garden soil in sun or partial shade.

**PLANT DETAILS:** Height 3–5 ft. Spacing — use as a dot plant.

**PROPAGATION:** Sow seed in March in gentle heat. Prick out into individual containers and eventually into 5 in. pots. Place a stake in the pot and retain this stake when planting out in May.

Eucalyptus globulus

# EUPHORBIA Snow on the Mountain

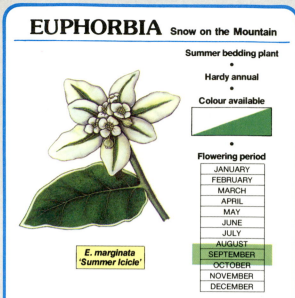

- Summer bedding plant
- Hardy annual
- Colour available

**Flowering period**

| | |
|---|---|
| JANUARY | |
| FEBRUARY | |
| MARCH | |
| APRIL | |
| MAY | |
| JUNE | |
| JULY | |
| AUGUST | |
| **SEPTEMBER** | |
| OCTOBER | |
| NOVEMBER | |
| DECEMBER | |

E. marginata 'Summer Icicle'

The Euphorbias or Spurges are a vast genus of plants, but only one is grown as a bedding plant. It is often recommended for the centre of the bed and is instantly recognisable. The fleshy green leaves of Snow on the Mountain have a white edge and the tiny flowers are surrounded by a ring of white, papery bracts. It is extremely easy to grow and is an excellent way of covering a patch of impoverished sandy soil where little else would thrive. It is often recommended as a cut flower, but remember that the white sap is extremely irritating to the skin and eyes. Dip cut ends in boiling water before placing in an arrangement and wear gloves when weeding self-sown plants.

**VARIETIES: E. marginata** (2 ft) is the species offered in the seed catalogues — the smaller variety **'Summer Icicle'** (1½ ft) is hard to find. The plants are bushy and upright, but you may have to provide support using twigs or pea sticks. The white flowers appear late in the season and are insignificant, but the variegated oval leaves and the large, white, petal-like bracts are an eye-catching foil for nearby reds and blues. Not popular in the U.K, but it is used in the U.S as a weed-controlling ground cover.

**SITE & SOIL:** Any well-drained garden soil will do — thrives best in infertile light land. Grow in sun or partial shade.

**PLANT DETAILS:** Height 1½–2 ft. Spacing 1 ft.

**PROPAGATION:** Sow seed in March in gentle heat. Plant out in late May.

Euphorbia marginata
'Summer Icicle'

# FELICIA Kingfisher Daisy

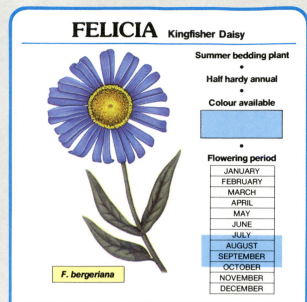

- Summer bedding plant
- Half hardy annual
- Colour available

**Flowering period**

| | |
|---|---|
| JANUARY | |
| FEBRUARY | |
| MARCH | |
| APRIL | |
| MAY | |
| JUNE | |
| JULY | |
| **AUGUST** | |
| **SEPTEMBER** | |
| OCTOBER | |
| NOVEMBER | |
| DECEMBER | |

F. bergeriana

A rarity, despite the beautiful kingfisher blue of its golden-centred Daisy-like flowers. It isn't particularly delicate but these South African plants do need full sun and well-drained soil. The dwarf Felicia bergeriana succeeds in windy and exposed situations, and when grown in sandy soil the flowers almost cover the foliage when the sun is shining. Unfortunately, as with other South African Daisies, the petals close up in dull weather. There are two species which can be used as bedding plants — seed is available for both from specialist nurseries and you will find F. bergeriana listed in some of the larger popular catalogues.

**VARIETIES: F. amelloides** is the taller species — it is more usually grown as a conservatory plant than an outdoor one and can grow 2 ft high if left unchecked. To avoid a straggly appearance the shoot tips should be removed from young plants. The flowers are about 1½ in. across and the leaves are bright green. Take cuttings in autumn and grow on as a house plant which will bloom during winter and early spring. **F. bergeriana** is a better bedding plant than its tall relative — the low-growing (4–6 in.) clumps of grey-green foliage are wide-spreading and bear ½ in. brilliant blue-turquoise flowers for several months. A good choice for rockery, window box or hanging basket. Dead-head regularly and water in dry weather.

**SITE & SOIL:** A well-drained site and full sun are essential.

**PLANT DETAILS:** Height 6 in. or 1½ ft. Spacing 9 in.

**PROPAGATION:** Sow seed in March in gentle heat. Plant out in late May.

Felicia amelloides
'Variegata'

Felicia bergeriana

# FUCHSIA Fuchsia

Summer bedding plant
·
Half hardy perennial
or
Hardy perennial
·
**Colours available**

·

**Flowering period**

| | |
|---|---|
| JANUARY | |
| FEBRUARY | |
| MARCH | |
| APRIL | |
| MAY | |
| JUNE | |
| **JULY** | |
| **AUGUST** | |
| **SEPTEMBER** | |
| OCTOBER | |
| NOVEMBER | |
| DECEMBER | |

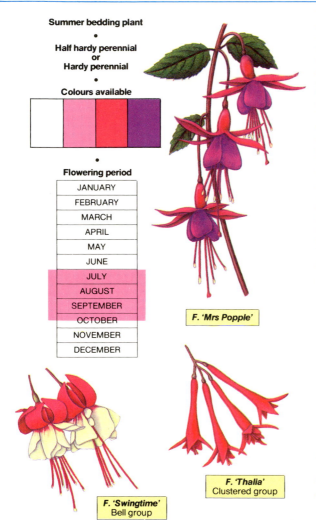

*F. 'Mrs Popple'*

*F. 'Thalia'*
Clustered group

*F. 'Swingtime'*
Bell group

The Fuchsia flower is a thing of beauty. The 4 swept-back sepals with the group of petals below give a bell-like effect — single varieties have 4 petals and the doubles have many more. Not all Fuchsias have this *Bell* pattern — the *Clustered* Fuchsias are long and tubular. There are many sorts of Fuchsia, ranging from tall shrubs to delicate greenhouse types — the varieties described here are the bedding ones which bear colourful flowers all summer long but which are usually (but not always) killed by frost. The ordinary Bush Fuchsia grows about 1–2 ft high and is quite easy to care for, but you must water in dry weather and occasional feeding is beneficial. To induce bushiness, pinch out the tips after 3 sets of leaves have been formed. A Standard Fuchsia makes an excellent dot plant when set out in June and then lifted for moving indoors in October — grow one by choosing a vigorous Bush variety and removing side shoots (but not leaves) from the leading shoot. Tie to a cane and remove the tip when the desired height has been reached and allow 5 or 6 strong shoots to develop to form the head of the standard. Remove leaves from the main stem. The final group is the Basket Fuchsia. There are a number of varieties — choose one of these trailers for a hanging basket.

**VARIETIES:** There are scores of **F. hybrida** varieties bearing large and colourful flowers. Bush Fuchsias with bell-like flowers include **'Avocet'** (red sepals, white petals), **'Alice Hoffman'** (red sepals, white petals), **'Bon Accord'** (white sepals, lilac petals), **'Royal Velvet'** (red sepals, purple petals), **'Ting-a-ling'** (red sepals and petals), **'Mission Bells'** (red sepals, purple petals), **'Mrs Popple'** (red sepals, purple petals), **'Rufus the Red'** (red sepals and petals) and **'Charming'** (deep pink sepals and petals) — there are many more. A few have colourful foliage — look for **'Golden Treasure'** (green and gold leaves) and **'Sunray'** (yellow, pink and green leaves). For a Clustered Fuchsia look for **F. triphylla** or its variety **'Thalia'**. Basket or Trailing Fuchsias include **'Cascade'** (white sepals, red petals), **'Marinka'** (red sepals, purple petals), **'Pink Galore'** (pink sepals, pale pink petals), **'Swingtime'** (red sepals, white petals) and **'Summer Snow'** (white sepals and petals). **'Tom West'** is the one with variegated foliage.

**SITE & SOIL:** Any well-drained garden soil will do — thrives in sun or light shade.

**PLANT DETAILS:** Height 1–2 ft. Spacing 1½ ft.

**PROPAGATION:** Seed mixtures are available but it is more usual to take softwood cuttings in spring or summer. Buy new plants in pots or as small seedlings for potting on before planting out in late May.

*Fuchsia 'Avocet'*

*Fuchsia 'Sunray'*

*Fuchsia 'Pink Galore'*

# GAILLARDIA Blanket Flower

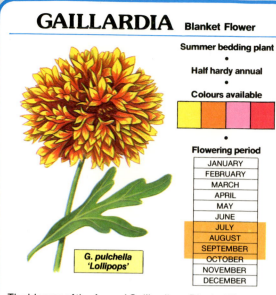

**Summer bedding plant**

•

**Half hardy annual**

•

**Colours available**

•

**Flowering period**

| | |
|---|---|
| JANUARY | |
| FEBRUARY | |
| MARCH | |
| APRIL | |
| MAY | |
| JUNE | |
| JULY | |
| AUGUST | |
| SEPTEMBER | |
| OCTOBER | |
| NOVEMBER | |
| DECEMBER | |

*G. pulchella*
*'Lollipops'*

The blooms of the Annual Gaillardia or Blanket Flower are large (3–5 in.) and the flowering period lasts from early July until the onset of the first frosts. It is excellent for cutting, but with all these virtues it still remains a bedding plant which is not often grown. Two problems are that the basic red and yellow blending or zoning is found in a number of other annuals and the growth habit is distinctly untidy. The introduction of the double Gaillardias should increase the popularity of this plant — you can buy 1 ft dwarfs and the ball-like flowers are extremely showy. Dead-head regularly and support tall varieties with a few twigs.

**VARIETIES:** **G. aristata** and **G. pulchella** bear a profusion of yellow, orange or red flowers. **'Torchlight'** (2½ ft) has very large yellow-edged red flowers — **'Blood-red Giants'** is deep red. **'Goblin'** (15 in.) is the dwarf of the group. Most Gaillardias are dark-centred singles or semi-doubles — choose instead the double-flowered **G. pulchella lorenziana** which produces colourful globular blooms made up of quilled petals. **'Gaiety'** is typical — 2 ft tall, with flowers in yellow, pink and red. **'Lollipops'** (cream, yellow and red) is a 1 ft dwarf variety with branching stems and grey-green leaves.

**SITE & SOIL:** Any well-drained garden soil will do — thrives in sun or light shade.

**PLANT DETAILS:** Height 1–2½ ft. Spacing 9 in.–1½ ft.

**PROPAGATION:** Sow seed in March in gentle heat. Plant out in late May.

Gaillardia 'Goblin'

# GAZANIA Gazania, Treasure Flower

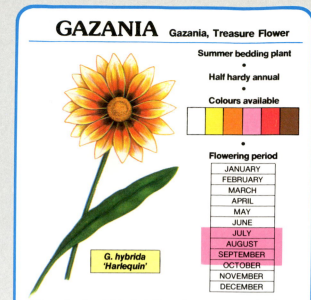

**Summer bedding plant**

•

**Half hardy annual**

•

**Colours available**

•

**Flowering period**

| | |
|---|---|
| JANUARY | |
| FEBRUARY | |
| MARCH | |
| APRIL | |
| MAY | |
| JUNE | |
| JULY | |
| AUGUST | |
| SEPTEMBER | |
| OCTOBER | |
| NOVEMBER | |
| DECEMBER | |

*G. hybrida*
*'Harlequin'*

It is understandable that Gazanias are appearing in an increasing number of gardens every year. The splash of colour on a sunny summer day is almost unrivalled in the world of annuals. Each large Daisy-like flower bears petals which arch backwards to reveal the central dark-coloured ring around the disc. The wide range of flower colours comes in all sorts of combinations — blends, stripes, contrasting zones etc. This is a plant for the edge of a sunny bed or rockery. It tolerates drought, salt-laden air and wind but it dislikes heavy soil and the flowers close up in dull weather and in the evening.

**VARIETIES:** The forms of **G. hybrida** offered are generally multi-coloured mixtures — all produce rosettes of attractive leaves which add to the display. **'Carnival'** has silvery-green leaves and the 1 ft plants bear bright medium-sized flowers. The largest blooms are borne by **'Sundance'** (1 ft) — these flowers are 4–5 in. across on well-grown plants. **'Mini-star'** (8–9 in.) can be bought as single colours (yellow, white etc) but it is more usual to buy a mixture. **'Harlequin'** (15 in.) is the tallest Gazania in the popular seed catalogues, and the new favourite is **'Chansonette'**. This free-flowering hybrid is compact (8–9 in.) — the green leaves have a silvery underside and the flowers are in many colours.

**SITE & SOIL:** Well-drained soil and a location in full sun are essential.

**PLANT DETAILS:** Height 8–15 in. Spacing 1 ft.

**PROPAGATION:** Sow seed in March in gentle heat. Plant out in late May.

Gazania hybrida
'Sundance'

Gazania hybrida
'Chansonette'

# GODETIA Godetia

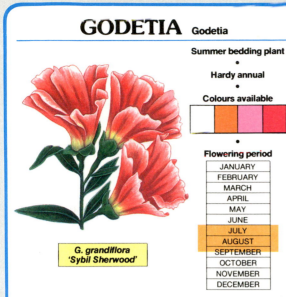

Summer bedding plant
•
Hardy annual
•
Colours available

Flowering period

| | |
|---|---|
| JANUARY | |
| FEBRUARY | |
| MARCH | |
| APRIL | |
| MAY | |
| JUNE | |
| **JULY** | |
| **AUGUST** | |
| SEPTEMBER | |
| OCTOBER | |
| NOVEMBER | |
| DECEMBER | |

*G. grandiflora 'Sybil Sherwood'*

A much-loved and easy-to-grow annual which can be raised by sprinkling seed over the ground in September or April and either thinning or transplanting in May. The large flowers (2–4 in. across) have fluted, papery petals and are borne freely for many weeks. Dwarf, intermediate and tall varieties are available — the tall ones require staking and all Godetias need watering when the weather is dry. Take care not to overfeed. These plants bear their blooms on top of upright leafy spikes — Clarkias (page 30) have quite a different flowering habit but the two are in fact very closely related and need similar conditions.

**VARIETIES:** The garden varieties are hybrids of **G. grandiflora**, a native of California. Buy **'Tall Double Mixed'** (2 ft) for the middle of the border — a mixture of white, pinks, oranges and reds. In the intermediate range there are a number of shorter and bushier varieties — **'Sybil Sherwood'** (salmon, edged white), **'Salmon Princess'** (salmon, cream centred) and **'Crimson Glow'** — all grow about 15 in. high. The showiest plants are **'Azalea-flowered Mixed'** (15 in.) which produce double and semi-double frilly flowers. For the front of the bed or border choose the single **'Dwarf Mixed'** (9 in.–1 ft) — a riot of colours in stripes, blends and picotees.

**SITE & SOIL:** Thrives best in light or medium soil which is slightly acid. Choose a sunny spot, although it will succeed in light shade.

**PLANT DETAILS:** Height 9 in.–2 ft. Spacing 9 in.–1 ft.

**PROPAGATION:** Sow seed in March under glass. Prick out into individual pots and plant out in mid May.

*Godetia 'Dwarf Mixed'*

# GRASSES Ornamental Grasses

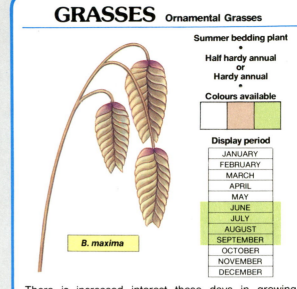

Summer bedding plant
•
Half hardy annual
or
Hardy annual
•
Colours available

Display period

| | |
|---|---|
| JANUARY | |
| FEBRUARY | |
| MARCH | |
| APRIL | |
| MAY | |
| **JUNE** | |
| **JULY** | |
| **AUGUST** | |
| **SEPTEMBER** | |
| OCTOBER | |
| NOVEMBER | |
| DECEMBER | |

*B. maxima*

There is increased interest these days in growing Ornamental Grasses and you will find an Ornamental Grass Mixture in many catalogues. They certainly provide an unusual feature for the informal bed or border and when dried make a useful addition to winter flower arrangements. Ornamental Grasses are raised from seed sown outdoors in spring where they are to grow or are sown in a nursery bed to be transplanted at the seedling stage. They are all grown for their decorative seed heads — always interesting but never colourful nor showy. Love them or hate them, they do provide a 'natural' look in the right situation. A word of warning — ripe seed falling on to the ground can give you a fine crop for years to come.

**VARIETIES:** Separate types can be bought from large or specialist seed companies. **Briza maxima** (1½ ft) or Quaking Grass is the most popular — the 1 in. lantern-like papery heads shake in the breeze. **Lagurus ovatus** or Hare's Tail Grass is more eye-catching — the 1½ ft stems are tipped by erect and furry 'rabbit tails'. **Agrostis nebulosa** (Cloud Grass) is quite different — cloud-like sprays of tiny, white seed heads on 1 ft stalks. **Coix lacryma-jobi** (Job's Tears) is a half hardy annual and much taller (3 ft) — pearl-like seeds hang from the reed-like stems.

**SITE & SOIL:** Any well-drained garden soil will do — thrives best in full sun.

**PLANT DETAILS:** Height 1–3 ft. Spacing 1–2 ft.

**PROPAGATION:** Sow hardy seed outdoors in March-May. Sow half hardy seed in March in gentle heat. Plant out in late May.

*Lagurus ovatus*

# GREVILLEA Silk Oak

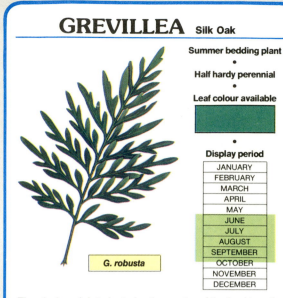

**Summer bedding plant**

•

**Half hardy perennial**

•

**Leaf colour available**

•

**Display period**

| | |
|---|---|
| JANUARY | |
| FEBRUARY | |
| MARCH | |
| APRIL | |
| MAY | |
| JUNE | |
| JULY | |
| AUGUST | |
| SEPTEMBER | |
| OCTOBER | |
| NOVEMBER | |
| DECEMBER | |

*G. robusta*

The choice of dot plants for the centre of the bed is rather limited — there are the classic flowering ones such as standard Fuchsias and Cannas but for a feathery effect the automatic selection is Kochia. There is, however, an alternative. Grevillea is raised quite easily from seed and it is not difficult to find a supplier. Alternatively you can buy a pot-grown specimen from your garden centre, but do make sure it is properly hardened off before bedding out in late May. The plant is hardy in only a few favoured areas — bring it indoors as a pot plant in winter and bed out again next year.

**VARIETIES: G. robusta** is the only species grown. Growth is tree-like and the foliage is graceful and ferny. The underside of the leaves is distinctly silky — hence the common name. In the first year the seedlings grow about 1–1½ ft tall — in 2 or 3 years you will have a lacy tree about 3 ft high — the peak display form for a dot plant for a large bed. After this stage the foliage starts to become coarse and so it is usual to cut back or discard the plant. A very unusual choice for a bedding plant — but a good one if you like to grow plants which are different.

**SITE & SOIL:** Any reasonable garden soil in sun or partial shade. Stake if necessary.

**PLANT DETAILS:** Height 2–3 ft. Spacing — use as a dot plant.

**PROPAGATION:** Sow seed in February–April in gentle heat. Prick out into 5 in. pots and plant out in late May.

*Grevillea robusta*

# GYPSOPHILA Baby's Breath

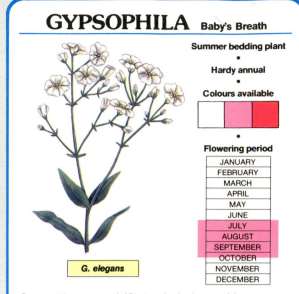

**Summer bedding plant**

•

**Hardy annual**

•

**Colours available**

•

**Flowering period**

| | |
|---|---|
| JANUARY | |
| FEBRUARY | |
| MARCH | |
| APRIL | |
| MAY | |
| JUNE | |
| JULY | |
| AUGUST | |
| SEPTEMBER | |
| OCTOBER | |
| NOVEMBER | |
| DECEMBER | |

*G. elegans*

Contrast is an essential feature in design, and these sprays of tiny flowers above fine grey-green foliage are used to provide contrast in both flower arrangements and in floral beds outdoors. The traditional partners are Sweet Peas indoors and brightly-coloured, large-flowered bedders outdoors. Gypsophila has its critics — the flowering period is usually quite short (despite the seed packet notes) and so successional planting is necessary to provide a July–October display. It also can look sparse if the blooms are not plentiful. Still, nobody can criticise it in a natural-looking setting such as a rockery or growing amongst the cracks in a stone wall. Do not overwater or overfeed.

**VARIETIES:** Do not confuse this plant with the herbaceous border perennial G. paniculata or the rockery perennial G. repens. Only one species of Annual Gypsophila is grown — **G. elegans**. White is the most popular colour and the best-known strain is **'Covent Garden'** (18 in.). **'Monarch'** is a rather shorter white variety and you can buy a seed mixture which produces white, pink and red flowers. You will have to search the catalogues for named coloured varieties — there are **'Shell Pink'** (15 in.) and **'Red Cloud'**. All Gypsophilas have thin stems and staking is sometimes advised, but canes look distinctly unsightly.

**SITE & SOIL:** Any well-drained, non-acid soil will do — choose a sunny spot.

**PLANT DETAILS:** Height 1–1½ ft. Spacing 1 ft.

**PROPAGATION:** Sow seed outdoors in September or April, or sow in February–March under glass. Plant out in May.

*Gypsophila elegans*
*'Covent Garden'*

# HEDERA Ivy

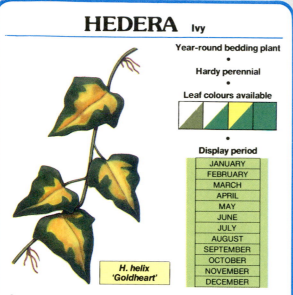

- Year-round bedding plant
- Hardy perennial

**Leaf colours available**

**Display period**

| |
|---|
| JANUARY |
| FEBRUARY |
| MARCH |
| APRIL |
| MAY |
| JUNE |
| JULY |
| AUGUST |
| SEPTEMBER |
| OCTOBER |
| NOVEMBER |
| DECEMBER |

*H. helix 'Goldheart'*

Once it would have been unthinkable to find Ivy listed as a bedding plant — its place was in a pot on the piano or clambering up fences or old trees as a perennial climber. It has been the rapid increase in container growing which has changed the picture. Decorative-leaved varieties can be bought cheaply from plant suppliers everywhere, and propagation of stem cuttings couldn't be easier. Ivy is an excellent edging plant for a container, window box or hanging basket. At the end of the season plants can be discarded or moved elsewhere, either indoors or out. Of course, Ivy has many rivals as a summer bedding plant, but as a trailing winter bedder it has few competitors.

**VARIETIES:** **H. helix** is the native Common Ivy with 3- or 5-lobed leaves. There are now many varieties available which offer added features and are better suited to garden use. The difference may be leaf shape — **'Ivalace'** is crinkled and **'Needlepoint'** has long and narrow leaves. It is better, however, to look for variegation rather than merely a different leaf shape. **'Glacier'** and **'Kholibra'** have white blotches and a white edge — **'Goldheart'** has a bright yellow centre. Choose **H. canariensis 'Gloire de Marengo'** for large leaves with creamy edges and red stems.

**SITE & SOIL:** Any reasonable garden soil in sun or partial shade.

**PLANT DETAILS:** Height 1–12 ft. Spacing 1–2 ft.

**PROPAGATION:** Stem cuttings at any time of the year.

*Hedera helix 'Glacier'*

*Hedera canariensis 'Gloire de Marengo'*

# HELIANTHUS Sunflower

*H. annuus*

- Summer bedding plant
- Hardy annual

**Colours available**

**Flowering period**

| |
|---|
| JANUARY |
| FEBRUARY |
| MARCH |
| APRIL |
| MAY |
| JUNE |
| JULY |
| AUGUST |
| SEPTEMBER |
| OCTOBER |
| NOVEMBER |
| DECEMBER |

*H. annuus 'Autumn Beauty'*

Giant Sunflowers have been loved by generations of children over the years and they are sometimes recommended for screening, but only Jack of the beanstalk fame could regard the coarse growth as attractive. For general display it is better to choose one of the more compact varieties which are usually more colourful and have flowers at a level where they can be seen at close quarters. Seeds may be sown 1 in. deep in April where they are to flower, but for earlier blooms it is necessary to raise seedlings under glass — see below. Despite the entry of the new varieties it is the mammoths which will remain popular as long as children and competitions exist — water weekly with a liquid fertilizer and stake firmly.

**VARIETIES:** The Annual Sunflowers are varieties of **H. annuus** and you should always check the height in the catalogue or on the packet before you buy. The 6–10 ft giants bear various names, such as **'Russian Giant'**, **'Tall Single'**, **'Giant Yellow'** and **'Giant Single'**. Flowers may be 1 ft across — leave over the winter to provide home-grown bird seed. **'Autumn Beauty'** (5 ft) is a fine medium-sized variety in yellow, orange or red — **'Velvet Queen'** is deep red with a black centre. Even shorter are **'Sunburst'** and **'Summer Sunshine'** but the baby is **'Teddy Bear'** (2 ft). Small, but the furry, double flowers measure 6 in. across.

**SITE & SOIL:** Any reasonable garden soil in a sunny position.

**PLANT DETAILS:** Height 2–10 ft. Spacing 1–3 ft.

**PROPAGATION:** Sow seed in March–April in gentle heat. Plant out in May.

*Helianthus annuus 'Sunburst'*

*Helianthus annuus 'Teddy Bear'*

# HELICHRYSUM Straw Flower

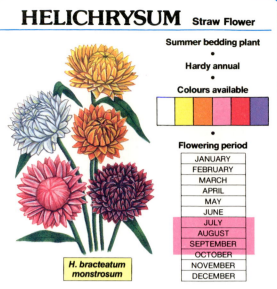

- Summer bedding plant
- Hardy annual
- Colours available

**Flowering period**

| | |
|---|---|
| JANUARY | |
| FEBRUARY | |
| MARCH | |
| APRIL | |
| MAY | |
| JUNE | |
| JULY | |
| AUGUST | |
| SEPTEMBER | |
| OCTOBER | |
| NOVEMBER | |
| DECEMBER | |

*H. bracteatum monstrosum*

The flowers have a distinct Double Daisy look, but there is an important difference. True petals are found only at the centre of each flower — the colourful display comes from the surrounding petal-like bracts. These bracts are crisp and strawy — Helichrysum is an 'Everlasting' flower. The stems are cut just before the blooms are fully open, the stalks are tied in bunches and then hung upside down in a cool dark place. When fully dry the flowers are removed and attached to florist wire.

**VARIETIES:** Until quite recently the only type which was commonly grown was **H. bracteatum monstrosum**. The flowers are 2–3 in. across and each 3 ft plant bears about 25 blooms. Mixtures are available as **'Tall Mixed'**, **'Double Mixed'** etc or you can buy single colours — **'Terracotta'**, **'White'**, **'Rose'** and so on. Unfortunately these tall plants are gaunt and unattractive, and the traditional place for Helichrysum was an out-of-sight spot for Everlasting flower production. The introduction of the dwarf (1 ft) and bushy **'Bright Bikini'** mixture means that it can now be used as an attractive bed or border plant. The star of this mixture is the glistening scarlet and gold **'Hot Bikini'**. A non-flowering but popular Helichrysum is **H. petiolatum** — an edging plant with grey-felted leaves.

**SITE & SOIL:** Any well-drained garden soil will do — thrives best in full sun.

**PLANT DETAILS:** Height 1 or 3 ft. Spacing 1 ft.

**PROPAGATION:** Sow seed in March in gentle heat. Plant out in May.

*Helichrysum 'Hot Bikini'*

*Helichrysum petiolatum*

# HELIOTROPIUM Heliotrope

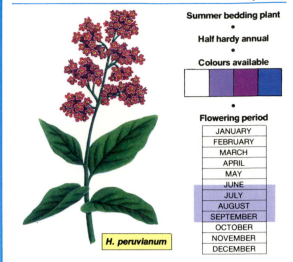

- Summer bedding plant
- Half hardy annual
- Colours available

**Flowering period**

| | |
|---|---|
| JANUARY | |
| FEBRUARY | |
| MARCH | |
| APRIL | |
| MAY | |
| JUNE | |
| JULY | |
| AUGUST | |
| SEPTEMBER | |
| OCTOBER | |
| NOVEMBER | |
| DECEMBER | |

*H. peruvianum*

A hundred years ago you would have found Heliotrope or Cherry Pie in countless gardens, but not now. It lives on in park bedding schemes but as a home bedding plant it has slipped out of the top twenty. It is a perennial shrub which is grown as a half hardy annual, and the range of varieties is strictly limited these days. Each individual flower is very small, but they are massed in large heads. Standards were once popular as centrepieces for formal beds and it has long been used as a cut flower. Now there is an additional role — to provide fragrance to tubs and other containers. Few bedding plants have Heliotrope's reputation for evening fragrance, even though some of the scent seems to have been lost over the years.

**VARIETIES:** Hybrids of **H. peruvianum** are available in several colours — **'White Lady'** (white), **'Lord Roberts'** (dark blue), **'Vilmorin's Variety'** (purple) etc. But these are bought as pot-grown plants raised from cuttings — only **'Marine'** (1½ ft, violet-purple, dark green wrinkled foliage) is listed in the seed catalogues. Flower clusters may reach 6 in. across — butterflies are attracted to the garden by this plant. **'Mini Marine'** is claimed to be an improvement.

**SITE & SOIL:** Any well-drained garden soil will do — thrives best in full sun.

**PLANT DETAILS:** Height 1–1½ ft. Spacing 1 ft.

**PROPAGATION:** Take cuttings from greenhouse plants in spring. Alternatively sow seed of 'Marine' in February-March in gentle heat. Plant out in early June.

*Heliotropium peruvianum 'Marine'*

# HIBISCUS Hibiscus

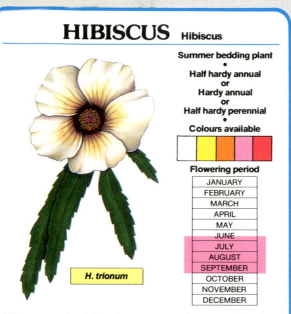

Summer bedding plant
•
Half hardy annual
or
Hardy annual
or
Half hardy perennial
•
Colours available

Flowering period

| JANUARY |
| FEBRUARY |
| MARCH |
| APRIL |
| MAY |
| JUNE |
| **JULY** |
| **AUGUST** |
| **SEPTEMBER** |
| OCTOBER |
| NOVEMBER |
| DECEMBER |

**H. trionum**

Hibiscus as a bedding plant may sound a strange idea, but advances in the past few years now make it practical. In fact you can choose between giant-sized flowers, medium-sized ones and even a decorative foliage variety. They can be raised from seed — one is a hardy annual but the others are half hardy types which must be discarded or brought inside before the frosts arrive.

**VARIETIES:** The large-flowered Hibiscus (**H. rosa sinensis**) sold in pots as house plants can be stood or bedded out in the garden during the summer months. Colours include white, yellow, orange, pink and red. Harden off before moving outdoors and then bring inside in September. The exotic Hibiscus to raise from seed is the F$_1$ hybrid **'Dixie Belle'**. Raise it like any other half hardy annual and bed out in a warm and sheltered spot in June to enjoy the white, pink and red saucer-sized flowers. **'Coppertone'** is another half hardy Hibiscus, but it is grown for its large, coppery-purple, Maple-shaped leaves. This 3 ft high Hibiscus makes an unusual and eye-catching dot plant. **H. trionum** or Annual Hibiscus (2 ft) is still another variation. It is a hardy annual which can be sown outdoors in April. The white or pastel flowers are 2–3 in. across and like other Hibiscus flowers last only for a single day.

**SITE & SOIL:** Any well-drained garden soil will do — thrives best in full sun.

**PLANT DETAILS:** Height 1–3 ft. Spacing 1 ft.

**PROPAGATION:** Sow seed of half hardy varieties in February in gentle heat. Prick out into pots and plant out in June.

*Hibiscus 'Dixie Belle'*

# IBERIS Candytuft

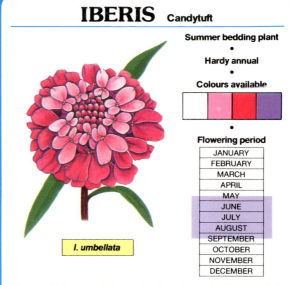

Summer bedding plant
•
Hardy annual
•
Colours available

•

Flowering period

| JANUARY |
| FEBRUARY |
| MARCH |
| APRIL |
| **MAY** |
| **JUNE** |
| **JULY** |
| **AUGUST** |
| **SEPTEMBER** |
| OCTOBER |
| NOVEMBER |
| DECEMBER |

**I. umbellata**

Candytuft is one of the easiest and most tolerant of all annuals — it withstands pollution, poor soil and cultivation by tiny fingers. It is usually sown in autumn or spring where it is to flower, but it can be raised indoors for bedding out in May. Massed in the front of a border or used as an edging along a path, this spreading, quick-growing plant produces 2 in. wide domed clusters of fragrant flowers. These blooms in sunny weather may be numerous enough to cover the lance-shaped leaves completely. Shear off the heads after blooming to prolong the flowering season.

**VARIETIES:** Nearly all types are varieties of **I. umbellata** and the old favourite is **'Fairy Mixed'**. These 6–9 in. high plants produce flowers in a range of pastel shades — for brighter blooms including rich purples and bright reds you should use **'Flash Mixed'** (9–15 in.). Single-colour varieties are listed in the catalogues — **'Red Flash'**, **'Pink Queen'** etc. Now for something different. The Hyacinth-flowered Candytuft (15 in.) bears spikes of long-lasting blooms on strong stems — there is a strong resemblance to miniature Hyacinths. Named varieties include **'Iceberg'**, **'White Empress'** and **'White Pinnacle'**.

**SITE & SOIL:** Any well-drained garden soil will do — thrives best in full sun.

**PLANT DETAILS:** Height 6–15 in. Spacing 9 in.

**PROPAGATION:** Sow where it is to flower. Alternatively sow seed in March under glass. Plant out in May.

*Iberis umbellata 'Fairy Mixed'*

*Iberis umbellata 'White Pinnacle'*

# IMPATIENS  Busy Lizzie

**Summer bedding plant**

•

**Half hardy annual**

•

**Colours available**

•

**Flowering period**

| JANUARY |
| FEBRUARY |
| MARCH |
| APRIL |
| MAY |
| JUNE |
| JULY |
| AUGUST |
| SEPTEMBER |
| OCTOBER |
| NOVEMBER |
| DECEMBER |

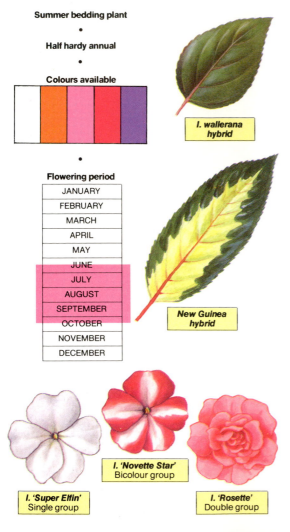

*I. wallerana hybrid*

*New Guinea hybrid*

*I. 'Super Elfin'*
Single group

*I. 'Novette Star'*
Bicolour group

*I. 'Rosette'*
Double group

For generations Busy Lizzie has been a popular house plant. It had no important place in the garden until the late 1970s, and then there was a remarkable change. Plant breeders produced the compact and showy $F_1$ hybrids, and gardeners found that nothing else gave solid sheets of colour for months on end when planted under trees or in damp shady places, although its main rival Begonia semperflorens gets close. Shade isn't essential — Impatiens stays in flower in a full sun situation during hot weather and it also comes into flower when seedlings are a few inches high. These virtues have made Busy Lizzie one of the top ten bedding plants in both Britain and the U.S. There are few real drawbacks, although you will have to water during dry spells and it is not an easy plant to grow from seed. The main criticism is that "there isn't much variation between the varieties". This was true at the start of the Impatiens revolution but not now. Orange and lilac have joined the familar white, pink and red flowers. There are now bicolours, double flowers and the bright-leaved New Guinea hybrids ... enough variation for anyone.

**VARIETIES:** There is a bewildering array of $F_1$ hybrids of **I. wallerana**, but they do fall into several distinct groups. The basic one for bedding plant use is the 8–10 in. high bushy group with the **'Super Elfin'** strain dominating the lists. You can buy single-colour types in white, red and pink or try the more unusual **'Salmon Blush'** or **'Blue Pearl'** — many people prefer a multicoloured mixture for bedding, hanging baskets or tubs. The **'Imp'** strain is quite similar but the flowers are rather larger — for the largest flowers (2 in. across) and the largest plants (1 ft high) look for **'Blitz'**. The varieties described so far are green-leaved, single-flowered and self-coloured. For bicoloured flowers with white stripes or centres there are **'Cinderella'**, **'Sparkles'**, **'Symphony Red Star'**, **'Starbright'** and the low-growing **'Novette Star'**. You can buy double varieties these days but do not expect too much — at least half of the plants you raise from seed will be single. Still they are something different and you will find **'Rosette'**, **'Double Duet'** and **'Confection'** in the catalogues. The Semi-trailing variety for hanging baskets is **'Futura'**. Showiest of all are the **New Guinea** hybrids — 1½ ft high plants with long leaves in mixtures of red, yellow and green. Look for **'Tango'** (leaves bronze, flowers orange) in the seed catalogues. The others you will find as plants for bedding out — **'Fanfare'** (leaves yellow/green, flowers pink), **'Arabesque'** (leaves yellow/red/green, flowers pink) etc.

**SITE & SOIL:** Any well-drained soil will do — thrives in sun or partial shade. Add organic matter before planting.

**PLANT DETAILS:** Height 6 in.–1½ ft. Spacing 6–9 in.

**PROPAGATION:** Sow seed in March under glass — germinates at 70°–75°F. Not easy — it is better to buy small seedlings for potting on. Plant out in late May.

Impatiens
'Super Elfin'

Impatiens
'Sparkles'

Impatiens
'Fanfare'

# IPOMOEA Morning Glory

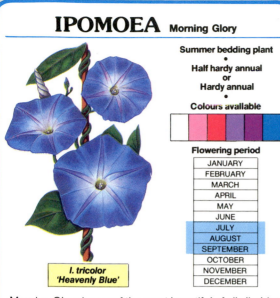

Summer bedding plant
•
Half hardy annual
or
Hardy annual
•
Colours available

**Flowering period**

| |
|---|
| JANUARY |
| FEBRUARY |
| MARCH |
| APRIL |
| MAY |
| JUNE |
| JULY |
| AUGUST |
| SEPTEMBER |
| OCTOBER |
| NOVEMBER |
| DECEMBER |

*I. tricolor*
*'Heavenly Blue'*

Morning Glory is one of the most beautiful of all climbing plants. The wiry stems twine around upright supports — trelliswork, pergolas, the branches of dead trees etc —and the large trumpet-like flowers appear throughout the summer months. Each one lasts for only a day, but they are borne continually and so there is the pleasure of being able to see new flowers open each morning. One problem — the foliage is not particularly dense and this means that Morning Glory is not an effective screening plant. Treat it as a decorative guest, not a work horse.

**VARIETIES:** **I. purpurea** (**Convolvulus major**) is a hardy annual which bears 3 in. purple trumpets in summer. The named types, however, are varieties of the half hardy perennial **I. tricolor** which is treated as a half hardy annual. Pride of place goes to **'Heavenly Blue'** — true blue trumpets which measure 3–5 in. across. **'Flying Saucers'** and **'Sapphire Cross'** are blue and white striped hybrids — **'Pearly Gates'** is white and **'Scarlett O'Hara'** bears large, red flowers. **'Minibar Rose'** is unusual — small variegated leaves with red flowers which are rosy-red edged with white. All can reach 8–10 ft — **'Scarlet Star'** is a rather delicate 4–5 ft dwarf.

**SITE & SOIL:** Any well-drained garden soil will do, but the site chosen must be sunny and sheltered.

**PLANT DETAILS:** Height 4–10 ft. Spacing 1½ ft.

**PROPAGATION:** Sow seed in individual pots in March under glass — warm conditions are necessary. Soak seed for 24 hours before sowing.

*Ipomoea tricolor*
*'Flying Saucers'*

*Ipomoea tricolor*
*'Scarlett O'Hara'*

# KALANCHOE Flaming Katy

Summer bedding plant
•
Half hardy annual
or
Half hardy perennial
•
Colours available

**Flowering period**

| |
|---|
| JANUARY |
| FEBRUARY |
| MARCH |
| APRIL |
| MAY |
| JUNE |
| JULY |
| AUGUST |
| SEPTEMBER |
| OCTOBER |
| NOVEMBER |
| DECEMBER |

*K. blossfeldiana*

You won't find this one in your books on garden flowers — it is regarded strictly as a house plant. You will have no difficulty in finding pots in the section of your garden centre devoted to indoor specimens. However, if you like the unusual in your window box, plant tub etc, then there is no reason why you should not bed out Flaming Katy in mid-late June and enjoy its neat growth habit and wide clusters of bright flowers for months. Buy the plants in flower and harden off before bedding out — don't assume hardening off isn't necessary just because the days are warm.

**VARIETIES:** The basic species is **K. blossfeldiana** — a bushy plant which can be bought in flower at any time of the year. It grows about 1–1½ ft high and the flower heads bear 25–50 tiny blooms. The oval leaves are fleshy and hybrids in many flower colours are available. If space is limited choose one of the 6 in. red dwarfs such as **'Tom Thumb'**, **'Vulcan'** or **'Compact Lilliput'**. If you are starting from seed, look for **'Mixed Swiss Hybrids'** — the flower clusters are in a range of very bright colours and measure up to 5 in. across. After the flowering season is over you can bring the plants indoors but the usual practice is to throw them away.

**SITE & SOIL:** Any well-drained garden soil will do — choose a sunny and sheltered location.

**PLANT DETAILS:** Height 6 in.–1½ ft. Spacing 9 in.

**PROPAGATION:** Buy plants from a garden centre or take cuttings in spring. Seed can be sown in early spring — germination temperature 70°–80°F. Plant out in June.

*Kalanchoe*
*'Mixed Swiss Hybrids'*

# KOCHIA  Burning Bush, Summer Cypress

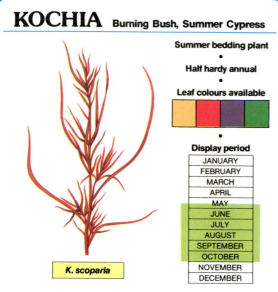

**K. scoparia**

Summer bedding plant
•
Half hardy annual
•
Leaf colours available

**Display period**

| JANUARY |
| FEBRUARY |
| MARCH |
| APRIL |
| MAY |
| **JUNE** |
| **JULY** |
| **AUGUST** |
| **SEPTEMBER** |
| **OCTOBER** |
| NOVEMBER |
| DECEMBER |

This foliage plant is a key feature of many bedding schemes — a group of three planted in the centre provides a welcome contrast to the low, flat sheets of colour below. Each plant is a neat, rounded bush densely covered with feathery leaves — it has a dwarf Conifer-like shape and staking is not usually necessary. Kochia has been a favourite dot plant for many years, but it can also be used as a temporary hedge or screen. Growth is rapid and regular shearing will do no harm. It will grow in most situations, but Kochia thrives best in a sunny and sandy locality.

**VARIETIES: K. scoparia** is the species grown as a bedding plant. The popular variety is **K. scoparia trichophylla** — this is the rather tall one with leaves which turn purple, bronze or brilliant red in autumn. Look for the novel form **'Acapulco Silver'** (3½ ft) if you want something different — the summer foliage is green tipped with silver and the colour changes to purple in September. Less popular than trichophylla is the variety **K. scoparia childsii**. This is not a 'Burning Bush' at all — the foliage of the compact (1½ ft) bush remains green all season long.

**SITE & SOIL:** Any well-drained garden soil will do — thrives in sun or light shade.

**PLANT DETAILS:** Height 1½–3½ ft. Spacing 2 ft.

**PROPAGATION:** Sow seed in February-March in gentle heat — do not cover seed with compost. Plant out in late May.

Kochia scoparia trichophylla

Kochia scoparia childsii

# LANTANA  Yellow Sage

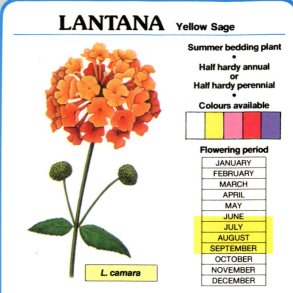

**L. camara**

Summer bedding plant
•
Half hardy annual
or
Half hardy perennial
•
Colours available

**Flowering period**

| JANUARY |
| FEBRUARY |
| MARCH |
| APRIL |
| MAY |
| JUNE |
| **JULY** |
| **AUGUST** |
| **SEPTEMBER** |
| OCTOBER |
| NOVEMBER |
| DECEMBER |

Lantana is one of the rarities which you will find scattered throughout this A-Z of bedding plants. It is not rare because of any special difficulty in cultivation — it has just failed to achieve recognition as a garden as well as a house plant. It is not uncommon in conservatories where its Verbena-like heads change colour as the tiny flowers mature. You can buy plants in pots from the house plant section of a garden centre — the standard form makes an excellent dot plant. However, it is quite easy to raise plants from seed sown in spring. Treat as an annual or keep the plants in their pots and move them indoors at the end of September.

**VARIETIES: L. camara** is the basic species. Named varieties are not available — seed is sold as a **'Hybrid Mixture'** and the resulting flower heads are globular and 1–2 in. across. Some may be all-yellow, others a blend of white and pale purple but the usual pattern is a yellow head which turns steadily red from the outer edge. Growth is bushy and the prickly stems bear rough wrinkled leaves. A novelty rather than a beauty — grow it if you like the unusual.

**SITE & SOIL:** Any well-drained garden soil in a sunny position will do.

**PLANT DETAILS:** Height 1½–2½ ft. Spacing 1½ ft.

**PROPAGATION:** Buy pot plants or sow seed in early spring in gentle heat. Alternatively take stem cuttings from indoor plants at any time of the year. Plant out in mid June.

Lantana camara

# LARKSPUR
### Annual Delphinium, Summer Delphinium

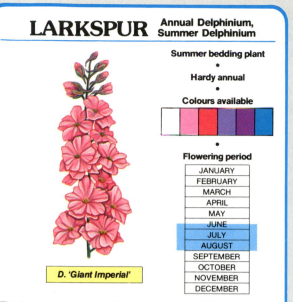

Summer bedding plant
•
Hardy annual

**Colours available**

**Flowering period**

| | |
|---|---|
| JANUARY | |
| FEBRUARY | |
| MARCH | |
| APRIL | |
| MAY | |
| JUNE | |
| JULY | |
| AUGUST | |
| SEPTEMBER | |
| OCTOBER | |
| NOVEMBER | |
| DECEMBER | |

**D. 'Giant Imperial'**

The Larkspur or Annual Delphinium is a relative of the tall and stately Delphiniums of the herbaceous border. The range of colours is equally wide but the plant and flower size are smaller. Larkspur is useful for massed planting, but you must choose a sheltered spot. The flower spikes are excellent for cutting and these plants have long been cottage garden favourites. The flowering season is often rather short.

**VARIETIES:** The true Larkspur appears to be a hybrid — **Delphinium ajacis** and **D. consolida** are involved, but the experts can't agree about all the parents. This hardy annual is usually bought as a mixture and sown in spring or autumn where it is to flower. The old favourite is **'Giant Imperial'** (3–4 ft) but it is more usual these days to buy one of the **'Hyacinth-Flowered'** mixtures. The **'Dwarf Hyacinth-Flowered'** is compact (1–1½ ft) and early flowering — the double blooms appearing in many shades. The **'Giant Hyacinth-Flowered'** is tall (2½–3½ ft) with unbranched stems tightly packed with semi-double and double blooms. As an alternative to Larkspur you can grow **D. chinensis** as a half hardy annual — look for **'Blue Butterfly'** (9 in.) or **'Tom Pouce'** (9 in.).

**SITE & SOIL:** Any well-drained garden soil will do — thrives in sun or light shade.

**PLANT DETAILS:** Height 9 in.–4 ft. Spacing 1–1½ ft.

**PROPAGATION:** The usual plan is to sow seed in autumn or spring where they are to flower. For bedding, sow seed in March and prick out into individual pots. Plant out in May.

Delphinium
'Giant Imperial'

# LAVATERA
### Annual Mallow

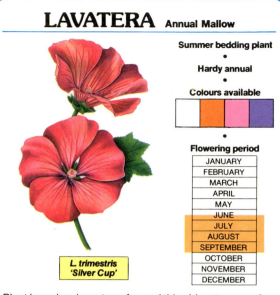

Summer bedding plant
•
Hardy annual

**Colours available**

**Flowering period**

| | |
|---|---|
| JANUARY | |
| FEBRUARY | |
| MARCH | |
| APRIL | |
| MAY | |
| JUNE | |
| JULY | |
| AUGUST | |
| SEPTEMBER | |
| OCTOBER | |
| NOVEMBER | |
| DECEMBER | |

**L. trimestris 'Silver Cup'**

Plant breeders have transformed this old cottage garden plant into a splendid bushy annual which is bold enough and bright enough to hold its own in a mixed border amidst showy perennials. It can also be used as a hedge or a dot plant in a bed of annuals. The trumpet-shaped flowers are 3–4 in. across and are recommended for cutting. Sow where they are to flower or plant out seedlings in spring — choose a sheltered spot. Stake tall-growing varieties and dead-head regularly to prolong the flowering season. The bushes need plenty of space and self-sown seedlings should be removed as they appear.

**VARIETIES:** **L. trimestris** has produced several excellent garden varieties which grow 3–4 ft high and produce pink flowers — **'Loveliness'** and **'Tanagra'** are examples. However, there are two compact varieties which dominate all the catalogues these days and both are very highly praised. **'Mont Blanc'** (2 ft) is the white-flowering one — shining flowers amid dark foliage. **'Silver Cup'** (2½ ft) is generally regarded as the best Lavatera — beautiful pink blooms borne all summer long. A new one is **'Ruby Regis'** (2 ft, rosy-red).

**SITE & SOIL:** Any reasonable garden soil will do — thrives in sun or light shade.

**PLANT DETAILS:** Height 2–4 ft. Spacing 2 ft.

**PROPAGATION:** The usual plan is to sow seed in autumn or spring where they are to flower. For bedding, sow seed in March and prick out into individual pots. Plant out in May.

Lavatera trimestris
'Loveliness'

Lavatera trimestris
'Mont Blanc'

# LIMNANTHES Poached Egg Flower

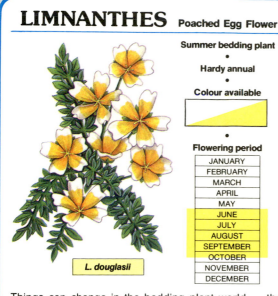

Summer bedding plant

•

Hardy annual

•

Colour available

•

**Flowering period**

| | |
|---|---|
| JANUARY | |
| FEBRUARY | |
| MARCH | |
| APRIL | |
| MAY | |
| JUNE | ■ |
| JULY | ■ |
| AUGUST | ■ |
| SEPTEMBER | ■ |
| OCTOBER | |
| NOVEMBER | |
| DECEMBER | |

*L. douglasii*

Things can change in the bedding plant world — the remarkable increase in popularity of Impatiens during the past few years illustrates the point. It is surprising, therefore, that Alyssum and Lobelia should maintain their dominance at the front of the bed or border as they have done since Victorian times. Limnanthes deserves a place here, but it appears in the catalogues and not along paths or in window boxes and containers. The ferny leaves are attractive, the flowers are borne in very large numbers and the blooms are attractive to wildlife. Flowering lasts all season long and the plants are hardy — perhaps white and yellow is an unattractive combination.

**VARIETIES:** You will find only one type of Limnanthes in the catalogues — **L. douglasii**, which came to Britain from California. The ferny foliage is pale green and the low-growing, spreading plants make excellent rockery specimens. The yellow petals of each flower have a distinct white edge — hence the common name. It is an easy plant to grow and the flowers cover almost all of the pale green foliage when grown in full sun. The fragrance is sweet but not strong.

**SITE & SOIL:** Any reasonable garden soil will do — thrives best in a sunny spot.

**PLANT DETAILS:** Height 6 in. Spacing 6 in.

**PROPAGATION:** Sow seed in March where they are to flower. For bedding, sow seed in February–March under glass. Plant out in May.

*Limnanthes douglasii*

# LIMONIUM Statice

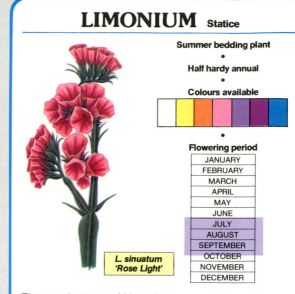

Summer bedding plant

•

Half hardy annual

•

Colours available

•

**Flowering period**

| | |
|---|---|
| JANUARY | |
| FEBRUARY | |
| MARCH | |
| APRIL | |
| MAY | |
| JUNE | |
| JULY | ■ |
| AUGUST | ■ |
| SEPTEMBER | ■ |
| OCTOBER | |
| NOVEMBER | |
| DECEMBER | |

*L. sinuatum 'Rose Light'*

The popular types of Limonium appear in the catalogues as Statice — perhaps the most popular of the 'Everlasting' flowers. The stems are cut when the flowers are fully open and bunches are tied with string and hung upside down in a cool place away from sunlight. The dried flowers retain their colour and are used for indoor decoration. Statice deserves wider use — the living blooms can be used for flower arranging and modern varieties are showy enough to be used in bedding schemes. Limonium withstands both dry soil and salt-laden air.

**VARIETIES: L. sinuatum** is the parent species of the many varieties used as Everlasting flowers. There is a basal rosette of leaves — above each rosette the erect winged stems appear, each with a 4 in. cluster of tiny, papery-petalled flowers. The usual practice is to buy a mixture — **'Pacific Mixed'**, **'Formula Mixed'**, **'Fortress Mixed'** etc or the dwarf **'Petite Bouquet'** (1 ft). Single-colour varieties are available — look for **'Gold Coast'** (yellow), **'Rose Light'** (pink), **'American Beauty'** (pink), **'Blue River'** (blue) and **'Midnight Blue'** (blue). **L. suworowii** is quite different — the flowering stems are tall spikes densely covered with tiny pink flowers. Good for flower arranging but not for drying.

**SITE & SOIL:** Any well-drained garden soil, but light or medium land is preferred. Choose a sunny spot.

**PLANT DETAILS:** Height 1–2 ft. Spacing 1 ft.

**PROPAGATION:** Sow in February–March in gentle heat. Plant out in late May.

*Limonium sinuatum*          *Limonium suworowii*

# LOBELIA Lobelia

Summer bedding plant
•
Half hardy annual
•
Colours available
•
Flowering period

| JANUARY |
| FEBRUARY |
| MARCH |
| APRIL |
| MAY |
| JUNE |
| JULY |
| AUGUST |
| SEPTEMBER |
| OCTOBER |
| NOVEMBER |
| DECEMBER |

**L. erinus 'Mrs Clibran Improved'**

Lobelia and Alyssum have been Britain's favourite edging plants for generations. The low mounds of Lobelia around beds, along paths and in tubs and window boxes are a basic feature of the summer garden scene, but they are more demanding than many less well-known annuals. Prolonged hot weather reduces the floral display and so does impoverished soil — for best results water thoroughly in dry weather, feed occasionally and shear off the tips of the plants after the first flush of flowers has faded. Give the plants a good start in life — transplant in small groups rather than singly and pinch out the tips of seedlings to induce bushiness.

**VARIETIES:** Blue remains the favourite colour of the Edging Lobelia (**L. erinus**). **'Mrs Clibran Improved'** is the old favourite with deep blue petals and a white eye — equally popular is the all-blue, bronzy-leaved **'Crystal Palace'**. The earliest is **'Blue Pearl'** — the usual pale blue one is **'Cambridge Blue'**. For other colours choose **'White Lady'** (white) or **'Rosamund'** (red) — for a mixture of colours sow **'String of Pearls'**. Grow the Trailing Lobelia (**L. erinus pendula**) in hanging baskets — **'Sapphire'** is the popular blue one — for mixed colours choose **'Cascade'** or **'Fountain Mixture'**.

**SITE & SOIL:** Any reasonable garden soil will do, but well-fed and moist land is preferred. Thrives in sun or light shade.

**PLANT DETAILS:** Height 4–6 in. Spacing 6 in.

**PROPAGATION:** Sow seed in January–March in gentle heat — do not cover with compost. Plant out in late May.

Lobelia erinus
'Cambridge Blue'

Lobelia erinus
'Rosamund'

# LUPINUS Annual Lupin

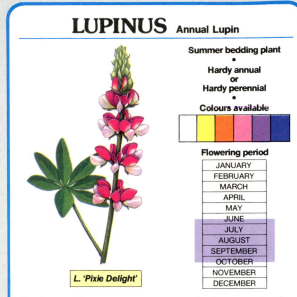

Summer bedding plant
•
Hardy annual
or
Hardy perennial
•
Colours available
•
Flowering period

| JANUARY |
| FEBRUARY |
| MARCH |
| APRIL |
| MAY |
| JUNE |
| JULY |
| AUGUST |
| SEPTEMBER |
| OCTOBER |
| NOVEMBER |
| DECEMBER |

**L. 'Pixie Delight'**

Lupins are known to everyone as herbaceous border perennials — the idea of growing them as bedding plants may seem strange. But Annual Lupins are offered in many seed catalogues and are well worth trying. You will not get the height, bloom size nor the bright colours of the stately Russell Lupin but the daintiness of 'Pixie Delight' is an advantage in a small plot and the beautiful blue of the Texas Bluebonnet cannot be matched by its larger perennial relatives. Some basic features are shared by both annual and perennial forms — flowering is poor in rich or alkaline soils and the seeds are poisonous.

**VARIETIES:** The Annual Lupins which are available are usually hybrids of a number of species, including **Lupinus hartwegii**, **L. luteus** and **L. pubescens**. The most popular hybrid is **'Pixie Delight'**, sometimes described as **'Pixie Strain'** or **'Pixy'**. These miniature Lupins grow about 1–1½ ft high and the blooms are white or a variety of pastel shades either as single colours or bicolours. If blue is your favourite colour, search for **L. subcarnosus** in the catalogues — it is the Texas Bluebonnet. The pyramid-shaped spikes are an intense and attractive blue. Some Perennial Lupins can be treated as annuals — try dwarf ones such as **'Lulu'** or **'Yellow Javelin'**.

**SITE & SOIL:** Any well-drained garden soil will do — acid land is preferred. Thrives in sun or light shade.

**PLANT DETAILS:** Height 1–2½ ft. Spacing 1–1½ ft.

**PROPAGATION:** Sow seed in February in gentle heat — chip seed before sowing. Plant out in May.

Lupinus
'Pixie Delight'

Lupinus
'Yellow Javelin'

# MARIGOLD
## African Marigold, French Marigold

**Summer bedding plant**

**Half hardy annual**

**Colours available**

**Flowering period**

| JANUARY |
| FEBRUARY |
| MARCH |
| APRIL |
| MAY |
| JUNE |
| JULY |
| AUGUST |
| SEPTEMBER |
| OCTOBER |
| NOVEMBER |
| DECEMBER |

*T. patula*

*T. patula*
**'Scarlet Sophia'**
French Marigold:
Double group

*T. patula*
**'Tiger Eyes'**
French Marigold:
Crested group

*T. patula*
**'Naughty Marietta'**
French Marigold:
Single group

*T. erecta*
**'Doubloon'**
African
Marigold

*T. 'Nell Gwynn'*
Afro-French
Marigold:
Single group

*T. 'Sunrise'*
Afro-French
Marigold:
Double group

French Marigolds are the most popular source of yellows and oranges in bedding schemes. These much-loved plants are easy to raise from seed, reliable under all sorts of conditions, long-flowering from June until the first frosts arrive and cheap to buy as seedlings for planting out in spring. There are some horticulturalists who regard the neat flower heads as the height of bad taste in the garden — love them or hate them, they are a fundamental feature of summer-flowering beds and containers. The first point to clear up is the confusion over naming. The half hardy Marigolds described here (not to be confused with the hardy Pot Marigold — page 25) are all species or varieties of Tagetes. The favourite one is T. patula (French Marigold) — lots of single, semi-double or double blooms on bushy plants about 9 in. high. T. erecta is the African Marigold — taller (1–3 ft), more upright and with fewer but larger flowers. Between the two are the hybrids of the French and African Marigold — the triploid hybrids known as Afro-French Marigolds. These recent introductions have larger blooms than the French ones but are more free-flowering and compact than the African sorts. There is one other species of Tagetes — the small T. signata listed in this book (page 76) and in the catalogues as Tagetes. These ferny-leaved plants are 6–9 in. high with masses of small single flowers. A few points about French and African Marigolds. Plant out before the flowers open — don't buy plants in full flower. Remove opened buds for the first couple of weeks after planting. Water when the weather is dry and keep watch for slugs as they can destroy young plants. Stake tall-growing varieties. Dead-head to prolong the display — it is not necessary for Afro-French varieties as they do not set seed.

**VARIETIES:** You will find scores of French Marigold varieties in the catalogues, with flowers ranging from white to deepest red and mahogany. The *Double* (or *Carnation*) types are now more popular than the *Single* French Marigolds which used to hold pride of place. Amongst the doubles look for the dwarf (6 in.) **'Boy'** series — **'Golden Boy'**, **'Harmony Boy'** (gold and red) and the **'Boy O' Boy'** mixture. **'Petite'** is another dwarf which is used for edging. Best of the doubles are found in the **'Sophia'** series — large (2 in.) blooms with fluted overlapping petals on 8–10 in. high bushy plants. The single types include the old favourite **'Naughty Marietta'** (1 ft, yellow and maroon), the smaller **'Dainty Marietta'**, **'Pascal'** and **'Disco'** (6 in.), the taller and large-flowered **'Silvia'** and **'Leopard'**, and the new **'Mischief'** (1 ft) series. In the *Crested* group of French Marigolds the petals in the centre of the flower are crowded and tightly rolled. Look for the popular and early-flowering **'Tiger Eyes'** (orange and red), **'Honeycomb'** (yellow and red), **'Queen Bee'** (red and yellow) and the **'Jacket'** series. The African Marigolds have double, ball-like blooms and they are generally grouped according to height. The *Tall* types reach 2–3 ft — in the catalogues you will find **'Doubloon'** (yellow, 5 in. flowers) and the **'Jubilee'** series in yellow and orange. The *Intermediate* types (1–2 ft) include the **'Perfection'**, **'Ladies'** and **'Calando'** series. The *Low* types (10–12 in.) are represented by **'Rhapsody'**, **'Sundance'** etc but the best ones are the **'Inca'** series with large, weather-resistant blooms. The Afro-French Marigolds grow 1–1½ ft high and the blooms measure about 3 in. across. **'Nell Gwynn'** is the popular single one — doubles include **'Sunrise'** (orange), **'Red Seven Star'** (red-brown), the **'Caribbean Parade'** and **'Solar'** mixtures and the early-flowering golden **'Showboat'**.

**SITE & SOIL:** Any reasonable garden soil will do — thrives best in full sun.

**PLANT DETAILS:** Height 6 in.–3 ft. Spacing 6 in.–1½ ft.

**PROPAGATION:** Sow seed in February–March in gentle heat. Plant out in late May. In mild areas seed can be sown outdoors in May.

# FRENCH MARIGOLDS

*Tagetes patula*
*'Golden Boy'*

*Tagetes patula*
*'Pascal'*

*Tagetes patula*
*'Honeycomb'*

# AFRICAN MARIGOLDS

*Tagetes erecta*
*'Perfection Gold'*

*Tagetes erecta*
*'First Lady'*

*Tagetes erecta*
*'Sundance'*

# AFRO-FRENCH MARIGOLDS

*Tagetes*
*'Nell Gwynn'*

*Tagetes*
*'Red Seven Star'*

*Tagetes*
*'Solar'*

# MATRICARIA Feverfew

**M. eximia 'Golden Ball'**

**M. eximia 'Ball's Double White'**

Summer bedding plant

•

Half hardy annual

•

Colours available

•

Flowering period

| JANUARY |
| FEBRUARY |
| MARCH |
| APRIL |
| MAY |
| JUNE |
| JULY |
| AUGUST |
| SEPTEMBER |
| OCTOBER |
| NOVEMBER |
| DECEMBER |

The ¾ in. flowers of Feverfew or Bachelor's Buttons are borne in flat heads. The single form (white petals around a central yellow disc) was popular in the formal beds of Victorian parks but these days the fully double forms are preferred. The compact plants are barely 1 ft high and the flowers look like miniature Chrysanthemums. The notched foliage has a pungent smell so this is not a flower for cutting, but it does make a colourful edging plant or a neat subject for a window box or small container.

**VARIETIES:** The experts can't agree whether the latin name should be **Matricaria eximia** or **Chrysanthemum parthenium**. The colour range is distinctly limited — yellow, white or a mixture of the two. The single varieties **'White Star'** and the golden-leaved **'aureum'** are not easy to find, but the double forms appear in most of the popular catalogues. Some are completely double without an outer ring of guard petals — the ball-like **'Golden Ball'** is the most popular one — the white **'Ball's Double White'** is uncommon. The usual pattern is a double flower with an outer ring of larger petals — varieties include **'Snow Ball'**, **'Snow Puffs'**, **'Snow Dwarf'** and **'White Gem'**.

**SITE & SOIL:** Any well-drained garden soil will do — thrives best in full sun.

**PLANT DETAILS:** Height 8 in.–1 ft. Spacing 1 ft.

**PROPAGATION:** Sow seed in February–March in gentle heat. Plant out in late May.

*Matricaria eximia 'Snow Dwarf'*

# MESEMBRYANTHEMUM
### Livingstone Daisy

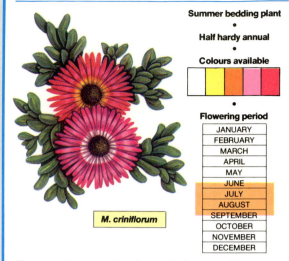

**M. criniflorum**

Summer bedding plant

•

Half hardy annual

•

Colours available

•

Flowering period

| JANUARY |
| FEBRUARY |
| MARCH |
| APRIL |
| MAY |
| JUNE |
| JULY |
| AUGUST |
| SEPTEMBER |
| OCTOBER |
| NOVEMBER |
| DECEMBER |

There are few carpeting plants which can rival this one for sheer brilliance. The glistening flowers look like large Daisies in an astonishing array of colours — apricot, buff, bright orange, snowy white, rosy red etc. The fleshy stems and tubular leaves are almost covered by the blooms ... but all this only applies to plants growing in sandy soil on a sunny day. In heavy soil, a shady site or a dull and wet summer, the Livingstone Daisy will not be worth the space it occupies. The blooms of this South African plant do not open unless the sun is shining. Put Slug Pellets around the seedlings and dead-head spent blooms regularly.

**VARIETIES:** **Mesembryanthemum criniflorum** is the latin name of the species sold as Livingstone Daisy. Quite a mouthful, but the scientists now want us to call it **Dorotheanthus bellidiformis**. It is available as a mixture of colours rather than single-colour varieties — the flowers are sometimes bicoloured with a contrasting pale-coloured inner zone. For something different grow **M. occulatus 'Lunette'** — the petals are clear yellow and the central disc is ruby red. It is early-flowering and less inclined to close in dull weather.

**SITE & SOIL:** The soil should be well-drained and sandy, and the site must be in full sun.

**PLANT DETAILS:** Height 4–6 in. Spacing 8 in.

**PROPAGATION:** Sow seed in March in gentle heat. Plant out in late May.

*Mesembryanthemum criniflorum 'Mixed'*

*Mesembryanthemum occulatus 'Lunette'*

# MIMULUS  Monkey Flower

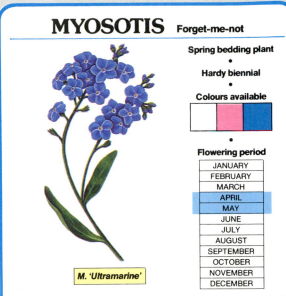

Summer bedding plant

•

Half hardy annual

•

Colours available

**Flowering period**

| JANUARY |
|---------|
| FEBRUARY |
| MARCH |
| APRIL |
| MAY |
| JUNE |
| JULY |
| AUGUST |
| SEPTEMBER |
| OCTOBER |
| NOVEMBER |
| DECEMBER |

*M. hybridus*

Shaded beds which get little sun and north-facing patios can pose a problem — Impatiens and Bedding Begonias are the popular bedding plants for such situations, but they can't provide yellows and oranges for these dull spots. Mimulus is a good solution but it is not popular — gardeners have not yet learnt just how useful and colourful the new F$_1$ hybrids can be. Flowering takes only 7–9 weeks from sowing. Grow them where shade and/or damp soil is a problem — window boxes, hanging baskets, rockeries, poolsides, beds etc. Dead-head to prolong the flowering season and do not let the soil dry out.

**VARIETIES:** Only the man who gave this plant its common name has ever seen the similarity between the open blotched or spotted trumpet-like flowers and the face of a monkey. Today's varieties are a great advance on the older types which were straggly and very fussy about growing conditions. **'Malibu'** is the baby — compact, dwarf (6 in.) and covered in masses of small blooms. You can buy single colours or a mixture. **'Calypso'** (9 in.) has the widest range of colours and types (plain, bicoloured, speckled, blotched etc). **'Viva'** (1 ft) is the tallest and showiest of the F$_1$ hybrids — the 2 in. trumpets are yellow heavily blotched with red. The only others you are likely to find listed are **'Royal Velvet'** and **'Queen's Prize'**.

**SITE & SOIL:** A soil which is not allowed to dry out is essential — some shade is desirable.

**PLANT DETAILS:** Height 6 in.–1 ft. Spacing 9 in.

**PROPAGATION:** Sow seed in March in gentle heat. Plant out in late May.

Mimulus
'Malibu Orange'

Mimulus
'Calypso Mixed'

# MYOSOTIS  Forget-me-not

Spring bedding plant

•

Hardy biennial

•

Colours available

**Flowering period**

| JANUARY |
|---------|
| FEBRUARY |
| MARCH |
| APRIL |
| MAY |
| JUNE |
| JULY |
| AUGUST |
| SEPTEMBER |
| OCTOBER |
| NOVEMBER |
| DECEMBER |

*M. 'Ultramarine'*

For generations Tulips growing above a blue carpet of Forget-me-nots have been a basic feature of British gardens in spring. Dwarf varieties of Myosotis for edging and underplanting are the favourite ones, but there are taller ones for growing in borders. All of them bear dense clusters of small flowers — blue is the most popular colour but both white and pink varieties are available. An easy plant to grow which will do well in sun or partial shade. The only requirements are well-drained soil and a watering can if the weather is dry. Self-sown seedlings will appear next year — welcome in some but not all situations.

**VARIETIES:** Nearly all garden Forget-me-nots are hybrids or varieties of **M. alpestris** — the tall-growing ones are thought to be derived from **M. sylvestris**. For traditional blue edging or planting under bulbs choose a compact (6 in.) variety such as the old favourite **'Ultramarine'** (rich blue) or **'Blue Ball'** (indigo). For a change you can try **'White Ball'** (white) or one of the pinks, such as **'Pink Gem'**, **'Carmine King'** or **'Rose Pink'**. Taller Forget-me-nots can be grown in a bed on their own or as clumps in a border. **'Blue Bouquet'** (1 ft) has unusually large flowers and is excellent for cutting — **'Royal Blue'** grows to the same height. The giant is **'Bluebird'** (1½ ft).

**SITE & SOIL:** Any reasonable garden soil will do — thrives best in light shade.

**PLANT DETAILS:** Height 6 in.–1½ ft. Spacing 6 in.–1 ft.

**PROPAGATION:** Sow seed in May or June — plant out in autumn.

Myosotis
'Royal Blue'

Myosotis
'Carmine King'

# NASTURTIUM

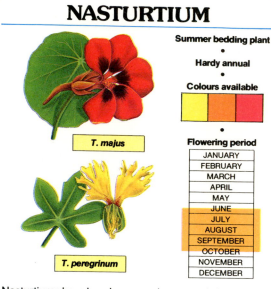

**T. majus**

**T. peregrinum**

- Summer bedding plant
- Hardy annual
- Colours available

**Flowering period**

| JANUARY |
| FEBRUARY |
| MARCH |
| APRIL |
| MAY |
| **JUNE** |
| **JULY** |
| **AUGUST** |
| **SEPTEMBER** |
| OCTOBER |
| NOVEMBER |
| DECEMBER |

Nasturtiums have long been used as annual climbers and trailers for clothing walls and fences, covering banks and hanging baskets and for draping over the edges of tubs and window boxes. The usual plan is to push the large seeds into the soil or compost in April where they are to flower. Nowadays they are also useful as groundwork plants for massed bedding or edging as there are varieties which form neat, low-growing mounds and bear their flowers above the foliage. These dwarfs provide a blaze of colour on impoverished, free-draining soil. Do not overfeed — spray against blackfly.

**VARIETIES:** Nasturtiums (latin name **Tropaeolum majus**) are grouped according to plant size. The *Climbers* grow up to 8 ft tall — look for the very vigorous **'Tall Mixed Hybrids'** and the red-speckled, orange-flowered **'Spitfire'**. The *Semi-trailer* (1–1½ ft) group is dominated by the **'Gleam'** hybrids — double or semi-double large flowers available as mixtures or in single colours. The compact *Dwarfs* grow 6–10 in. high and the new favourite here is **'Whirlybird'** — the semi-double, spurless flowers face upwards and are held well above the foliage. Others include **'Alaska'** (white-speckled foliage), **'Jewel Mixture'** (semi-double), **'Empress of India'** (dark red) and **'Peach Melba'** (red-blotched, yellow). The Canary Creeper (**T. peregrinum**) is a climber with small, yellow flowers.

**SITE & SOIL:** Thrives in sandy soil in full sun or partial shade.

**PLANT DETAILS:** Height 6 in.–8 ft. Spacing 6 in.–1½ ft.

**PROPAGATION:** For bedding, sow seed in February in gentle heat. Plant out in May.

Tropaeolum
'Whirlybird Mixed'

# NEMESIA Nemesia

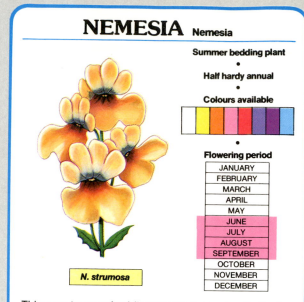

**N. strumosa**

- Summer bedding plant
- Half hardy annual
- Colours available

**Flowering period**

| JANUARY |
| FEBRUARY |
| MARCH |
| APRIL |
| MAY |
| **JUNE** |
| **JULY** |
| **AUGUST** |
| **SEPTEMBER** |
| OCTOBER |
| NOVEMBER |
| DECEMBER |

This easy-to-grow bedding plant has remained in the top ten for many years — the main reason is the vast range of colours of the 1 in. wide blooms. A good mixture will provide flowers from pure white to dark purple with a scattering of bicolours and tricolours. Some will be plain, but others will be spotted or edged with contrasting colours. An added benefit is the short time between sowing and flowering but a definite disadvantage is the short time of blooming if the summer is hot and dry. A second planting may be necessary to cover the whole of the early June to late September flowering period stated on the seed packet. Keep plants well watered in dry weather and cut back once the first flush is over.

**VARIETIES:** N. strumosa has given rise to many garden varieties and hybrids, most of which grow about 10 in. tall. You can buy single colours such as the pale blue **'Blue Gem'** and red **'Fire King'**. The most novel Nemesia is the variety with flowers which have the top half red and the bottom half white — it is sold as **'St. George'** or **'Mello Red & White'**. But most people buy a mixture and the most popular one is **'Carnival'**, noted for its large flowers. Other mixtures include **'Funfair'** (bright colours), **'Triumph'** (small flowers) and **'Sparklers'** (many bicolours and tricolours).

**SITE & SOIL:** Any reasonable garden soil will do — thrives best in sun or light shade and lime-free land.

**PLANT DETAILS:** Height 9 in.–1 ft. Spacing 6 in.

**PROPAGATION:** Sow seed in March–April in gentle heat. Plant out in late May.

Nemesia strumosa
'Mello Red & White'

Nemesia strumosa
'Carnival Mixed'

# NEMOPHILA Californian Bluebell

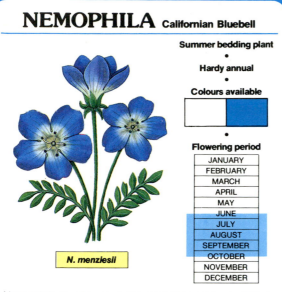

Summer bedding plant
•
Hardy annual
•
Colours available

Flowering period

| JANUARY |
| FEBRUARY |
| MARCH |
| APRIL |
| MAY |
| JUNE |
| **JULY** |
| **AUGUST** |
| **SEPTEMBER** |
| OCTOBER |
| NOVEMBER |
| DECEMBER |

**N. menziesii**

Nemophila is a low-growing carpeting annual which is waiting to be discovered as a bedding plant. The mounds of pale feathery leaves seldom grow taller than 1 ft high and the large Buttercup-like flowers are borne from June until the arrival of the first frosts if the conditions are right. This calls for adding organic matter to the soil before planting and watering copiously if the weather is dry. Think about Nemophila if you have beds to edge or boxes to fill on the north side of the house.

**VARIETIES:** There are just two varieties offered for sale these days. In some catalogues you won't find either — the popular lists generally include one — **N. menziesii**, which is sometimes listed as **N. insignis** or Baby Blue Eyes. The flowers are about 1½ in. across and the sky blue petals have a prominent white base — a useful ground cover plant for humus-rich soil in which many bedding plants would be all leaf with few flowers. Comprehensive catalogues also include the other variety **N. maculata** or Five Spot. Each of the white petals of the 1 in. flowers bears a large purple spot at the edge. A small plant, growing 6–9 in. high.

**SITE & SOIL:** Any reasonable garden soil will do, but moisture-retaining land is preferred. Thrives in sun or partial shade.

**PLANT DETAILS:** Height 6 in.–1 ft. Spacing 6 in.

**PROPAGATION:** Prefers to be sown in April where it is to flower. For bedding, sow seed in March in gentle heat. Plant out in May.

Nemophila menziesii

# NICOTIANA Tobacco Plant

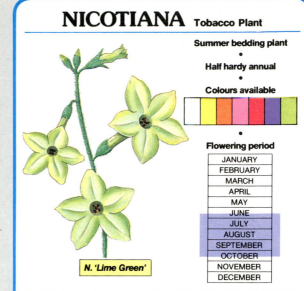

Summer bedding plant
•
Half hardy annual
•
Colours available

Flowering period

| JANUARY |
| FEBRUARY |
| MARCH |
| APRIL |
| MAY |
| JUNE |
| **JULY** |
| **AUGUST** |
| **SEPTEMBER** |
| OCTOBER |
| NOVEMBER |
| DECEMBER |

**N. 'Lime Green'**

N. alata (sometimes listed as N. affinis) is the old-fashioned Tobacco Plant. Its glory is the intense fragrance at sunset, but it isn't much to look at. The tall, branching stems need staking and the drooping flowers do not open during the day. Plant breeders have dramatically changed the picture during the past 20 years. The most popular form of Nicotiana today is the 1 ft dwarf — flowers face upwards and are open during the day, the colours are bright and they are much more resistant to bad weather. But, alas, much of the fragrance has gone. Two tips — dead-head regularly and spray against greenfly.

**VARIETIES:** You can still buy **N. alata** (3 ft) but you are much more likely to find some of its hybrids in the catalogues. The **'Domino'** series is the F$_1$ hybrid which leads the field — day-opening and dwarf (1 ft). Buy a mixture or a single colour — red, white, pink, lime green etc are available. Less expensive but not quite as good is the F$_2$ hybrid **'Roulette'** series. **'Nikki'** is another 1 ft dwarf in a number of colours — the modern tall hybrids which open during the day are the **'Sensation'** series (2–3 ft). Others you will find in the catalogues include **N. 'Lime Green'** (2½ ft, yellowish-green) and **'Crimson Rock'** (2 ft, red).

**SITE & SOIL:** Any well-drained garden soil will do — thrives in sun or light shade.

**PLANT DETAILS:** Height 9 in.–3 ft. Spacing 9 in.–1½ ft.

**PROPAGATION:** Sow seed in March in gentle heat. Plant out in late May.

Nicotiana 'Domino White'

Nicotiana 'Sensation Mixed'

# NIGELLA Love-in-a-mist

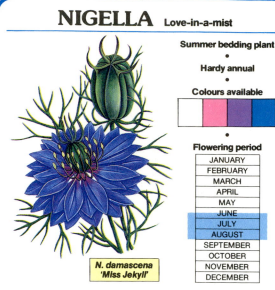

Summer bedding plant
•
Hardy annual

**Colours available**

**Flowering period**

| JANUARY |
| FEBRUARY |
| MARCH |
| APRIL |
| MAY |
| JUNE |
| JULY |
| AUGUST |
| SEPTEMBER |
| OCTOBER |
| NOVEMBER |
| DECEMBER |

*N. damascena 'Miss Jekyll'*

Love-in-a-mist describes the way the pastel flowers peep through the finely-cut foliage. The blue varieties have been grown in gardens for hundreds of years, but these days you are more likely to find a multicoloured mixture listed in the catalogue. It is an easy plant to grow and is quite undemanding, but for top results you should incorporate organic matter in the soil before planting and dead blooms should be cut off to prolong the flowering season. Even with care this season will not be long — 6–8 weeks at best. Resow or replant if you want flowers in late summer or autumn.

**VARIETIES:** The popular types are varieties of **N. damascena** — 1–1½ ft high bushy plants which should be supported with twiggy sticks. **'Miss Jekyll'** is the sky blue old favourite — **'Persian Jewels'** is a mixture of white, pink, lavender and blue flowers. Both make excellent plants for an old world look in informal plantings and they are widely used as cut flowers. The decorative seed heads are also used for arranging — cut the stems and hang to dry when the seed pods have turned brown. In some catalogues you will find a larger plant — **N. hispanica** (2 ft). The large blue flowers have a near-black centre with red stamens.

**SITE & SOIL:** Any well-drained garden soil will do — thrives in sun or light shade.

**PLANT DETAILS:** Height 1–2 ft. Spacing 9 in.

**PROPAGATION:** Sow in autumn or early spring where it is to flower as it does not like transplanting. For bedding, sow in peat pots in March and plant out in May.

*Nigella damascena 'Persian Jewels'*

# PALM

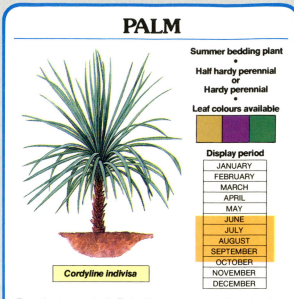

Summer bedding plant
•
Half hardy perennial
or
Hardy perennial

**Leaf colours available**

**Display period**

| JANUARY |
| FEBRUARY |
| MARCH |
| APRIL |
| MAY |
| JUNE |
| JULY |
| AUGUST |
| SEPTEMBER |
| OCTOBER |
| NOVEMBER |
| DECEMBER |

*Cordyline indivisa*

Few plants can rival a Palm if you want to provide a tropical look to a bed or a large container. Two are hardy in mild areas, but even with these you can expect some to die in a severe winter. The best plan is to keep the plant in its pot and bed out in June as a centrepiece. The pot should then be lifted and brought indoors before the first frosts arrive. Shelter from strong winds and water during dry weather. Each spring remove some of the surface compost and replace with fresh material.

**VARIETIES:** There are 2 True Palms which can be used for summer display outdoors — both are hardy under average winter conditions in the South and West but can be used as bedding plants in all parts of the country. The Chinese Windmill Palm (**Trachycarpus fortunei**) has large fan-shaped leaves at the top of a thick trunk — the European Fan Palm (**Chamaerops humilis**) has similar fan-shaped leaves but is a smaller plant. The False Palms are more popular — the ones you will see in park bedding schemes are **Cordyline australis** (Cabbage Palm) with sword-like leaves on a branched trunk, its variety **'Purpurea'** with red-purple leaves and **C. indivisa** with sword-like leaves on an unbranched trunk. Specimens are usually 3–4 ft tall.

**SITE & SOIL:** Any potting compost will do — thrives in sun or partial shade.

**PLANT DETAILS:** Height 2–5 ft. Spacing — use as a dot plant.

**PROPAGATION:** Sow seed in March in gentle heat — plant out next year. It is usually a better idea to buy a pot plant from a reputable supplier.

*Cordyline australis*

# PANSY

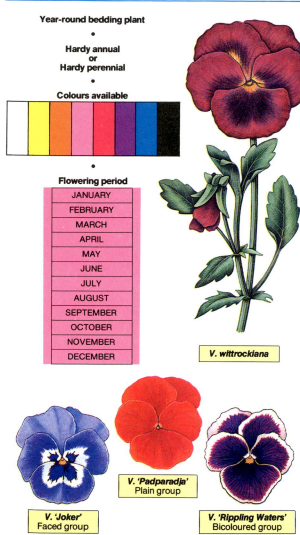

**Year-round bedding plant**

•

**Hardy annual**
or
**Hardy perennial**

•

**Colours available**

•

**Flowering period**

| JANUARY |
| FEBRUARY |
| MARCH |
| APRIL |
| MAY |
| JUNE |
| JULY |
| AUGUST |
| SEPTEMBER |
| OCTOBER |
| NOVEMBER |
| DECEMBER |

**V. wittrockiana**

**V. 'Joker'**
Faced group

**V. 'Padparadja'**
Plain group

**V. 'Rippling Waters'**
Bicoloured group

With care and the proper choice of varieties it is quite possible to have Pansies in flower during every month of the year. These plants are invaluable for pockets at the front of the border, in gaps left by bedding plants which have reached the end of their flowering span and for massed planting in ground to be covered, ranging from a large bed to a window box. The dividing line between the Pansy and the Viola is not a clear one, but you will usually find them on different pages of the seed catalogue. Pansies are generally taller and less compact. The flowers are larger and more rounded than Violas and the petals tend to be blotched in some way. The flower stems are shorter and so is their life span if grown as a perennial. Pansies can be expected to be in bloom for 4 to 6 months and no other flower has such a wide colour span, ranging from pure white to almost jet black — only green is missing. Faced varieties have a large dark marking ('face' or 'mask') at the centre of the bloom — plain ones are self-coloured and bicolours bear two distinct shades. Dead-head the stems regularly, protect from slugs and greenfly, and water in dry weather.

**VARIETIES:** Pansies are varieties of **Viola wittrockiana** and there are scores to choose from. The *Winter-flowering* group is sown in summer for flowering in November to May — the major display is usually in the spring. The **'Universal'** strain dominates this group — buy as a mixture or as a faced, plain or bicoloured variety. The only other popular type for winter display is **'Floral Dance'** — a mixture of rather small flowers. The *Summer-flowering* group is sown in spring for flowering in summer and autumn and nearly all Pansies belong here. Mixtures are popular — for the largest flowers (4 in. across) grow **'Majestic Giants'** and for a range of attractive plain Pansies choose **'Clear Crystals Mixed'**. The old-fashioned faced variety **'Swiss Giants'** remains popular, but for many people a plain variety is preferred. Look for **'Forerunner Tangerine'** (orange), **'Azure Blue'** (clear blue), **'Black'** (velvety near-black) and **'Padparadja'** (vermilion). The F$_1$ hybrid **'Imperial'** strain is widely grown, and so are the novelties which appear each year. **'Joker'** is pale blue with a dark blue face and **'Love Duet'** is cream with a rose face. **'Rippling Waters'** has deep purple flowers with a distinct white edge and **'Jolly Joker'** is an eye-catching purple and orange bicolour.

**SITE & SOIL:** Any reasonable garden soil in sun or partial shade.

**PLANT DETAILS:** Height 6–9 in. Spacing 9 in.–1 ft.

**PROPAGATION:** Sow seed of Winter-flowering varieties in June–July in a nursery bed or cold frame. Plant out in autumn. Summer-flowering varieties are sown in February–April under glass. Plant out in May.

Viola 'Universal Mixed'

Viola 'Swiss Giants'

Viola 'Imperial Pink'

# PELARGONIUM Geranium

**Summer bedding plant**
•
**Half hardy perennial**
•
**Colours available**

•

**Flowering period**

| |
|---|
| JANUARY |
| FEBRUARY |
| MARCH |
| APRIL |
| MAY |
| JUNE |
| JULY |
| AUGUST |
| SEPTEMBER |
| OCTOBER |
| NOVEMBER |
| DECEMBER |

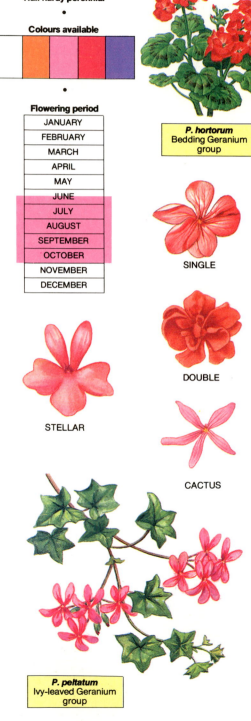

**P. hortorum**
Bedding Geranium group

SINGLE

DOUBLE

STELLAR

CACTUS

**P. peltatum**
Ivy-leaved Geranium group

Once it was quite simple. In spring we bought pot-grown Pelargoniums (popular name Geraniums) for bedding out in late spring. These had been raised from cuttings by the nurseryman and we in turn took cuttings in late summer for new plants to put out next year. There were the bright red 'Paul Crampel', the snowy 'Queen of the Whites' etc, and some of these Zonal Pelargoniums had multicoloured leaves which were even brighter than the flowers. Things have now changed with the introduction of F$_1$ hybrids which can be raised from seed. These days it is possible to raise your own plants in large numbers, and the range of varieties in the catalogues is impressive. Listed below are some of the various types, but new ones continue to appear. You will have to read the current catalogues each year if you want to keep up to date. Whether home-grown or shop-bought, the pots should be watered a few hours before planting and make sure that the Geraniums have been hardened-off properly. Plant firmly and pinch out the growing tips occasionally to increase the bushiness of the plants. Geraniums can withstand dry conditions better than most plants — constant watering is an easy way to kill them. So water only if dry weather is prolonged and remember to feed occasionally with a potash-rich fertilizer. You must remove the flower stalks once the blooms have faded if you want a prolonged flowering season — this is especially important with some of the new varieties. Before the first frosts arrive carefully dig up the plants and shake off the soil around the roots. Pot them up singly in Seed and Cutting Compost, using pots which are no larger than necessary to house the roots. Keep in an unheated room and only water if the leaves begin to flag. In spring move to a well-lit spot and increase the amount of water.

**VARIETIES:** The *Bedding Geraniums* make up by far the largest group of **Pelargonium hortorum** hybrids. Some of the plants on offer at garden centres will have been raised from cuttings. The usual height is 1–1½ ft and the leaves may or may not be prominently zoned with horseshoe-shaped markings. Well-known single varieties grown from cuttings include '**Paul Crampel**' and '**Pandora**' (red) and the pink '**Elaine**'. All the doubles are raised from cuttings — look for '**Josephine**' (red), '**Hermione**' (white) and '**Mrs Lawrence**' (pink). Nowadays many shop-bought plants are raised from seed, and you will find a large selection in the catalogues. There are some excellent basic reds such as '**Ringo Deep Scarlet**', '**Red Elite**' and '**Cheerio Scarlet**'. '**Orange Appeal**' is claimed to be the first true orange, '**Cherie**' is salmon, '**Hollywood White**' is pure white. For a white-eyed Geranium choose the pink '**Hollywood Star**' or the red '**Bright Eyes**'. The '**Gala**' series is noted for sturdy plants with large flower heads — even more compact (8 in.) is the dark-leaved '**Video**' series. The latest introductions include the *Multibloom/Floribunda* Group with a number of varieties ('**Sensation**', '**Pinto**' etc) which are very early and bear an unusually large number of flower heads. Some of these Bedding Geraniums (e.g '**Picasso**') have prominent dark markings on the leaves, but for really decorative foliage you should pick a *Fancy-leaved Geranium* such as '**Mrs Henry Cox**', '**Caroline Schmidt**' or '**Happy Thoughts**' — all are raised from cuttings. A new group is the *Spreading Geraniums* — the '**Breakaway**' varieties are basal branching which means that the stems spread out, making them useful for containers and hanging baskets. The true trailing types are the *Ivy-leaved Geraniums* which are varieties of **P. peltatum**. Examples include '**Ville de Paris**' (salmon), '**Red Mini Cascade**', '**Snow Queen**', '**Lilac Gem**' and the bicoloured '**Harlequin**' series. There is just one ('**Summer Showers**') which can be raised from seed.

**SITE & SOIL:** Any well-drained garden soil will do — thrives in sun or light shade.

**PLANT DETAILS:** Height 6 in.–1½ ft. Spacing 9 in.–1 ft.

**PROPAGATION:** Sow seed in January–February at 70°–75°F — plant out in late May. Take stem cuttings in July or August and grow on in a cool greenhouse until the danger of frost has passed.

*Pelargonium hortorum*
'Red Elite'

*Pelargonium hortorum*
'Hollywood Star'

*Pelargonium hortorum*
'Sensation'

*Pelargonium hortorum*
'Mrs Henry Cox'

*Pelargonium hortorum*
'Caroline Schmidt'

*Pelargonium hortorum*
'Happy Thoughts'

*Pelargonium peltatum*
'Harlequin Alpine Glow'

*Pelargonium peltatum*
'Red Mini Cascade'

*Pelargonium peltatum*
'Summer Showers'

# PETUNIA   Petunia

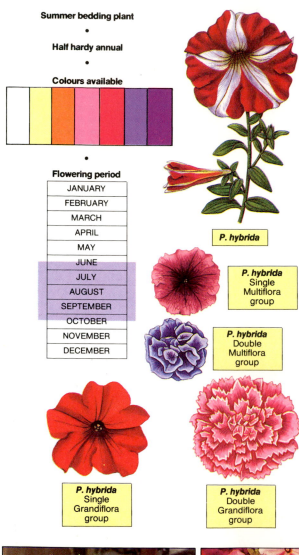

**Summer bedding plant**

•

**Half hardy annual**

•

**Colours available**

**Flowering period**

| |
|---|
| JANUARY |
| FEBRUARY |
| MARCH |
| APRIL |
| MAY |
| JUNE |
| JULY |
| AUGUST |
| SEPTEMBER |
| OCTOBER |
| NOVEMBER |
| DECEMBER |

*P. hybrida*

*P. hybrida*
Single
Multiflora
group

*P. hybrida*
Double
Multiflora
group

*P. hybrida*
Single
Grandiflora
group

*P. hybrida*
Double
Grandiflora
group

The modern F$_1$ hybrids have become great favourites — they are grown in vast numbers in containers, window boxes and hanging baskets as well as in beds and borders. Once all you could buy was a straggly plant with dull pink flowers which much preferred a warmer climate than ours. Now there is a wide range of flower colours and sizes. Growth is much more even these days, and modern varieties bear showy, funnel-shaped blooms which may be self-coloured, multicoloured, picoteed with a broad white edge or striped to give a star-like effect. These flowers may be single or double and petal edges may be smooth or deeply ruffled. Petunias love hot and dry conditions — the display can be disappointing in prolonged wet weather. Where possible buy plants before they have come into flower and pinch out the tips when the stems are 4–6 in. high. Protect with Slug Pellets and when in full flower feed with a potash-rich fertilizer. Dead-head regularly and cut back if they become too straggly.

**VARIETIES:** There are 2 main groups of **P. hybrida** — the Multifloras and the Grandifloras. The *Multifloras* are the ones to choose for bedding — the flowers are quite small (2 in. across) but they are borne in large numbers and stand up to rain much better than the larger ones. The **'Dwarf Resisto'** (1 ft) series is the most popular one and regarded by many as the best. The plants resist rain and wind remarkably well — look for **'Resisto Rose'**, **'Resisto Iced Blue'** (striped), **'Resisto Blue'** etc. Other reliable ones include the **'Carpet'** series. For heavily-veined flowers pick **'Plum Crazy'** — **'Starfire'** is the brightest red-and-white striped one. Double Multifloras are available — **'Cherry Tart'**, **'Delight'** etc with Carnation-like blooms. They are not as reliable as the single ones. *Grandifloras* bear much larger flowers (4–5 in. across) than Multifloras but the plants are generally straggly, the flowers are not borne freely and they are damaged by rain — use for containers rather than bedding out. Good singles include **'Colour Parade'**, **'Picotee'**, **'Telstar'** (striped), **'Blue Frost'**, **'Red Cloud'** and the heavily-veined **'Daddy'** series. There are large ruffled doubles (**'Bouquet'**, **'Giant Victorious'**, **'Purple Pirouette'** etc) — rain protection is essential with these varieties. A third group, the *Floribundas*, has appeared — the **'Mirage'** series is a Multiflora-Grandiflora cross. For hanging baskets grow one of the **'Cascade'**, **'Supercascade'** or **'Balcony'** series.

**SITE & SOIL:** Any well-drained garden soil will do, but light land is preferred. Choose a sunny site.

**PLANT DETAILS:** Height 6 in.–1½ ft. Spacing 9 in.–1 ft.

**PROPAGATION:** Sow seed in January–March under glass. Not easy — germination temperature of 70°–75°F is required. Do not cover seed. Plant out in late May.

Petunia 'Resisto Iced Blue'

Petunia 'Colour Parade'

Petunia 'Bouquet'

# PENSTEMON Beard Tongue

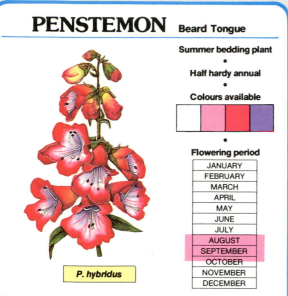

- Summer bedding plant
- Half hardy annual
- Colours available

**Flowering period**

| | |
|---|---|
| JANUARY | |
| FEBRUARY | |
| MARCH | |
| APRIL | |
| MAY | |
| JUNE | |
| JULY | |
| **AUGUST** | |
| **SEPTEMBER** | |
| OCTOBER | |
| NOVEMBER | |
| DECEMBER | |

*P. hybridus*

It is odd that this imposing plant has not become popular as a rival to the universally-grown Antirrhinum. The modern varieties of Penstemon listed below can be grown as half hardy annuals, although in most parts of Britain it is quite safe to plant out properly-hardened off seedlings in late April. Compared with Antirrhinums there is the disadvantage of yellows and oranges being absent, but on the credit side the tubular blooms are larger and open faced, and some of the bicolours are quite spectacular. The flowering season starts rather late but it does continue until late autumn.

**VARIETIES:** You will find one or more of 3 varieties of **P. hybridus** in most catalogues — some sadly do not list any. The most popular Penstemon for bedding is **'Skyline'** — a bushy and compact plant (1–1½ ft) with attractive blooms massed all round the stout flowering stems. **'Bouquet'** (1½–2 ft) is rather bolder with flowers which cover the whole of the Penstemon colour range. The tallest Penstemon is **'Monarch'** — the 2½ ft plants provide the brightest bicolours. This one is used in parks and other public plantings as a dot plant — 'Skyline' is recommended for groundwork planting. All the varieties can be used as bright but short-lived cut flowers.

**SITE & SOIL:** Any well-drained garden soil will do — thrives best in full sun.

**PLANT DETAILS:** Height 1–2½ ft. Spacing 9 in.–1½ ft.

**PROPAGATION:** Sow seed in gentle heat in February. Plant out in late April or May.

*Penstemon 'Skyline'*

# PHACELIA Phacelia

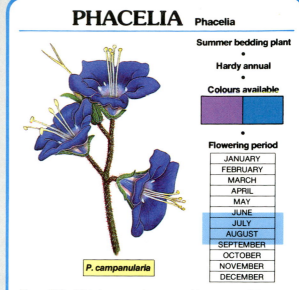

- Summer bedding plant
- Hardy annual
- Colours available

**Flowering period**

| | |
|---|---|
| JANUARY | |
| FEBRUARY | |
| MARCH | |
| APRIL | |
| MAY | |
| JUNE | |
| **JULY** | |
| **AUGUST** | |
| SEPTEMBER | |
| OCTOBER | |
| NOVEMBER | |
| DECEMBER | |

*P. campanularia*

You will find this low-growing annual in many catalogues but in very few gardens. This is a shame because the flowers, which are 1 in. wide upturned bells, are an intense Gentian blue. The colour is almost unique amongst bedding plants and it really is no trouble to grow. Phacelia is quite hardy and flowering takes place within 2 months of sowing. The reddish stems creep and branch, the greyish foliage is fragrant when crushed and the flowers bear bright yellow stamens which clearly stand above the blue petals. Plant Phacelia as an edging along a path or in clumps in the rockery.

**VARIETIES:** The only species which you are likely to find in popular catalogues is **P. campanularia**. There will rarely be a choice — the only one listed will be the 6–10 in. blue-flowering dwarf which does so well in poor, sandy soil. A few specialist seedsmen offer the taller hybrid **'Blue Bonnet'** which grows about twice as high and has the same bright blue flowers. These specialist catalogues may also offer other species of Phacelia. **P. viscida** (1½ ft) bears its Gentian blue flowers in long spikes. **P. tanacetifolia** (2½ ft) does not have the true blue effect — its bell-shaped flowers are mauve.

**SITE & SOIL:** Any well-drained garden soil will do, but light land is preferred. Thrives in sun or light shade.

**PLANT DETAILS:** Height 6 in.–2½ ft. Spacing 6 in.–1 ft.

**PROPAGATION:** Sow in autumn or early spring where it is to flower as it does not like transplanting. For bedding, sow in peat pots in March or April and plant out in May.

*Phacelia campanularia*

*Phacelia tanacetifolia*

# PHLOX Annual Phlox

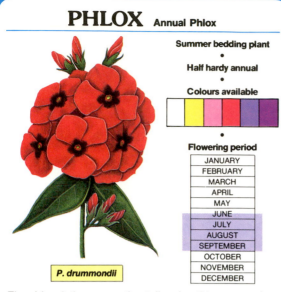

- Summer bedding plant
- Half hardy annual
- Colours available

**Flowering period**

| | |
|---|---|
| JANUARY | |
| FEBRUARY | |
| MARCH | |
| APRIL | |
| MAY | |
| JUNE | |
| JULY | |
| AUGUST | |
| SEPTEMBER | |
| OCTOBER | |
| NOVEMBER | |
| DECEMBER | |

*P. drummondii*

The old varieties were rather tall and untidy — nowadays there are dwarfs with bright flowers which may be smooth edged or distinctly star-like. Many colours are available, although true yellow is rare. The bloom may be a single colour, but some varieties produce a large number of flowers which have a distinct central eye in a different colour. The flower heads are tightly massed and measure about 4 in. across. An easy plant to grow but avoid overwatering. Use the dwarf types for edging, containers or in the rockery. Put down Slug Pellets if ragged holes appear in the leaves and dead-head regularly.

**VARIETIES:** The various forms of Annual Phlox are varieties of **P. drummondii**. For a tall old-fashioned type look for **'Brilliant'** (1½ ft) — each flower bears a distinct eye. Another rather tall type with eyed flowers is **'Large-flowered Mix'** (1–1½ ft). The most popular dwarf is the large-flowered **'Beauty Mixed'** or **'Dwarf Beauty'** (6–9 in.) — for eyed flowers choose **'Cecily'** (6 in.). Rather taller and brighter is **'Carnival'** — a 1 ft Phlox noted for the gay colours of the display. A lovely novelty is **'Twinkles'** (6 in.) which bears masses of starry flowers with sharply-cut petals. Another starry Phlox but even more compact is **'Petticoat'** (4 in.).

**SITE & SOIL:** Any well-drained garden soil will do — thrives best in full sun.

**PLANT DETAILS:** Height 4 in.–1½ ft. Spacing 6 in.–1 ft.

**PROPAGATION:** In mild areas sow seed outdoors in April. For bedding, sow seed in gentle heat in February–March. Plant out in late May.

Phlox drummondii 'Beauty Mixed'

Phlox drummondii 'Twinkles'

# PLUMBAGO Cape Leadwort

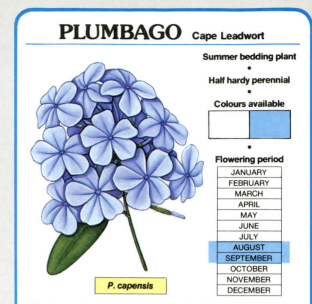

- Summer bedding plant
- Half hardy perennial
- Colours available

**Flowering period**

| | |
|---|---|
| JANUARY | |
| FEBRUARY | |
| MARCH | |
| APRIL | |
| MAY | |
| JUNE | |
| JULY | |
| AUGUST | |
| SEPTEMBER | |
| OCTOBER | |
| NOVEMBER | |
| DECEMBER | |

*P. capensis*

Plumbago is sometimes regarded as too tender for growing as a garden plant outdoors, but this popular conservatory climber can be used as an out-of-the-ordinary dot plant in a summer bedding scheme or as a specimen plant in a container. The plant itself is not attractive — the straggly stems require support. It is the colour of the flowers which earns Plumbago a place in the garden — the star-faced tubular flowers are an unusual sky blue and are borne in large clusters. The 2 in. long leaves are grey below.

**VARIETIES:** There is just one species — **P. capensis**, sometimes listed as **P. auriculata**. You can try to grow it as a half hardy annual, sowing seed under glass in January for planting out when the danger of frost has passed and hopefully enjoying the flower heads in late summer. However, the chances of success are not great and it is a much better plan to buy a plant in flower from your local garden centre and then carefully harden off before planting outdoors in June. Lift and bring back indoors before the arrival of the first frosts. Trim back old shoots in early spring and bed out again in summer. A white variety (**alba**) is available but is not worth growing.

**SITE & SOIL:** Any well-drained garden soil will do — full sun is essential.

**PLANT DETAILS:** Height 3–4 ft. Spacing — use as a dot plant.

**PROPAGATION:** Buy as a pot-grown specimen — plant out in June or July.

Plumbago capensis

# POLYANTHUS

**Spring bedding plant**

•

**Hardy perennial**

•

**Colours available**

•

**Flowering period**

| JANUARY |
| FEBRUARY |
| MARCH |
| APRIL |
| MAY |
| JUNE |
| JULY |
| AUGUST |
| SEPTEMBER |
| OCTOBER |
| NOVEMBER |
| DECEMBER |

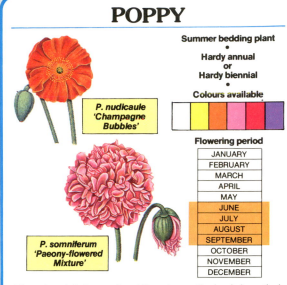

*P. variabilis*

If you want a brightly coloured carpet of bedding plants in spring, then you must turn to the Universal Pansy (page 61) or Polyanthus. This latter plant, a cross between the Common Primrose and the Cowslip, has given rise to some splendid strains which bear massed flowers borne on stout stems, each bloom measuring up to 2½ in. across. Place twigs between the plants in early spring to keep the birds away — put down Slug Pellets if large holes appear in the leaves. Use for groundwork planting, edging etc — there may be a second flush in autumn, but the usual plan is to lift the plants in mid–late May to make room for summer bedding.

**VARIETIES:** This hybrid may be listed as **Primula variabilis** or **P. polyantha**. The **'Pacific Giants'** have the largest flowers, but they are not fully winter hardy. For maximum winter reliability, wide colour range and large blooms the best choice is the $F_1$ hybrid **'Crescendo'**. For the most ornate flowers choose **'Gold Lace'** — a golden-eyed red bloom with yellow-edged petals. There are a number of single-colour varieties, even a green one (**'Chartreuse'**), but most catalogues offer only mixtures. All of these varieties grow 9–12 in. high.

**SITE & SOIL:** Any moisture-retentive soil will do — thrives best in partial shade.

**PLANT DETAILS:** Height 9 in.–1 ft. Spacing 1 ft.

**PROPAGATION:** Sow seed in April–June — plant out in autumn. Raising Polyanthus from seed is not easy — consider buying seedlings or divide established clumps for bedding out in September or October.

*Polyanthus 'Pacific Giants'*

# POPPY

**Summer bedding plant**

•

**Hardy annual**
**or**
**Hardy biennial**

•

**Colours available**

•

**Flowering period**

| JANUARY |
| FEBRUARY |
| MARCH |
| APRIL |
| MAY |
| JUNE |
| JULY |
| AUGUST |
| SEPTEMBER |
| OCTOBER |
| NOVEMBER |
| DECEMBER |

*P. nudicaule*
*'Champagne*
*Bubbles'*

*P. somniferum*
*'Paeony-flowered*
*Mixture'*

There is a daintiness about Poppies — the buds bow their heads, the petals flutter in the breeze and the flowers are short-lived. But they are not delicate at all — they are quite hardy, easy to grow and do not need staking. There are singles (cup-shaped with four overlapping petals) and doubles (ball-like with many crowded petals). There are perennial, biennial and annual varieties.

**VARIETIES:** The most popular Poppies are the annual ones, descended from the Corn Poppy **Papaver rhoeas**. The well-known Shirley Poppies (2 ft, double) belong here — so does the much shorter **'Mother of Pearl'** (1 ft, unusual pastel colours). **P. somniferum** (the Opium Poppy) is much taller and bolder — choose **'Paeony-flowered Mixture'** for its 4 in. wide double blooms. All the annuals are best sown where they are to flower — they do not like transplanting. The biennial **P. nudicaule** (Iceland Poppy) is a bedding plant — treat it as a biennial (see below) or an early-sown annual. Look for **'Sparkling Bubbles'** (2 ft, mixed colours), **'Matador'** (1½ ft, 5 in. wide scarlet flowers) and **'San Remo'** (2 ft, mixed colours). Iceland Poppy is a good cut flower — sear ends with a match.

**SITE & SOIL:** Any reasonable garden soil will do — thrives in sun or light shade.

**PLANT DETAILS:** Height 9 in.–2½ ft. Spacing 9 in.–1 ft.

**PROPAGATION:** For bedding, sow seed of annuals under glass in March. Plant out in May. Biennials should be sown in July for planting out in autumn — they can also be sown under glass in January for planting out in April to bloom in the same year.

*Papaver nudicaule 'San Remo'*

# PORTULACA Sun Plant

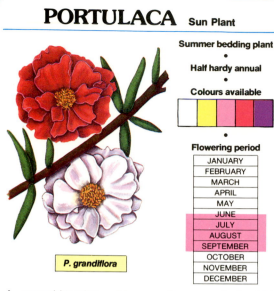

**Summer bedding plant**
•
**Half hardy annual**
•
**Colours available**
•
**Flowering period**

| | |
|---|---|
| JANUARY | |
| FEBRUARY | |
| MARCH | |
| APRIL | |
| MAY | |
| JUNE | |
| JULY | |
| AUGUST | |
| SEPTEMBER | |
| OCTOBER | |
| NOVEMBER | |
| DECEMBER | |

**P. grandiflora**

A ground-hugging, wide-spreading succulent which provides a summer-long colourful display if the conditions are right. The reddish stems bear clusters of long fleshy leaves which in a sunny season can be almost covered by the saucer-shaped flowers. These blooms are often ruffled and the petals have a distinctive silky sheen. This is one to plant at the front of a sunny bed or border or in an unshaded rockery — look for another plant if your soil is heavy or if the site is in shade for even a short period during the day. Take care not to overwater and avoid overfeeding — water only when the plants appear to be wilting.

**VARIETIES:** **P. grandiflora** is the popular species. A number of varieties are available — the flowers are generally 1 in. wide, semi-double and bear prominent yellow stamens. Single varieties are now out of favour. The favourite one offered for bedding out in spring is the $F_2$ hybrid **'Calypso'** — a 6–8 in. many-coloured mixture producing plants with a 1 ft spread. The baby of the group is **'Minilaca'** (4 in.). Unfortunately most types close their flowers when the weather is dull or wet. There are two varieties which claim to stay open when the sun isn't shining — **'Sundance'** (6 in., 1½ in. wide flowers) and **'Cloudbeater'** (6 in., 1 in. wide flowers).

**SITE & SOIL:** Well-drained sandy soil and full sun are essential.

**PLANT DETAILS:** Height 4–8 in. Spacing 6 in.–1 ft.

**PROPAGATION:** Sow seed in gentle heat in February–March. Take care not to overwater — Portulaca is prone to damping-off disease. Plant out in late May.

*Portulaca grandiflora 'Sundance'*

# PRIMULA Primrose

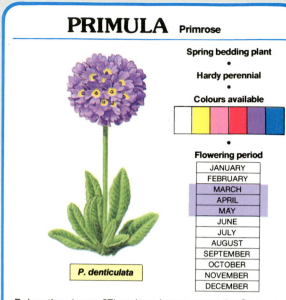

**Spring bedding plant**
•
**Hardy perennial**
•
**Colours available**
•
**Flowering period**

| | |
|---|---|
| JANUARY | |
| FEBRUARY | |
| MARCH | |
| APRIL | |
| MAY | |
| JUNE | |
| JULY | |
| AUGUST | |
| SEPTEMBER | |
| OCTOBER | |
| NOVEMBER | |
| DECEMBER | |

**P. denticulata**

Polyanthus (page 67) and to a lesser extent the Common Primrose are widely used as bedding plants which are set out in autumn and lifted in May if the site is needed for summer bedding. Other members of the Primula genus are rarely used for this purpose — they are either cultivated as indoor pot plants or as perennials for outdoor use in the border or rockery. There are two unusual species, however, which can be planted out in autumn for a spring display as an alternative to Polyanthus. Like all Primulas these types need a humus-rich soil and partial shade.

**VARIETIES:** The Common Primrose (**P. vulgaris**) grows 4–6 in. high — it blooms a little later than Polyanthus and is less reliable. **P. denticulata** is the Drumstick Primrose — the 1 ft stems produce 3 in. wide ball-shaped flower heads bearing many yellow-eyed blooms. Lavender is the usual colour, but in a mixture you will also find white, pink and red. The Japanese or Candelabra Primrose (**P. japonica**) is different — here the blooms are borne in a series of whorls up the stem. It grows about 2 ft high and a number of named varieties are available. There is **'Miller's Crimson'** and **'Postford White'** — you can also buy a white/pink/red mixture. P. japonica is perhaps the easiest Primula to raise from seed.

**SITE & SOIL:** Any moist garden soil containing organic matter will do — thrives best in partial shade.

**PLANT DETAILS:** Height 4 in.–2 ft. Spacing 9 in.–1 ft.

**PROPAGATION:** Raising plants from seed is difficult — buy pot-grown specimens for bedding out in autumn.

*Primula japonica*

*Primula vulgaris*

# PYRETHRUM Pyrethrum

- Summer bedding plant
- Half hardy perennial
- Leaf colours available

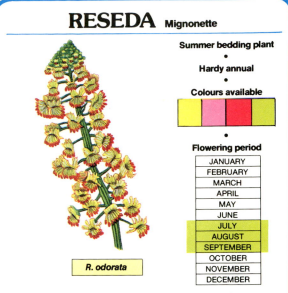

P. ptarmicaeflorum

**Display period**

| JANUARY |
| FEBRUARY |
| MARCH |
| APRIL |
| MAY |
| JUNE |
| JULY |
| AUGUST |
| SEPTEMBER |
| OCTOBER |
| NOVEMBER |
| DECEMBER |

The Pyrethrum of the herbaceous border has no place here — plants sown from seed do not flower in the first year. The bedding plant Pyrethrums are grown for their foliage — silvery-grey or golden. P. ptarmicaeflorum is the usual one — a perennial which is generally raised as an annual each year from seed. It is used as an edging plant or as a divider between brightly-coloured flowers in beds or borders. It is quite similar to but not as popular as Cineraria maritima (page 30) — the yellow-leaved Pyrethrum is even less likely to be found in gardens or the catalogues.

**VARIETIES:** P. ptarmicaeflorum is aptly called Silver Feather. The silvery leaves are finely divided and have a distinctly feathery appearance. The maximum height is about 1 ft and a sunny site is needed to ensure that the overall effect is silvery and not green. P. aureus is listed as Golden Moss or Golden Ball — small mounds of mossy foliage which is yellow or golden. Growth is always neat and rarely exceeds 4 in. — Golden Moss is an excellent choice for carpet bedding. Small Chrysanthemum-like flowers may appear — white-petalled and yellow-centred. These may be removed so that the foliage display is not impaired.

**SITE & SOIL:** Any reasonable garden soil will do — thrives best in full sun.

**PLANT DETAILS:** Height 4 in. or 1 ft. Spacing 6–8 in.

**PROPAGATION:** Sow seed in gentle heat in January–March. Plant out in late May.

Pyrethrum ptarmicaeflorum

# RESEDA Mignonette

- Summer bedding plant
- Hardy annual
- Colours available

R. odorata

**Flowering period**

| JANUARY |
| FEBRUARY |
| MARCH |
| APRIL |
| MAY |
| JUNE |
| JULY |
| AUGUST |
| SEPTEMBER |
| OCTOBER |
| NOVEMBER |
| DECEMBER |

About 200 years ago vast numbers of these plants were grown in London and Paris. It was not for their appearance — untidy stems with clusters of tiny greenish flowers. The attraction was the fragrance — it was said that a few plants could perfume a whole room. This beloved cottage garden plant is still recommended for planting under a window or near a door so that the evening fragrance can be enjoyed. Growth is upright at first and then spreading, its small flowers appearing in cone-like trusses. The flowering season is disappointingly short in a hot and dry summer.

**VARIETIES:** There is just one species — R. odorata. Breeders have tried to improve the floral display over the years and a number of named varieties can be found in the catalogues. The yellow and pink 'Machel' appears to be the favourite one — others include the green and red 'Red Monarch' and the red 'Goliath'. However, it is better to choose for maximum scent and not colour — choose 'Sweet Scented', 'Fragrant Beauty' or 'Giant'. They say that the fragrance is only a pale shadow of the heady perfume of Mignonettes in Victorian days, but we shall never know.

**SITE & SOIL:** Any reasonable garden soil will do — add lime if it is acid. Thrives in sun or light shade.

**PLANT DETAILS:** Height 1 ft. Spacing 9 in.

**PROPAGATION:** The usual plan is to sow seed in April where they are to flower. For bedding, sow seed in March and plant out in May.

Reseda odorata 'Giant'

# RICINUS Castor Oil Plant

**Summer bedding plant**

•

**Half hardy perennial**

•

**Leaf colours available**

•

**Display period**

| | |
|---|---|
| JANUARY | |
| FEBRUARY | |
| MARCH | |
| APRIL | |
| MAY | |
| JUNE | ▮ |
| JULY | ▮ |
| AUGUST | ▮ |
| SEPTEMBER | ▮ |
| OCTOBER | |
| NOVEMBER | |
| DECEMBER | |

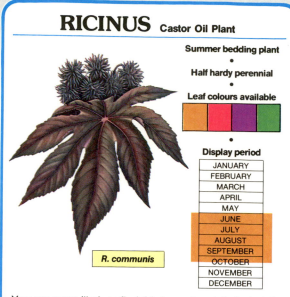

*R. communis*

You are more likely to find this imposing dot plant at the centre of a bed in a park or other public place than in a home garden. The round and spiky seed pods which appear in late summer are sometimes colourful, but Ricinus is grown for its large leaves. This palmate foliage is 1 ft or more across — glistening green, bronze or purple. Grow it as a half hardy annual and feed regularly after planting out. Take care — the seeds are poisonous and this plant will not thrive in an exposed northern site. Tall plants should be staked.

**VARIETIES:** R. communis is the only species grown but the varieties offered differ from catalogue to catalogue. The giant is **'Zanzibarensis'** and is in a number of lists — the imposing stem reaches 6 ft and the large leaves are a blend of bronze, green and purple with pale-coloured midribs. At the other end of the scale is the compact **'Mizuma'** which rarely exceeds 3 ft. Leaves are green, but both veins and stems are red. **'Gibbsonii'** (4 ft, dark red foliage) is perhaps the most colourful, but the popular variety is **'Impala'**. This 4 ft plant bears a crown of bronzy-red leaves above the lower bronzy-green foliage. The seed pods are red. Use this one as a back of the border plant if there is a space to fill.

**SITE & SOIL:** Any well-drained garden soil will do — thrives best in full sun.

**PLANT DETAILS:** Height 3–6 ft. Spacing — use as a dot plant.

**PROPAGATION:** Sow seed in peat pots in March in a heated propagator. Plant out in late May.

Ricinus communis
'Mizuma'

# ROSA Miniature Rose

**Summer bedding plant**

•

**Hardy perennial**

•

**Colours available**

•

**Flowering period**

| | |
|---|---|
| JANUARY | |
| FEBRUARY | |
| MARCH | |
| APRIL | |
| MAY | |
| JUNE | |
| JULY | ▮ |
| AUGUST | ▮ |
| SEPTEMBER | ▮ |
| OCTOBER | |
| NOVEMBER | |
| DECEMBER | |

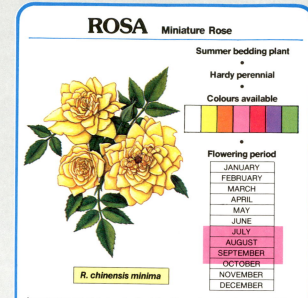

*R. chinensis minima*

It may seem strange to find the Rose in a book on bedding plants, but the Miniature or Fairy Rose is an excellent subject for containers or edging along a bed or border. The ½–1½ in. blooms are similar to their large outdoor relatives. You will find fragrance, a wide range of colours and a variety of growth habits including bushes, climbers and standards. Little care is needed — bed out in autumn or spring, using shop-bought or home-raised plants. Feed occasionally, spray against pests or diseases and lift in autumn if the site is needed for spring bedding.

**VARIETIES:** You will find a good selection of **Rosa chinensis minima** hybrids in the rose catalogues and at large garden centres. Look for **'Angela Rippon'** (double, carmine pink, fragrant, 12 in.), **'Starina'** (double, vermilion, fragrant, 10 in.), **'Pour Toi'** (double, creamy white, no fragrance, 8 in.), **'Cinderella'** (double, silvery-pink, slight fragrance, 10 in.), **'Stars 'n Stripes'** (double, striped red and white, no fragrance, 15 in.) and **'Coralin'** (double, orange-red, no fragrance, 15 in.). Just a few — you will find many more in the lists. You may be able to buy seed from rose growers and nurseries — only mixtures are available but they are easily raised for flowering in the first season.

**SITE & SOIL:** Any reasonable soil will do — thrives best in full sun.

**PLANT DETAILS:** Height 6 in.–1½ ft. Spacing 1 ft.

**PROPAGATION:** Buy plants in flower or take cuttings in spring — plant out in autumn or spring. Sow seed in February under glass. Plant out in May.

Rosa
'Angela Rippon'

Rosa
'Coralin'

# RUDBECKIA Cone Flower

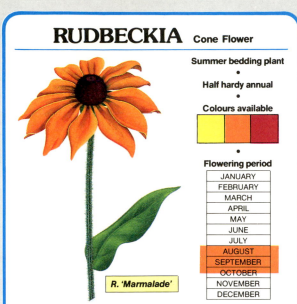

Summer bedding plant

•

Half hardy annual

•

Colours available

•

**Flowering period**

| |
|---|
| JANUARY |
| FEBRUARY |
| MARCH |
| APRIL |
| MAY |
| JUNE |
| JULY |
| **AUGUST** |
| **SEPTEMBER** |
| OCTOBER |
| NOVEMBER |
| DECEMBER |

*R. 'Marmalade'*

Rudbeckia is just one of several bedding plants which bear large Daisy-like flowers in yellow, orange or mahogany red on stout stems. The main feature of this one is that there is a prominent cone-shaped disc at the centre — usually but not always brown or near-black. The blooms generally appear late in the season but they are usually very large and plentiful. The tall ones are suitable for the middle or back of the border, but nowadays there are 1 ft dwarfs to give colour to the smallest bed. Stake tall varieties — keep watch for slugs. A fine flower for indoor display — immerse cut ends in boiling water for about half a minute before arranging.

**VARIETIES: R. hirta** comes in many varieties and hybrids — the 2½–3 ft popular giant is the Gloriosa Daisy **'Giant Tetraploid Mixed'** with its saucer-sized flowers. **'Marmalade'** (2 ft) has beautiful orange petals and a prominent purple-black cone — **'Irish Eyes'** grows to about the same height but its cone is green, as you would expect from its name. **'Rustic Dwarfs'** (2 ft) has 4–6 in. flowers in gold, bronze, deep red and a variety of bicolours, but the modern one which has attracted much interest is the 1 ft **'Goldilocks'** which flowers in July and bears semi-double or double flowers.

**SITE & SOIL:** Any well-drained garden soil will do — thrives in sun or light shade.

**PLANT DETAILS:** Height 1–3 ft. Spacing 1–2 ft.

**PROPAGATION:** Sow seed in February under glass. Plant out in mid–late May.

*Rudbeckia 'Rustic Dwarfs'*

*Rudbeckia 'Goldilocks'*

# SALPIGLOSSIS Painted Tongue

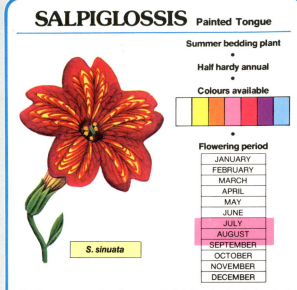

Summer bedding plant

•

Half hardy annual

•

Colours available

•

**Flowering period**

| |
|---|
| JANUARY |
| FEBRUARY |
| MARCH |
| APRIL |
| MAY |
| JUNE |
| **JULY** |
| **AUGUST** |
| SEPTEMBER |
| OCTOBER |
| NOVEMBER |
| DECEMBER |

*S. sinuata*

Seeing a group of well-grown Salpiglossis plants in a hot and dry summer has made many a gardener write down the name as a must for bedding out next year. Few other annuals can rival its exotic appearance — velvety, trumpet-shaped flowers with prominent veins in contrasting colours — yellow on dark red, deep purple on yellow and so on. Unfortunately its exotic appearance goes with exotic tastes — Salpiglossis will not thrive in wet soil nor in dry sandy ones, it suffers very badly on exposed sites and it needs a warm summer to show its full glory. Still, all you have to lose is a packet of seed and the challenge is well worthwhile.

**VARIETIES: S. sinuata** is the garden species and the variety to go for is the $F_1$ hybrid **'Splash'**. The 1½ ft plants are quite bushy, but still require support with twigs like all other varieties. A host of flowers in brilliant colour appear in midsummer — the $F_2$ hybrid **'Bolero'** is less expensive, rather taller (2 ft) but rather less free-flowering. The tallest plants (2½ ft) and the widest flowers (2 in.) are produced by **'grandiflora'** — at the other end of the scale are the 1 ft dwarfs **'Festival'** and **'Flamenco'**.

**SITE & SOIL:** Well-drained garden soil and a sunny, sheltered site are essential.

**PLANT DETAILS:** Height 1–2½ ft. Spacing 9 in.–1 ft.

**PROPAGATION:** Sow seed in January–February in gentle heat. Plant out in late May.

*Salpiglossis sinuata 'Splash'*

# SALVIA Sage

**Summer bedding plant**

•

**Half hardy annual**
or
**Hardy annual**
or
**Hardy biennial**

•

**Colours available**

**Flowering period**

| |
|---|
| JANUARY |
| FEBRUARY |
| MARCH |
| APRIL |
| MAY |
| JUNE |
| JULY |
| AUGUST |
| SEPTEMBER |
| OCTOBER |
| NOVEMBER |
| DECEMBER |

**S. splendens**

**S. patens**

**S. horminum**

The most popular Salvia by far is the Scarlet Sage which can be seen in any street during the summer months. Its traditional use has been to provide the red in red, white and blue bedding schemes where the cost of Geraniums is prohibitive. Many purists find the erect spikes of fiery red flowers far too vulgar for their taste, but the plant still remains in the top ten list of bedding plants. Pinch out the tips of seedlings to induce bushiness and plant out when flowers have started to colour. Remember to feed and water when necessary. Now for something quite different. S. horminum is grown for its coloured leaves and bracts — it is a hardy annual which can be sown outdoors in spring or autumn or raised by the half hardy annual technique as for the Scarlet Sage. There are also two blue Salvias which should be more widely grown. S. farinacea produces long-lasting displays of dainty flowers on erect spikes. The other blue (S. patens or the Gentian Sage) is also a half hardy annual and is the other extreme to the Scarlet Sage — some gardeners feel that the blue flowers scattered between the leaves provide too subtle an effect. Clary (S. clarea) is a biennial for the border or cottage garden rather than the formal bed — 3 ft stems bearing papery rose or blue bracts.

**VARIETIES:** S. splendens (Scarlet Sage) carries a mass of tubular blooms at the top of 1 ft stems. The bright red **'Blaze of Fire'** was once the only one you could find, but not any more. The dark green leaved varieties with red flowers have become popular — **'Vanguard'**, **'Red Riches'**, **'Flarepath'** and the dark red **'Firecracker'**. **'Tom Thumb'** is the 6 in. dwarf. Red is not the only colour — you can buy **'Laser Purple'** or a salmon, pink, cream, lilac and red mixture such as **'Phoenix'** or **'Dress Parade'**. The red shades need full sun but partial shade is better for the pastel mixtures. **S. horminum** (1½ ft) is a bushy plant — varieties include **'Pink Lady'** (pink bracts) and **'Blue Beard'** (purple bracts). The flower heads can be dried for flower arranging. **S. farinacea** grows about 2 ft tall — most catalogues list only **'Victoria'** which bears long-lasting spikes of blue-purple flowers on blue stalks, but you can find white-flowering varieties such as **'Silver'** and **'Porcelaine'** in specialist catalogues. **S. patens** (2½ ft) is usually sold only as the species. It has blue flowers — you might find the variety **'Cambridge Blue'** which is much paler.

**SITE & SOIL:** Any reasonable garden soil will do — Scarlet Sage thrives best in full sun.

**PLANT DETAILS:** Height 6 in.–3 ft, depending on the species. Spacing 9 in.–1½ ft.

**PROPAGATION:** Sow seed in February–March — germination temperature 70°–75°F. Plant out in late May.

Salvia splendens
'Phoenix'

Salvia horminum
'Pink Lady'

Salvia farinacea
'Victoria'

# SCABIOSA Sweet Scabious

Summer bedding plant

•

Hardy annual

•

Colours available

•

Flowering period

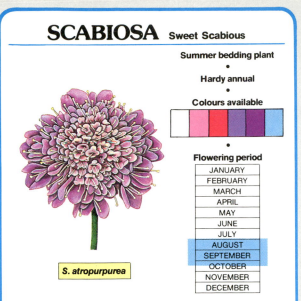

S. atropurpurea

| |
|---|
| JANUARY |
| FEBRUARY |
| MARCH |
| APRIL |
| MAY |
| JUNE |
| JULY |
| **AUGUST** |
| **SEPTEMBER** |
| OCTOBER |
| NOVEMBER |
| DECEMBER |

The fluffy round flower heads look rather like a Cornflower — in the U.S the common name is the Pincushion Flower. The colour range is wide — white right through to deepest red. Once there was a strong fragrance, hence the English common name, but this has been almost lost in the modern varieties. An easy plant to grow which is quite hardy but it is distinctly unhappy in prolonged wet weather. Sweet Scabious is generally grown in beds or borders for summer colour, but there is one species which is grown just for drying and the unusual flower heads are used in flower arrangements.

**VARIETIES:** **S. atropurpurea** is the species grown for bedding. In the catalogues you will find **'Dwarf Double Mixed'** (1½ ft) with flowers in a mixture of several colours. **'Double Large-flowered Mixed'** (2½ ft) has flowers in a similar range of colours but here staking is required. Occasionally you may find single-colour varieties such as **'Blue Moon'** and **'Rose Cockade'**, but mixtures are much more popular. These varieties can be dried for indoor use, but it is more usual these days to buy a variety of **S. stellata** (**'Drumstick'**, **'Paper Moon'** etc) for this purpose. Let the flowers dry on the plant — the 3 in. wide papery bronze heads are most unusual.

**SITE & SOIL:** Any non-acid well-drained soil will do — choose a sunny spot.

**PLANT DETAILS:** Height 1½–2½ ft. Spacing 1 ft.

**PROPAGATION:** Sow seed in March under glass. Plant out in May.

Scabiosa atropurpurea
'Double Large-flowered Mixed'

Scabiosa stellata
'Paper Moon'

# SCHIZANTHUS Poor Man's Orchid

Summer bedding plant

•

Half hardy annual

•

Colours available

•

Flowering period

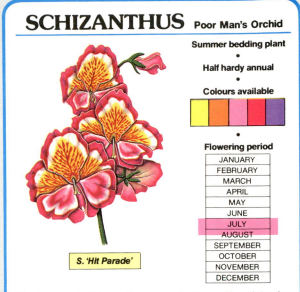

S. 'Hit Parade'

| |
|---|
| JANUARY |
| FEBRUARY |
| MARCH |
| APRIL |
| MAY |
| JUNE |
| **JULY** |
| AUGUST |
| SEPTEMBER |
| OCTOBER |
| NOVEMBER |
| DECEMBER |

Perhaps only Schizanthus can challenge the claim by Salpiglossis to be the most exotic of all annual bedding plants. Each bloom looks like a miniature Orchid, streaked and spotted in a variety of colours. These flowers are borne in large numbers above pale green ferny foliage — an ideal bedding plant by the sound of it. It is rarely seen, however, as Schizanthus is regarded as an indoor plant rather than an outdoor one, but it can be grown outdoors quite easily if you follow the rules. Pick a spot which is in full sun and sheltered from cold winds, and make sure that it is free-draining — Schizanthus is a good plant for container growing in a peat-based compost. It is recommended as a cut flower.

**VARIETIES:** Named varieties of **S. wisetonensis** are available in the catalogues. Avoid the tall ones such as the **'Magnum Hybrids'** (3 ft) which are much better in the conservatory — go instead for a dwarf variety which has proved its worth as an outdoor plant. You can try **'Hit Parade'** (1 ft) or **'Star Parade'** (6 in.) if you wish but the two which the experts recommend for outdoors are the bushy and free-flowering **'Angel Wings'** (1½ ft) or the shorter-growing **'Bouquet'** (9 in.).

**SITE & SOIL:** A well-drained soil is essential — thrives best in full sun.

**PLANT DETAILS:** Height 6 in.–1½ ft. Spacing 9 in.–1 ft.

**PROPAGATION:** Sow seed in pots in March in gentle heat. Plant out in late May.

Schizanthus
'Bouquet'

# STOCK

**Spring/summer bedding plant**

**Half hardy annual**
or
**Hardy annual**
or
**Hardy biennial**

**Colours available**

**Flowering period**

| |
|---|
| JANUARY |
| FEBRUARY |
| MARCH |
| APRIL |
| MAY |
| JUNE |
| JULY |
| AUGUST |
| SEPTEMBER |
| OCTOBER |
| NOVEMBER |
| DECEMBER |

**M. incana**
Ten Week Stock

**M. bicornis**
Night-scented Stock

**M. incana**
Brompton Stock

Once millions of people grew these plants in formal beds and in cottage gardens, but these days they are more often bought as cut flowers for indoor use rather than being grown as bedding plants outdoors. The problem is that there is much confusion over the use of the various types and the task of raising double-flowered plants from seed may call for careful temperature control. In addition the annual types tend to have a relatively short flowering period and the biennials need some winter protection in the colder areas of the country. Still, the great charm of Stocks remains — densely-clustered flowering spikes above soft grey-green foliage and a fragrance which fills the air. There are several types from which to make your choice (see below) and you will find some strains are offered as 'selectable' seed. With these it is necessary to reduce the temperature to 45°–50°F after germination. Dark-leaved seedlings will produce only single plants and should be discarded — prick out the yellowish-green seedlings which will grow into double-flowered plants.

**VARIETIES:** The first group of **Matthiola incana** is made up of the *Ten Week Stocks* — half hardy annuals which are sown in February or March in gentle heat and then planted out in late May for a June–August display. A **'Dwarf Ten-Week Mixture'** (1 ft) will produce a high proportion of doubles. For earlier flowers pick a **'Trysomic Seven-Week Mixture'** — for taller (1½–2 ft) but later-flowering plants choose **'Beauty of Nice'**. The most imposing types are the Column Stocks which grow 2–3 ft high — look for **'Giant Imperial'** or the selectable **'Giant Excelsior'** strain. The second group is another important one — the *Brompton Stocks*. These are biennials, sown outdoors in May–July and then pricked out into small pots before overwintering in a cold frame. Plant out in February–March for an April–May display. The usual height of the bushy, branching plants is 1½ ft — selectable strains are available. The third group is only a small one. It contains the *East Lothian Stock* — dwarf (1 ft) plants which look like small Brompton Stocks and can be grown as either half hardy annuals or biennials. Selectable strains are not available, but most plants are double. The fourth group is quite different from the others. This is the *Night-scented Stock* (**M. bicornis**) — a hardy annual which is sown in spring where it is to flower. The 1 ft plants bear insignificant blooms which close during the day, but at night the fragrance is outstanding.

**SITE & SOIL:** Any well-drained garden soil which is not acid will do — thrives in sun or light shade.

**PLANT DETAILS:** Height 1–3 ft. Spacing 9 in.–1½ ft.

**PROPAGATION:** Follow the hardy annual, half hardy annual or biennial technique depending on the variety chosen — see above.

Matthiola incana
'Giant Excelsior'

Matthiola incana
'Brompton Stock'

Matthiola incana
'East Lothian Stock'

# SWEET PEA

**Summer bedding plant**

**Hardy annual**

**Colours available**

**Flowering period**

| |
|---|
| JANUARY |
| FEBRUARY |
| MARCH |
| APRIL |
| MAY |
| JUNE |
| JULY |
| AUGUST |
| SEPTEMBER |
| OCTOBER |
| NOVEMBER |
| DECEMBER |

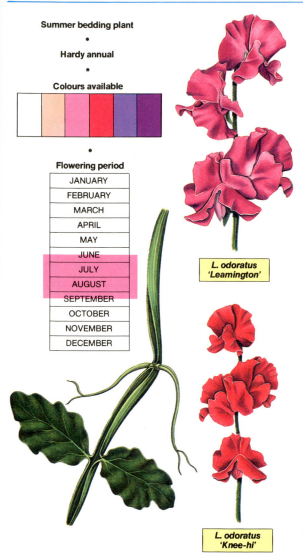

**L. odoratus 'Leamington'**

**L. odoratus 'Knee-hi'**

It was the Victorian railway workers who turned the Sweet Pea (latin name Lathyrus odoratus) from a rather plain climber which had come from Sicily in 1699 into a popular garden plant. Many varieties appeared in the catalogues of the day, but the range nowadays is much greater. Of course the tall climbers remain the favourite group, but you can buy knee-high ones and even dwarfs which do not require support. The colour span is vast, from white to almost black with only the true yellows missing. Unfortunately some of the old-fashioned fragrance has been lost in the newer types, and so many gardeners prefer the dainty and small-flowered ones which are renowned for their scent. There are several books devoted entirely to Sweet Peas, but these are only for exhibitors. For them thorough soil preparation is essential, sowing and planting are carefully timed and protection against both weather and pests is important. For the ordinary gardener who just wants a colourful screen or a source of cut flowers the Sweet Pea is a much easier plant to grow. Just soak the seed overnight and sow in pots or open soil. Pinch out the tips when the stems are about 4 in. high, provide support for the tendrils and water thoroughly in dry weather. Remove dead blooms regularly.

**VARIETIES:** For tall plants and large flowers choose *Standard* varieties — climbers which will grow 5–8 ft high. If you are growing for exhibition use the cordon method — train a single stem up each cane and remove all unnecessary growth such as tendrils and side shoots. For garden display choose a highly fragrant variety and grow over a wigwam of canes or against a frame of trellis or plastic netting. The *Spencer* varieties dominate the catalogues and our gardens — well-known ones include **'Air Warden'** (orange-scarlet), **'Winston Churchill'** (crimson), **'Swan Lake'** (white), **'Leamington'** (lavender), **'Sheila McQueen'** (orange-salmon) and **'Mrs R Bolton'** (pink). For fragrance choose **'The Doctor'** (mauve) or **'Ballerina'** (pink), but for maximum fragrance move away from the Spencers and buy an **'Old-fashioned Mixture'** or the oldest variety of all — **'Painted Lady'** (red and white). For more flowers per stem than you will find on a Spencer variety the choice should be one of the **'Galaxy'** strain or a **'Royal'** variety. The *Hedge* varieties such as **'Knee-hi'**, **'Jet Set'**, **'Snoopea'** and **'Supersnoop'** are much more compact, growing 2–3 ft high and needing little support. The 1 ft high *Dwarf* varieties need no support at all — look out for **'Bijou'**, **'Patio'** and **'Little Sweetheart'**. Shortest of all is the 6 in. tall carpeting variety **'Cupid'**.

**SITE & SOIL:** Any well-drained soil in a sunny position.

**PLANT DETAILS:** Height 6 in.–8 ft. Spacing 6 in.–1 ft.

**PROPAGATION:** Sow seed in pots in October and overwinter in a cold frame — plant out in March or April. Alternatively sow seed outdoors in March or April.

*Lathyrus odoratus 'Air Warden'*

*Lathyrus odoratus 'Jet Set'*

*Lathyrus odoratus 'Cupid'*

# SWEET WILLIAM

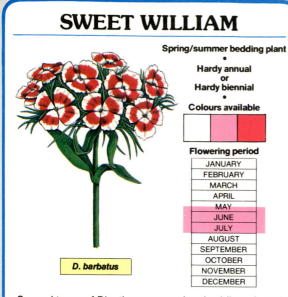

Spring/summer bedding plant
•
**Hardy annual
or
Hardy biennial**
•
**Colours available**

**Flowering period**

| | |
|---|---|
| JANUARY | |
| FEBRUARY | |
| MARCH | |
| APRIL | |
| MAY | |
| JUNE | |
| JULY | |
| AUGUST | |
| SEPTEMBER | |
| OCTOBER | |
| NOVEMBER | |
| DECEMBER | |

**D. barbatus**

Several types of Dianthus are used as bedding plants in the garden — D. barbatus or Sweet William is the one which produces densely-packed, flattened heads of sweet-smelling Pink-like flowers. These blooms bridge the gap between the spring- and the traditional summer-flowering bedding plants. No cottage garden would be without this old favourite — but it has a place in every garden for window boxes, containers, rockeries, beds and borders. There are tall ones and dwarfs, singles and doubles as well as annuals and biennials. Obviously there is a Sweet William for you.

**VARIETIES:** For tall (1½–2 ft) **D. barbatus** choose **'Single Flowered Mixed'** if you want a variety of colours — for single colours pick **'Albus'** (white), **'Scarlet Beauty'** (red) or **'Newport Pink'** (salmon-pink). **'Harbinger'** is a May-flowering mixture and **'Double Flowered Mixed'** produces double and semi-double flowers. Many people prefer the bicoloured form with a distinct eye — buy the **'Auricula-eyed Mixture'** (2 ft). The traditional dwarf for rockery or window box is **'Indian Shot'** (6 in.) — there are also **'Summer Beauty'** and the annual types **'Roundabout'** (9 in.) and **'Wee Willie'** (6 in.). They bloom in August — much later than the standard May–July flowering period associated with Sweet Williams.

**SITE & SOIL:** Any well-drained garden soil which is not acid will do — choose a sunny spot.

**PLANT DETAILS:** Height 6 in.–2 ft. Spacing 9 in.–1 ft.

**PROPAGATION:** Sow biennial seed in May or June — plant out in autumn. For annuals sow seed in March — plant out in May.

*Dianthus barbatus*
'Scarlet Beauty'

# TAGETES Tagetes

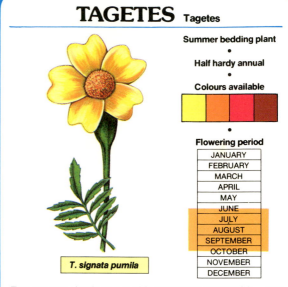

Summer bedding plant
•
**Half hardy annual**
•
**Colours available**
•

**Flowering period**

| | |
|---|---|
| JANUARY | |
| FEBRUARY | |
| MARCH | |
| APRIL | |
| MAY | |
| JUNE | |
| JULY | |
| AUGUST | |
| SEPTEMBER | |
| OCTOBER | |
| NOVEMBER | |
| DECEMBER | |

**T. signata pumila**

Tagetes are a lowly group of the half hardy Marigolds — the larger ones are described on page 54. Lowly perhaps, but these plants are colourful from June until the first frosts arrive and have been popular as edging plants for generations. 'Dainty' is the descriptive word you will find in many catalogues — the plants are compact and rounded with leaves which are usually pale and always finely divided. The single flowers are small but they are borne in large numbers and may cover almost all the foliage. An easy and trouble-free plant to grow, but avoid overfeeding and overwatering.

**VARIETIES:** Tagetes are varieties of **T. signata pumila** (**T. tenuifolia pumila**). The seed lists have been dominated by the **'Gem'** series for many years. The favourite one is **'Golden Gem'** (6 in., tiny golden-yellow blooms) — you will also find **'Orange Gem'**, **'Yellow Gem'** and the taller and more eye-catching **'Tangerine Gem'** (9 in.). New varieties are beginning to challenge the 'Gem' dominance. **'Paprika'** (6 in.) is quite distinctive — gold-edged red flowers borne above dark green foliage. **'Ornament'** (8 in.) is maroon — **'Ursula'** (8 in.) is golden-yellow with deep orange markings. The mixture to buy is **'Starfire'** (6–9 in.) — yellows, oranges and browns with many bicolours.

**SITE & SOIL:** Any reasonable garden soil will do — thrives best in full sun.

**PLANT DETAILS:** Height 6–9 in. Spacing 6–9 in.

**PROPAGATION:** Sow seed in February–March in gentle heat. Plant out in late May.

*Tagetes signata pumila*
'Tangerine Gem'

*Tagetes signata pumila*
'Paprika'

# THUNBERGIA Black-eyed Susan

Summer bedding plant

•

Half hardy annual

•

Colours available

•

Flowering period

| JANUARY |
| FEBRUARY |
| MARCH |
| APRIL |
| MAY |
| JUNE |
| **JULY** |
| **AUGUST** |
| **SEPTEMBER** |
| OCTOBER |
| NOVEMBER |
| DECEMBER |

**T. alata**

Thunbergia is more usually regarded as a conservatory climber than a bedding plant, but it will grow happily outdoors if the site is sunny and sheltered and if the soil or compost is free-draining. A plant, then, for southern or western districts where it can be used for twining up posts or other supports, or left to trail over banks and walls. It grows rapidly, the showy flowers standing out above the arrow-shaped leaves. These blooms are funnel-shaped and measure about 2 in. across — they are borne singly from the axils of the leaves.

**VARIETIES: T. alata** is the species which is grown in the garden and conservatory. It is a vigorous climber, reaching 10 ft or more. The petals are cream, yellow, pale brown or orange and the throat is dark purple, giving a black-eye effect. For garden use it is usual to buy a variety with a more controlled growth habit — the only one you are likely to find is **'Susie'**. This reaches about 4–6 ft and the flowers are white, yellow or orange. The black eye is often but not always present. **'Angel Wings'** is hard to find — the large white flowers have a yellow eye.

**SITE & SOIL:** Any well-drained garden soil will do — full sun is essential.

**PLANT DETAILS:** Height 4–6 ft. Spacing 2 ft.

**PROPAGATION:** Sow seed in pots in March in gentle heat. Plant out in late May.

*Thunbergia alata*
*'Susie'*

# TITHONIA Mexican Sunflower

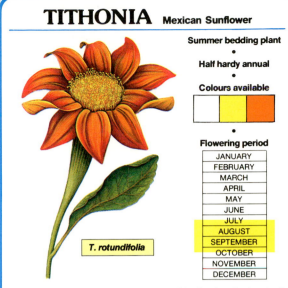

Summer bedding plant

•

Half hardy annual

•

Colours available

•

Flowering period

| JANUARY |
| FEBRUARY |
| MARCH |
| APRIL |
| MAY |
| JUNE |
| JULY |
| **AUGUST** |
| **SEPTEMBER** |
| OCTOBER |
| NOVEMBER |
| DECEMBER |

**T. rotundifolia**

A big and bold plant for the centre of the bed or the back of the border — there is a 2½ ft tall variety where space is limited and a 5–6 ft one to cover a sizeable and unsightly area. The blooms are eye-catching and look like a large Dahlia, but the foliage is quite different and the flowers are slightly fragrant. This is not a plant for everyone — it needs protection from strong winds and requires a sunny spot. Stake tall-growing plants and protect young growth from slugs. Cut when flowers are beginning to open to provide unusual material for flower arranging — sear the ends before placing in water.

**VARIETIES:** The basic species is **T. rotundifolia**, sometimes listed as **T. speciosa**. The orange-red petals are yellow underneath and there is a central yellow disc. Under good conditions it will grow 5 ft or more — there is a less vigorous variety **'Torch'** which has similar colouring but does not exceed 4 ft. **'Yellow Torch'** has all-yellow flowers. The one you are most likely to find in the catalogues is the orange-flowering **'Goldfinger'** which grows about 2½ ft high.

**SITE & SOIL:** Any well-drained garden soil will do — full sun is essential.

**PLANT DETAILS:** Height 2½–6 ft. Spacing — use as a dot plant.

**PROPAGATION:** Sow seed in pots in March in gentle heat. Plant out in late May or early June.

*Tithonia rotundifolia*
*'Yellow Torch'*

# URSINIA Ursinia

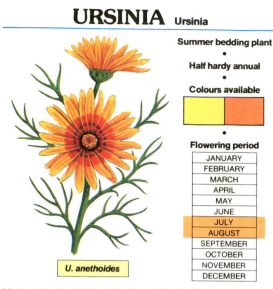

**Summer bedding plant**
•
**Half hardy annual**
•
**Colours available**
•
**Flowering period**

| JANUARY |
| FEBRUARY |
| MARCH |
| APRIL |
| MAY |
| JUNE |
| **JULY** |
| **AUGUST** |
| SEPTEMBER |
| OCTOBER |
| NOVEMBER |
| DECEMBER |

*U. anethoides*

Yet another bedding plant from South Africa with Daisy-like flowers. These blooms are large (about 2 in. across) and are attractively zoned. They do not close up as readily as Arctotis and Mesembryanthemum in dull weather and the massed heads above the fragrant, ferny foliage in midsummer are certainly eye-catching. But Ursinia has never become popular — the colour range is limited and the flowering period is quite short. It also needs warm and dry conditions if it is to flourish — consider this one only if you have a patch of sandy soil to cover. Tall plants should be supported by means of branched twigs.

**VARIETIES:** The choice is strictly limited. You will find the species **U. anethoides** in some catalogues, and all you will be offered is the **'Special Hybrids'** mixture. The plants are bushy and the pale green leaves are finely divided. The petals are usually orange, but flowers with yellow petals occasionally appear. In the centre of each flower is a golden disc separated from the orange or yellow of the petals by a distinct brown, red or deep maroon band. The central disc turns purple as the flower ages. Textbooks sometimes list single-colour varieties such as **'Sunstar'**, but you will have to search for a supplier.

**SITE & SOIL:** Thrives in light, well-drained soil — full sun is essential.

**PLANT DETAILS:** Height 1–1½ ft. Spacing 9 in.

**PROPAGATION:** Sow seed in March in gentle heat. Plant out in late May.

*Ursinia anethoides*
*'Special Hybrids'*

# VERBENA Verbena

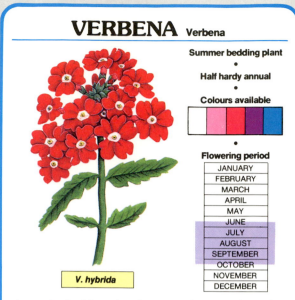

**Summer bedding plant**
•
**Half hardy annual**
•
**Colours available**
•
**Flowering period**

| JANUARY |
| FEBRUARY |
| MARCH |
| APRIL |
| MAY |
| **JUNE** |
| **JULY** |
| **AUGUST** |
| **SEPTEMBER** |
| OCTOBER |
| NOVEMBER |
| DECEMBER |

*V. hybrida*

A popular bedding plant for generations, much used in window boxes, tubs, hanging baskets and as an edging for beds and borders. The plants are low-growing with either an upright or spreading growth habit. The small Primrose-like flowers, usually fragrant and white-eyed, are borne in globular clusters which measure about 2 in. across. Seed germination is often slow and erratic — try to keep the temperature at 60°–65°F at this time. Many people prefer taking cuttings as the way to propagate Verbena at home. Add organic matter to the soil, pinch out the tips of young plants, dead-head regularly and water in dry weather.

**VARIETIES:** **V. hybrida** varieties are available in a range of colours, but the usual practice is to buy a mixture. **'Derby'** (1 ft) is the one to choose if you want upright plants — **'Tropic'** is another upright Verbena. If you want maximum ground cover choose a spreading one such as **'Springtime'** or **'Showtime'**. One of the smallest and most compact Verbenas is **'Sparkle Mixed'** (6 in.). For a bright splash of a single colour pick one of the reds — **'Blaze'**, **'Showtime Belle'** or **'Sandy Scarlet'**. Other single colours include **'Amethyst'** (blue) and **'Delight'** (pink). **V. venosa** (1½ ft) is different — it has heads of rosy-purple flowers.

**SITE & SOIL:** Any well-drained garden soil will do — thrives best in full sun.

**PLANT DETAILS:** Height 6 in.–1½ ft. Spacing 1 ft.

**PROPAGATION:** Sow seed in March in gentle heat. Plant out in late May. Alternatively take cuttings in autumn.

*Verbena hybrida*
*'Springtime'*

*Verbena venosa*

# VINCA Madagascar Periwinkle

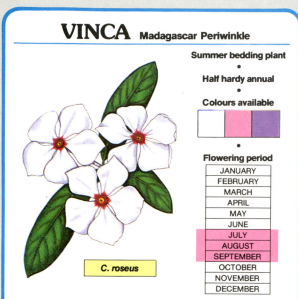

Summer bedding plant
•
Half hardy annual
•
Colours available

**Flowering period**

| JANUARY |
|---|
| FEBRUARY |
| MARCH |
| APRIL |
| MAY |
| JUNE |
| JULY |
| AUGUST |
| SEPTEMBER |
| OCTOBER |
| NOVEMBER |
| DECEMBER |

*C. roseus*

The lists of best-selling bedding plants in Britain and the U.S are remarkably similar, but there is one outstanding difference. Vinca is in the American top ten — in this country it is virtually unknown as an outdoor plant. It looks quite similar to the bedding Impatiens varieties which have become so popular, but it is more tolerant of hot and dry conditions. Try this one as a change if your garden is in the South and rather sheltered. Like Impatiens it is a good ground cover plant, but it can also be used in containers, hanging baskets and for edging.

**VARIETIES:** There is some confusion over names. The latin name is **Catharanthus roseus**, although it is often listed as **Vinca rosea**. Its proper common name is Madagascar Periwinkle, but it is often sold as Vinca. You will usually be offered a mixture — **'Magic Carpet'** (or **'Carpet'**) — 6–8 in. bushy plants with glossy dark green leaves and white, pink or rose flowers. Make sure you choose a variety recommended for bedding as well as pot culture — suitable types include **'Peppermint Cooler'**, **'Peppermint Parasol'**, **'Little Pinkie'** and **'Little Bright Eyes'**. You will have to raise it from seed — seedlings are not offered in spring by garden centres.

**SITE & SOIL:** Any well-drained garden soil will do — thrives in sun and light shade.

**PLANT DETAILS:** Height 6 in.–1 ft. Spacing 1 ft.

**PROPAGATION:** Sow seed in March in gentle heat. Plant out in early June.

*Catharanthus roseus*
*'Peppermint Parasol'*

# VIOLA Viola

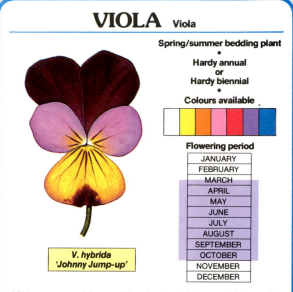

Spring/summer bedding plant
•
Hardy annual
or
Hardy biennial
•
Colours available

**Flowering period**

| JANUARY |
|---|
| FEBRUARY |
| MARCH |
| APRIL |
| MAY |
| JUNE |
| JULY |
| AUGUST |
| SEPTEMBER |
| OCTOBER |
| NOVEMBER |
| DECEMBER |

*V. hybrida*
*'Johnny Jump-up'*

Violas are small Pansy-like plants which stay in bloom for about 6 months and are generally self-coloured, although varieties which are faced (dark central blotch) or whiskered (dark lines radiating from the centre) can be bought. The bloom is generally less rounded than a Pansy and some types are much more like a Violet. Violas are perennials, but they are generally grown as annuals (sow in spring for June–October flowering) or as biennials (sow in summer for March–August flowering). Grow them in the same way as Pansies (see page 61) — use them for bedding, containers, window boxes and in the rockery. Keep watch for pansy sickness (see Foot Rot page 116) if they are grown in the same spot year after year.

**VARIETIES:** Violas have complex parentage — they may be listed under **V. williamsii**, **V. tricolor**, **V. cornuta** or **V. hybrida**. Popular ones include **'Prince Henry'** (deep purple), **'Arkwright Ruby'** (red), **'Chantreyland'** (apricot yellow) and **'Blue Heaven'** (mid blue). **'Johnny Jump-up'** is an old-fashioned tricolour and **'Pretty'** is an eye-catching yellow and purple bicolour. The novelty ones are **'Bambini'** and **'Funny Face'** — a distinct yellow face and dark whiskers are set against variously coloured backgrounds to give a cat-like appearance.

**SITE & SOIL:** Any reasonable garden soil in sun or partial shade.

**PLANT DETAILS:** Height 6–8 in. Spacing 6 in.

**PROPAGATION:** Sow seed in February–April under glass — plant out in May. For spring flowering sow seed in May–July under glass or in open ground — plant out in September.

*Viola hybrida*
*'Chantreyland'*

*Viola hybrida*
*'Bambini'*

# WALLFLOWER

**Spring bedding plant**

•

**Hardy biennial**

•

**Colours available**

•

**Flowering period**

| |
|---|
| JANUARY |
| FEBRUARY |
| MARCH |
| APRIL |
| MAY |
| JUNE |
| JULY |
| AUGUST |
| SEPTEMBER |
| OCTOBER |
| NOVEMBER |
| DECEMBER |

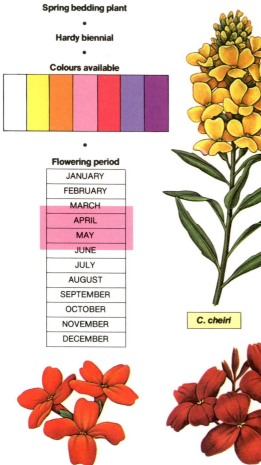

**C. cheiri**

**C. allionii
'Orange Queen'**

**C. cheiri
'Vulcan'**

In countless gardens up and down the country the only spring bedding plant to match the Tulips and Daffodils for height and colour is the Wallflower. Yellow and red may be the favourite colours, but the range extends from creamy white to near-black, and there are varieties which are as low as 9 in. and as tall as 2 ft. All branch freely and the flowers of many varieties are sweetly scented — this fragrance is most noticeable in the evening. When raising your own Wallflowers choose a nursery bed which has not been used for plants belonging to the Cabbage family. Work peat into the soil and sow the seeds in summer. Do not let the ground dry out and pinch out the tips of the seedlings before moving them to their final quarters in late autumn. Remember to plant firmly. In early spring remove any side shoots which have been broken by wind or snow. The Wallflower is an easy plant to grow and is fully hardy. Its basic needs are good drainage and a non-acid soil which is free from club root disease. The display, however, is greatly influenced by the quality of the planted seedlings — make sure you get sturdy, bushy plants and not thin, weedy specimens if you buy rather than raise your own.

**VARIETIES:** The ordinary Wallflower is **Cheiranthus cheiri** and many varieties are available. For small beds, edging or window boxes choose the baby of the group — **'Tom Thumb Mixed'** (9 in.). Rather taller but still smaller than the average Wallflower is the **'Bedder'** series. You can buy a mixture or separate colours — **'Primrose Bedder'**, **'Orange Bedder'**, **'Scarlet Bedder'** etc. For general bedding there is a large number of varieties which grow about 1½ ft high. Most catalogues include the popular ones such as **'Cloth of Gold'** (golden yellow), **'Blood Red'** and **'Vulcan'** (deep red) and the vermilion ones **'Fire King'** and **'Scarlet Emperor'**. There are many others, such as **'Primrose Monarch'**, **'Ivory White'** and the very dark **'Purple Queen'**. **'Harlequin'** produces some bicolours and **'Fair Lady'** contains a range of pastel shades. The tallest Wallflower is the **'Double-flowered Branching Mixture'** (2 ft). All the above varieties bloom between March and mid May — for May to June flowering and an eye-catching display of orange blooms choose the Siberian Wallflower (**C. allionii**) which is listed as Cheiranthus in many catalogues. **'Orange Queen'** (1 ft) is the most popular variety.

**SITE & SOIL:** Any free-draining garden soil with adequate lime will do. Choose a sunny spot.

**PLANT DETAILS:** Height 9 in.–2 ft. Spacing 9 in.–1 ft.

**PROPAGATION:** Sow seed outdoors in May–June and plant out seedlings in October where they are to flower.

*Cheiranthus cheiri*
'Orange Bedder'

*Cheiranthus cheiri*
'Tom Thumb Mixed'

*Cheiranthus allionii*

# ZEA Ornamental Maize

Summer bedding plant
•
Half hardy annual
•
Leaf colours available

Display period

| | |
|---|---|
| JANUARY | |
| FEBRUARY | |
| MARCH | |
| APRIL | |
| MAY | |
| JUNE | |
| JULY | ■ |
| AUGUST | ■ |
| SEPTEMBER | ■ |
| OCTOBER | |
| NOVEMBER | |
| DECEMBER | |

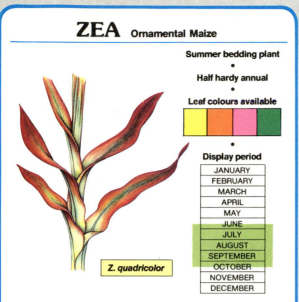

**Z. quadricolor**

These bold plants with colourful foliage make successful dot plants in a bedding scheme because they remain attractive throughout the season. Ornamental Maize is quite often used in park displays — the upright stems bear gracefully arching leaves which are invariably striped — white, cream, yellow, orange or red depending on the variety and growing conditions. There are also varieties which produce colourful cobs for display on the living plant or for drying for indoor decoration. Zea needs a sheltered spot and fertile soil. Make sure the plants are thoroughly hardened off before planting out when all danger of frost has passed. Water thoroughly in dry weather.

**VARIETIES:** There are two basic types listed in the catalogues. **Z. japonica** bears green leaves with narrow white or cream stripes — **Z. quadricolor** has broad pink and yellow stripes. Both grow about 4–5 ft tall — plant singly as a dot plant or in a group of 3 or 5. Some seed companies offer **'Harlequin Mixed'** — striped leaves in various colours. For multicoloured cobs (yellow, orange, red and blue grains) grow **Z. 'Amero'**. Even more novel is **'Strawberry Corn'** (3 ft) — strawberry-shaped cobs bearing strawberry-coloured grains.

**SITE & SOIL:** Any well-drained garden soil which has been fed will do — thrives in full sun.

**PLANT DETAILS:** Height 3–5 ft. Spacing — use as a dot plant.

**PROPAGATION:** Sow seed singly in pots in March in gentle heat. Plant out in early June.

*Zea quadricolor*

# ZINNIA Zinnia

Summer bedding plant
•
Half hardy annual
•
Colours available

Flowering period

| | |
|---|---|
| JANUARY | |
| FEBRUARY | |
| MARCH | |
| APRIL | |
| MAY | |
| JUNE | |
| JULY | ■ |
| AUGUST | ■ |
| SEPTEMBER | ■ |
| OCTOBER | |
| NOVEMBER | |
| DECEMBER | |

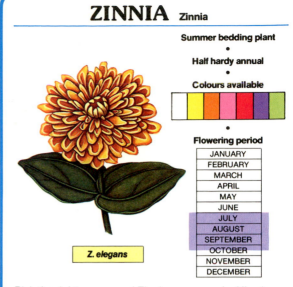

**Z. elegans**

Pick the right season and Zinnias are superb. All colours apart from blue are available, and the Daisy-like heads are single, semi-double or double. Massive blooms as large as Dahlias, small buttons like Double Daisies — you will find both and all types in between in the vast array of flower types, colours and shapes which are available. But Zinnia is happier in the U.S than in Britain — it dislikes prolonged cool and wet weather. Wind is not usually a problem but it suffers in poor soil. Staking is rarely necessary. Cut blooms last well in water.

**VARIETIES:** Parentage is rather complex — **Z. angustifolia**, **Z. elegans** and **Z. haageana** are involved in the varieties listed in the catalogues. For maximum display choose the big ones — **'Dahlia-flowered Mixed'** or **'State Fair'** (5 in. wide blooms on 2½ ft plants). At the other end of the scale there are **'Thumbelina'** (6 in. high with small button-like flowers which stand up to wet weather), **'Hobgoblin'** (10 in.) and **'Peter Pan'** (10 in. with large flowers). **'Chippendale'** (2 ft) has yellow-edged blooms and the $F_1$ hybrid **'Ruffles'** (2 ft) has flowers with a multitude of petals. **'Persian Carpet'** (1 ft) is a mixture of bicoloured blooms. The green one is **'Envy'** (1½ ft).

**SITE & SOIL:** Any compost-enriched soil will do — thrives best in full sun.

**PLANT DETAILS:** Height 6 in.–2½ ft. Spacing 6 in.–1½ ft.

**PROPAGATION:** Sow seed singly in pots in March in gentle heat. Plant out in early June.

*Zinnia 'Dahlia-flowered Mixed'*

*Zinnia 'Hobgoblin'*

# CHAPTER 4

# USING BEDDING PLANTS

Some plants, such as ornamental trees, are grown for their attractive shape and permanence. Others, like Roses, are cultivated for the beauty of their individual blooms. Bedding plants are providers of **colour** — colour which may be strident or muted and which is usually derived from the flowers but may be a feature of the foliage.

It has been traditional to fill beds and borders with a number of different varieties of bedding plants to produce a multicoloured display. Bedding out in this way began more than a century ago and will no doubt continue for many more years, but there are other ways of using them. They can be grown as small groups to provide bright splashes of colour amongst perennial plants and they can be used to fill containers. Nowadays tubs and hanging baskets are seen everywhere, and the horticultural history books of the future will certainly tell of the popular container-growing movement which began in the 1980s.

## WHERE TO USE BEDDING PLANTS

### *In open ground*

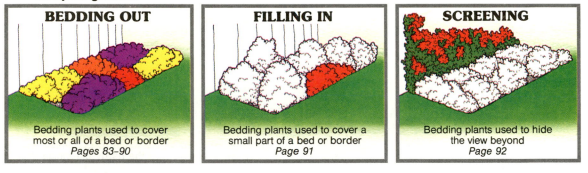

**BEDDING OUT**

Bedding plants used to cover most or all of a bed or border
*Pages 83–90*

**FILLING IN**

Bedding plants used to cover a small part of a bed or border
*Page 91*

**SCREENING**

Bedding plants used to hide the view beyond
*Page 92*

### *In containers*

**POTS & TROUGHS**

Bedding plants used to cover the soil or compost in a free-standing container
*Pages 93–95*

**WINDOW BOXES**

Bedding plants used to cover the soil or compost in a container attached to the base of a window
*Pages 96–97*

**HANGING BASKETS**

Bedding plants used to cover the soil or compost in a container suspended from a hook or bracket
*Pages 98–99*

## WHEN TO USE BEDDING PLANTS

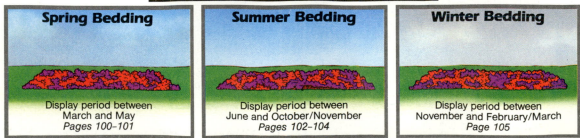

**Spring Bedding**

Display period between March and May
*Pages 100–101*

**Summer Bedding**

Display period between June and October/November
*Pages 102–104*

**Winter Bedding**

Display period between November and February/March
*Page 105*

# BEDDING OUT

Bedding plants used to cover
most or all of a bed or border

Devoting a bed or border *entirely* to bedding plants is not usual nowadays. Totally bedded-out areas do, of course, occur in parks, street plantings and tiny front gardens but the more popular approach is to have a scatter of perennials in the area to be bedded. For a spring display the Wallflowers, Polyanthus, Daisies or Forget-me-nots share the land with Daffodils, Tulips and other bulbs. In summer the popular bedding plants such as Marigolds, Alyssum, Ageratum and Begonias cover the ground beneath standard Roses and other shrubs in countless gardens.

## TYPES OF BEDDING OUT

### The 6 steps to success

**1** **CHOOSE A SUITABLE SITE** In most cases you will have to make do with beds and borders which already exist. If you are able to choose the site then pick a spot in an open, sunny position which is protected from strong winds. Only a restricted group of plants are suitable for shady sites — see page 104.

**2** **CHOOSE A SIMPLE SHAPE** Avoid too many small beds and reject complex outlines. Beds cut in lawns should have simple shapes — square, rectangle, circle or oval.

**3** **READ THE COLOUR CHAPTER** (pages 106–109) The choice of colours is a matter of personal preference but there are one or two rules which you really should follow. Do not plant a multicoloured mixture of one bedding plant right next to a mixture of another — break up groups of kaleidoscope mixtures with single-colour varieties. Another general rule is to use some greys or whites here and there between bold patches of bright colours.

**4** **READ THE A–Z CHAPTER** (pages 14–81) Look through the pictures and text and write down a wish list of the ones which appeal to you. There is nothing wrong with the ever-popular ones but do think about a few unusual ones if you know that seeds or plants are available to you. Make sure that the ones on your list are suitable, bearing in mind location, soil type, flowering period, height etc.

**5** **DRAW UP A PLAN** Yes, do this with a piece of paper, pen and coloured pencils. Don't draw in too many groups of different plants— even in formal bedding it is nearly always a good idea to have just a limited number of bedding plant varieties. Try to have a mixture of shapes — spires such as Antirrhinum, Stocks and Salvia next to sheets such as Pansy, Begonia and Petunia.

**6** **WRITE UP YOUR SHOPPING LIST** Not all the plants from your wish list can be fitted into your plan. Once you have made your selection it will be necessary to go back to the A–Z chapter to check up on recommended spacing. From this you will be able to calculate how much seed or how many seedlings you will have to buy.

**BED**

A bed is a planted area designed to be viewed from all sides. A *flower bed* is the traditional home for bedding plants, but these days there are usually other types present such as hardy perennials and bulbs. In an *island bed* the hardy perennials are dominant with bedding plants grown in pockets between them.

**BORDER**

A border is a planted area designed to be viewed from one, two or three sides but not from all angles. A *flower border* is made up of a selection from herbaceous border plants, bedding plants and bulbs. A *mixed border* consists of a selection from shrubs, conifers, herbaceous border plants, bulbs etc together with pockets filled with bedding plants.

# Formal Bedding

There is no precise definition of formal bedding. A basic feature, of course, is the strictly geometrical arrangement of the plants — easy to spot when the effect is neat and symmetrical but much less easy to detect when the arrangement is a jumble of abstract shapes. There is, however, a second feature of formal bedding which is also important — the desired effect is to have *all* the plants in bloom at the same time. This requirement may be easy to achieve in a large, open garden but can be difficult in a small plot close to the house where the uneven lighting of the bed or border can result in a highly variable display from sun-loving varieties. There is a third property which separates formal from informal bedding — the boundaries between the different plants are quite distinct with no attempt at blending of different plants to provide a 'natural' look.

### Points to Remember

- Formal bedding is really only successful when the whole bed or border is devoted to it — symmetrically placed shrubs or herbaceous perennials may not be a drawback but a scatter of randomly-placed bushes will certainly ruin the effect.

- The effect is also spoilt if gaps appear in the rows or blocks of plants. Always have some spares growing in an out-of-the-way part of the garden for replacement planting if you want to make sure that your formal bedding scheme is always in tip-top condition.

- Single rows of plants have a place in edging and in long and narrow borders but in most cases it is better to use blocks of plants rather than bed- or border-long strips.

- The evenness of both growth and time of flowering associated with $F_1$ hybrids make them especially useful in formal bedding schemes.

## THE STANDARD GARDEN BEDDING SCHEME

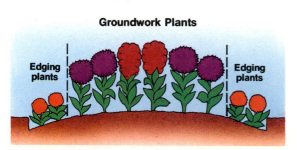

**Groundwork Plants**

**Edging plants**

**Edging plants**

This is the bedding scheme seen in millions of suburban gardens in circular beds in the front garden or in long rectangular beds flanking the driveway. Most of the bed is filled with **groundwork plants** — medium-height varieties reaching 8 in.–2 ft. Growing amongst them may be a central or a neat line of trees or shrubs. At the outer edge are set the low-growing **edging plants** —Alyssum, Lobelia, Tagetes, Limnanthes, Ageratum etc. Styles have not greatly changed over the years — Impatiens and Begonia have come in and Calceolaria and Heliotrope have gone out. Cost is usually a controlling factor — unusual plants may be chosen for a tub or hanging basket as only a few specimens are required, but inexpensive types are generally picked when large numbers have to be bought for a bed or border.

*A standard garden bed — a colourful but uninspired collection of African Marigold, Salvia and Lobelia*

# THE STANDARD PARK BEDDING SCHEME

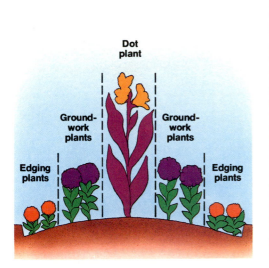

**Dot plant**

**Ground-work plants**

**Ground-work plants**

**Edging plants**

**Edging plants**

The large beds and borders planted out each year in public gardens and around our towns illustrate formal bedding at its best or in all its bad taste depending on your point of view. Schemes vary enormously, from occasional examples of blanket bedding (page 89) to the ornate complexity of carpet bedding (page 88). The basic standby of the professional gardener, however, is the park bedding scheme. It generally covers a more extensive area than the standard garden bedding scheme and unusual bedding plants such as Chlorophytum and Iresine are sometimes included. There are other differences from the front garden plot but the fundamental one is the regular incorporation of **dot plants** within the scheme. These plants are set at the centre of circular and square schemes or are planted several feet apart in rectangular and oval beds. They are grown singly or in groups and are tall enough to stand above the surrounding **groundwork plants** which in turn grow above the **edging plants** at the rim of the bed or border.

Height is not the only feature of a successful dot plant — both colour and leaf form should contrast with the surrounding plants. A large-leaved Canna or Ricinus will act as a foil to feathery-leaved types such as Marigolds, and the grey-leaved Centaurea candidissima can be used where the groundwork plants are brightly coloured. It is this combination of extra height and contrasting form which makes dot plants the focal points of standard park bedding schemes.

| Edging Plants | | Groundwork Plants | | Dot Plants | |
|---|---|---|---|---|---|
| Dwarf plants up to 8 in. | | Medium-height plants 8 in.-2 ft | | Tall plants with showy leaves or flowers | |
| *Examples:* | | *Examples:* | | *Examples:* | |
| Alyssum | Dwarf Impatiens | Pelargonium | Calceolaria | Standard Fuchsia | Abutilon |
| Pansy | Limnanthes | Petunia | Bedding Dahlia | Standard Pelargonium | Amaranthus |
| Lobelia | Dwarf Nasturtium | Salvia | Nemesia | Standard Heliotrope | Ricinus |
| Ageratum | Nemophila | French Marigold | Zinnia | Standard Lantana | Tall Antirrhinum |
| Tagetes | Phacelia | Larkspur | Wallflower | Canna | Musa |
| Dwarf Antirrhinum | Phlox | Aster | Mimulus | Kochia | African Marigold |
| Iberis | Dwarf Verbena | Bedding Begonia | Clarkia | Zea | Cordyline |

*The park-style bed — Salvia, Cineraria, Bedding Begonia with Ageratum at the edge and Musa in the middle*

# Informal Bedding

As with formal bedding the whole or most of the bed or border is covered with bedding plants. The similarity stops there. With informal bedding there is no attempt to arrange the plants into geometrical shapes or straight lines — they are set out in groups in the same way as hardy perennials in an herbaceous border. Some overlapping is allowed to occur to add to the air of informality. In addition it is not necessary to select plants which will all be in bloom at the same time. In fact it is a definite advantage to aim for a succession of flowering periods when making your selection.

Landscape designers prefer informal to formal bedding from the artistic point of view, but there are also several practical reasons for choosing the informal approach. The plants of a single variety within the group need not all flower at the same time or grow to the same height — even if the plants should fail they can be quite simply replaced without spoiling the overall pattern of the bed.

Even more important is the fact that a year-round display can be achieved without having to clear the whole area between spring and summer bedding and then between summer and winter bedding. The usual site is a front-garden bed or border which contains a few herbaceous perennials or shrubs. Spring bedders are planted in groups in autumn — Wallflowers, Bellis, Myosotis etc together with Daffodils and Tulips. As the spring bedders come to the end of their life the clumps are cleared and the spaces are planted with the summer-flowering types — hardy annuals first and then the delicate types in the spots vacated by late-spring bloomers such as Sweet William. The display of summer bedders comes to an end between August and November — the early gaps can be filled with late flowerers such as Asters. The late autumn gaps are used for winter bedding plants like Universal Pansies and Winter Heather and for the spring-flowering types to start the cycle again.

## SUBTROPICAL BEDDING SCHEME

The subtropical bed or border was one of the display features of the large Victorian garden. The owner proudly showed off the plants from his greenhouses — pots of delicate exotics were planted out for the summer months and then brought back in during the frost-prone months. The keystone of the collection was the tall and large-leaved group — Banana, Canna, Rubber Plant, Ricinus, Tree Fern, Agave etc. Bold hardy plants such as Gunnera and Cortaderia were sometimes used, and at the front were set the small exotics such as Iresine, Coleus, Perilla etc. The subtropical bed has declined in popularity but it is still occasionally seen in botanical gardens and large parks. You can create one for yourself if you have a sunny and protected spot — for maximum effect aim for a jumble of conservatory plants with interesting foliage in a wide range of colours and plant heights.

*A riot of jumbled colour — African & French Marigolds, Geranium, Nicotiana, Antirrhinum, Abutilon, Kochia, Verbena and so on*

# Raised Bedding

It is one of the principles of garden design that a flat and uninteresting plot can be improved by having plants growing at different levels. The rockery and the window box have been used for generations to achieve this effect and more recently both the patio tub and the hanging basket have become popular.

The raised bed is perhaps the most satisfactory way of raising plants above ground level — unlike the container it is truly part of the garden and it can be large enough to provide an impressive display of bedding plants.

A number of walling materials are available — choose the one which is most in keeping with the setting. It should be attractive in its own right or you should plan to cover it with trailing plants. Choose a spot away from trees and draw a plan. The area should not be too large — you must be able to reach the centre without having to climb on to the wall. The height is up to you, but 3 ft is generally considered to be the maximum. The walls must be firm, especially if a large amount of soil is to be retained. A concrete foundation is needed for brick, concrete or stone — sink part of the bottom course below ground level. Wooden walling material must be treated with a preservative and should be firmly embedded into the soil.

When the walling is complete, break up the soil at the bottom of the bed and add a layer of bricks or rubble. Cover with peat or old growing bag compost and then fill with good-quality garden soil. Wait a couple of weeks before planting. The area around the bed should be paved if it joins the lawn — grass growing against a wall is difficult to trim.

**Brick**

**Reconstituted stone**

**Railway sleepers**

**Rustic poles**

Many types of walling material are suitable — stone, brick, concrete blocks, railway sleepers, peat blocks, reconstituted stone blocks, rustic poles, stout timber boards and pre-cast concrete sections

Stagger rectangular blocks to increase stability

The wall face can be planted with rockery perennials if dry walling (no mortar between stones) or peat blocks are used. Plant as you go when building the wall

## The advantages of Raised Bedding

- Small and dainty plants are much easier to see and the perfume of fragrant ones is more noticeable. Miniature Roses and bedded-out house plants take on a new dimension.
- Planting, weeding and dead-heading are easier to do — very important if you are elderly or disabled.
- Drainage is improved — plant roots can be kept away from the high water table in clay soil.
- The area is contained — weeds can't creep in from the surrounding area and the bedding plants can't creep out.
- Attractive pendant plants can be grown to hang over the edge, adding another design element to the bed.
- Children and dogs do not run over the surface — a problem which can occur with surface beds.

# Carpet Bedding

True carpet bedding has a precise definition — it is the bedding out of dwarf plants with coloured foliage into complex patterns which may resemble an Oriental carpet. It is hardly practical at all these days, although a variation (picture bedding) is seen in park plantings in tourist towns — coats of arms, animals, birds or simple messages created with a range of low-growing flowering and foliage plants.

In true carpet bedding there was little or no place for flowering plants. The spark for this type of display was the introduction of a number of brightly-coloured foliage plants into Europe in the 1860s. During the 1870s carpet beds appeared everywhere — giant ones at Kew and Hampton Court and tiny ones in the front gardens of suburban villas.

Although much despised after the First World War, the carpet bed did offer a number of advantages when compared with the standard floral bedding scheme, and these advantages remain. The display is not harmed by the weather and it lasts all season long. In addition the colours are more muted as they are derived from leaves and not flowers, and gaps do not appear when flowering seasons come to an end. But there is one enormous drawback which led to the disappearance of this style from home gardens — it is extremely laborious.

The area to be planted is dug and carefully cleared of all perennial weed roots. The surface is raked smooth — it may be left horizontal or it may be domed to improve the display. After firming the bed is allowed to settle for at least a couple of weeks and then the pattern is marked out by creating furrows with a stick — the furrows are filled with silver sand. The spaces between are then planted in mid June — close planting is essential so that little soil is seen, and sometimes but not always the plants are left in their pots.

It is maintenance which is so laborious — each week the bed must be tended so that flower buds are removed, excess growth is checked and failed plants are replaced. Regular watering is necessary if the plants have been kept in their pots and the lines between the various types must be kept sharp or the effect is lost.

Many different sorts of plants were used in carpet bedding when the style was in its heyday, but nowadays some of them are extremely hard to find. Eight favourite ones are illustrated on this page. In late Victorian times it became fashionable to use foliage dot plants in carpet beds — popular ones were Yucca, Iresine, Agave, Cordyline, Coleus and Abutilon.

*Alternanthera amoena*

*Calocephalus brownii*

*Echeveria glauca*

*Iresine herbstii*

*Sagina boydii*

*Saxifraga moschata*

*Sedum lydium*

*Sempervivum tectorum*

# Blanket Bedding

The concept could not be simpler — the whole of the bed or border is filled with a single variety. Just one colour may be involved, such as Pelargonium 'Paul Crampel', Petunia 'Resisto Blue' and Begonia semperflorens 'Illumination', or a mixture may be grown — Impatiens 'Super Elfin Mixed', Antirrhinum 'Floral Carpet' etc.

The blanket bed is the very opposite of the carpet bed — supremely simple. Because of this it has its critics and is often regarded as too dull for general use. This may be true for a small front garden where more points of interest are required, but it certainly does not apply where large areas of land have to be covered. The appearance of a single-variety, irregular-shaped bedded meadow can be spectacular and is often seen in Scandinavia and some other European countries. A small raised bed often looks better when planted with a single variety rather than with groups of different bedding plants, and there is one area where blanket bedding is clearly superior to other styles. Circular beds under large and leafy trees are difficult or impossible homes for nearly all bedding plants — the answer is to cover the area with either a variety of Impatiens or Bedding Begonia.

An impressive bank of Bedding Begonias — blanket bedding at its best

# Vertical Bedding

The height of bedding-out skill or the ultimate in bad taste — both views have been expressed on vertical bedding. It all began in the early 1900s as a development of the carpet bed idea — 3-dimensional beds began to appear in public parks.

A piece of sculpture was made out of wire netting and filled with soil — flower vases and crowns were the most popular designs. The surface was then carpet-bedded and dot plants were placed around the base to form a piece of living sculpture. These beds were regarded with interest by the park visitors but the horticultural world did not like this odd approach — these sculptured beds died out nearly everywhere after the First World War. Exceptions are the Priory Gardens in Bath where nursery rhyme schemes are created each year and the Chelsea Flower Show where 3-D bedding displays have been a feature for many years.

Until recently vertical bedding had no practical use and certainly did not have a place in the home garden. The advent of Impatiens as a popular bedding plant has changed the picture — compost-filled screens covered with this bedding plant can be seen in the streets of Switzerland and other Continental countries.

A version of this screen can be made as a garden feature. Drive four stout wooden stakes into the ground so that about 9 in. is below the surface and 2 ft above. Wrap plastic netting around the posts to form a mesh box — attach the netting to the posts with wire. Line the inside with black polythene and fill with potting compost — insert two 1-ft long cardboard tubes during this filling process. Cut small holes in the polythene and plant Impatiens seedlings in early June.

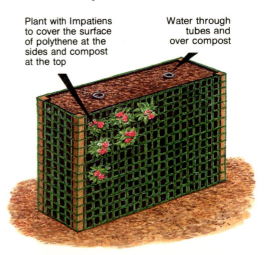

A bedding plant Teddy Bear at the Glasgow National Garden Festival

Plant with Impatiens to cover the surface of polythene at the sides and compost at the top

Water through tubes and over compost

# Picture Bedding

Picture bedding developed quite quickly following the introduction of carpet bedding (see page 88) — in picture bedding a range of low-growing plants are used to produce an illustration. A large colour palette is often required which means that flowering plants as well as foliage ones have to be used.

We do know that the first picture beds appeared in the 1870s, but there is no record of the original design. However, the first well-known picture bed is described in the horticultural history books — it portrayed a set of six butterflies in Crystal Palace Park in London in 1875. From then on the picture bed became the vehicle by which park superintendents throughout the country showed off their skill.

Flowers, animals, nursery rhymes and fairy story scenes, 'Keep Britain Tidy', 'Recycle Waste', 'Britain Can Take It' have all been illustrated by means of Alyssum, Echeveria, Lobelia, Cerastium and the rest over the years. The most consistent design in city parks has been the municipal coat of arms, but important anniversaries seem to be equally popular when they arise. Royal events, such as coronations and weddings, are of course never to be missed.

Picture bedding had its place in private grand gardens for a time when monograms and coats of arms were displayed florally, but the style was quite quickly left to public parks. There is, of course, no place for picture bedding in the ordinary home garden, but traditionally there is an exception. Coronations and the Armistices at the end of two World Wars have produced picture beds in front gardens from Aberdeen to Torquay.

The most spectacular picture bed is the floral clock — that great delight of the seaside town parks department. However, it did not begin in a seaside town — the first one in Britain was created in Edinburgh at the beginning of this century.

*Winning entry in the Gardener's Royal Benevolent Society Competition*

*A 'cascade' of bedding plants tumbling between the rocks at Stoke Garden Festival*

*A traditional floral clock at Weston-Super-Mare*

# FILLING IN

Bedding plants are usually associated with the massed planting of beds or borders (pages 83–90) or filling containers (pages 93–99). Less obvious, perhaps, but equally important in many gardens is their role in filling in. This is the provision of colours by planting one or more groups of bedding plants in a bed or border which is dominated by other subjects.

The first type of filling in is **pocket planting**, where gaps are left deliberately and are filled in each year with spring- or summer-flowering plants. This is a general pattern found in millions of front gardens throughout the country. The strip of ground around the lawn is a mixed border of roses, shrubs, herbaceous perennials, a tree or two and a number of pockets reserved for Wallflowers in the spring which are then replaced by Bedding Dahlias, Marigolds, Geraniums and the rest for summer flowering. Rockeries are sometimes treated in the same way with gaps reserved for dwarf annuals such as Bellis, Calandrinia, Felicia, Gypsophila, Iberis, Mimulus, Pansy etc.

Another type of filling in is **emergency planting** where an unsightly gap appears amongst shrubs or in the herbaceous border. Bedding plants are used to provide foliage and colour. The classic situation is the border in August when most herbaceous perennials are past their display period and the stretch of plants can look distinctly dull. The two natural late flowerers are Asters and Bedding Dahlias and both are extremely useful for filling late-summer gaps. Others with a good reputation for this purpose are Cosmos, Salvia, Verbena, Chrysanthemum frutescens and Clarkia. Of course, you will have to plan ahead for this emergency planting — you can't just go along to the garden centre in late summer and expect to find pots of bedding plants. The plan must be to keep some reserve plants in pots for use as gaps occur, and they certainly will appear if the summer is hot and dry.

The final type of filling in is **new garden planting**. In a new border, trees and herbaceous plants are set at recommended distances which to the beginner may seem ridiculously far apart. For instance a couple of Forsythia bushes need to be planted 4 ft apart, and that leaves a large expanse of bare earth beneath. The easiest way to provide colour is to plant bulbs in autumn and then bedding plants in summer in the spaces between the newly-planted woody or herbaceous perennials. This annual filling in ceases when the trees, shrubs or perennials become mature specimens. A word of warning about new garden planting. You must never grow bedding plants which are tall enough or vigorous enough to compete with the developing shrubs or border perennials for light or space.

*Pocket planting in a conifer border*

*Pocket planting in a rock garden*

*Winter Heather and Ornamental Cabbage filling in between newly-planted shrubs*

# SCREENING

The reasons for creating living screens in the garden are many and varied. The most usual purpose of growing screening plants is to provide privacy around the boundary, and bedding plants play only a minor role. The point is that the screen must be permanent, and that means using dense and shrubby plants which are perennials and may be evergreen (Box, Yew), semi-evergreen (Privet) or deciduous (Beech, Rose etc). Sometimes a tall hedge may seem unattractive or a fence of wire, brick or wood may seem dull. In these cases climbing bedding plants can be planted at the base and are then trained or left to clamber against the permanent screen in order to give summer colour.

A more common use for annual climbers is to provide open screens within the garden to act as attractive dividers between various sections — vegetable gardens are sometimes screened off from the rest of the plot in this way. Other uses are to cover dead trees and to add interest to dull expanses of house walls.

There are several climbing bedding plants from which to make your choice but in most cases one of the big two is selected — Nasturtium or Sweet Pea. Nasturtium (page 58) has dense foliage when the plants are grown closely together and so has good covering power — use it to cover chain-link fencing, old shrubs or a dull Privet hedge. 'Tall Mixed Hybrids' will provide a mass of yellow, orange and red single flowers if the soil is not too rich. The Canary Creeper (Tropaeolum peregrinum) bears pale green lobed leaves and lemon-yellow flowers. Sweet Peas (page 75) have a different role — they are much more delicate in appearance, growth habit and cultural needs, and are used to provide trellis or netting cover within the garden. Three other climbers are described in the A–Z guide. Ipomoea (page 49) bears beautiful trumpet-like flowers but its lack of dense foliage means that it will decorate trelliswork or a pergola but will not keep out prying eyes. Cobaea (page 31) bears large violet bells and the trendrils on the stems will cling to trellis, branches etc — but it is not for everyone as it hates shade, wind and heavy soil. Thunbergia (page 77) is another climbing bedding plant which hates shady or exposed situations, but put it where it will be happy and the twining stems will reach 5 ft or more and produce a succession of black-throated yellow flowers.

Not all screening plants are climbers — a line of bushy annuals can provide an effective screen if the growth is dense and they are set close together. Kochia (page 50) can be used to provide a temporary and inexpensive 3 ft high hedge prior to planting a permanent one in autumn. Helianthus (page 45) is another non-climbing type used for screening where taller plants are required — the bushy variety 'Holiday' is a better choice than the standard 'Russian Giant' or 'Tall Single'.

*The Tropaeolum peregrinum screen*

*The Ipomoea tricolor screen*

*The Kochia scoparia screen*

# POTS & TROUGHS

Bedding plants used to cover the soil or compost in a free-standing container

In the 1980s the idea of 'outdoor living' took hold in millions of homes throughout the country. No longer was the garden just a place to be worked in and then admired from the kitchen window — it was a place to be lived in during the summer. So the patio became popular, and the sales of barbecues and outdoor furniture rose dramatically. At the same time plants were brought into this outdoor living area, and 'container gardening' became fashionable.

As a result both the number and variety of free-standing containers have increased greatly during the past decade, and now pots, troughs and tubs filled with bedding plants are to be seen on balconies, patios and porches everywhere. But the idea is not new. The Hanging Gardens of Babylon were a vast collection of containers; terracotta pots filled with Gillyflowers (Dianthus caryophyllus) were a feature of Elizabethan gardens.

In a tiny garden the display from containers may be more important than the open ground features, but in most cases the pots and troughs are restricted to a number of well defined areas. These free-standing containers should be chosen with care (see below) and may be used singly or grouped with others. When grouping it is usually wise to have a limited range of container *types* (wood, plastic etc) but a distinct range of container *sizes* — wide and tall ones with smaller pots around them. The experts tell us that an odd number is better than 2, 4 etc.

Your container garden should never be empty. The summer bedding display (pages 102–104) in some pots and troughs should be followed by spring bedding (pages 100–101) and in other containers by winter bedding (page 105).

## Choosing a pot or trough

- **Is it large enough?** Large containers do not have to be watered as frequently as small ones, and you will need considerable planting space if you propose to use a bold dot plant (see page 95) surrounded by several other varieties. Containers with vertical sides will need less frequent watering than those with sharply sloping sides.
- **Is it attractive enough?** Remember that the pot or trough may be devoid of flowers for part of the year. Make sure the material is in keeping with the house and style of garden. Ornate pots may be out of place in a small modern garden and plain plastic is certainly out of place in a large old-world one. Bright plastic colours are undesirable almost everywhere.
- **Is it strong and durable enough?** Not generally a problem with shop-bought pots and troughs, but it can be with odd objects pressed into service. Will it hold the weight of compost required and is the surface truly weatherproof?
- **Is it free-draining enough?** There should be at least one hole (½ in. or more across) every 4–6 in.

## Displaying pots & troughs

FRONT DOOR & PORCH An excellent place for containers — either singly or as a pair of matched pots. Careful selection and maintenance are essential as display must always be in first class condition

BALCONY Trailing plants to grow over the container and climbing plants to clothe the railings are widely grown. Use a light-weight container and peat-based compost. Exposure to strong winds can be a problem

PATH OR STEPS LINER A line of identical pots or troughs can enhance the appearance of a plain walkway or a flight of steps

PATIO The favourite place these days for free-standing containers. The starkness of bare walls and paving slabs is relieved by the presence of bedding plants — in turn the bedding plant display is improved by the plain surroundings

FOCAL POINT A large and attractive container or a group of containers can be used to provide a focal point. Both the pot and the plants must be in scale with the surroundings

## The advantages of Container Gardening

- **Ground is not needed** Paved areas, pathways, water-logged soil etc will support containers — you don't even need a garden. Plants can be grown right next to the house and patios can be decorated.
- **Display is improved** Small and dainty plants are easier to see — the various types can be grown at different levels by grouping pots together. Arrangements can be easily altered. Attractive pendant plants can be grown, and so can delicate types requiring the protection of a wall.
- **Some of the work is easier** There is no digging — in addition planting, weeding and dead-heading are easier to do as no stooping is involved. But some jobs are more tedious — watering can be a chore in dry weather.
- **Plants not suited to your soil can be grown** Your soil may be cold, heavy and badly drained, making it unsuitable for many bedding plants. With container growing you use a compost which is known to be suitable for the varieties involved.
- **Less chance of pest damage** Plants get some protection against slugs and soil pests.
- **Eyesores can be hidden** Manhole covers can be masked and plain front doors can be transformed with flower-filled containers.

# Types

## METAL
Many old planters were made of lead, iron or copper — no longer popular. Paint inside with Arbrex.

## 'SCRAPYARD'
Many scrap items can be used — demolition yards provide some. Chimney pots, old sinks and baths, old car tyres etc.

## WOOD
Extremely practical — fits into most situations. Shop-bought or do-it-yourself, make sure that the wood is properly treated before use. The most popular form is the half-barrel. Check that the boards are not split and metal bands are secure.

## NOVELTY
The range of unusual containers is enormous — wheelbarrows, coal scuttles, litter baskets etc.

## STONE
Natural stone containers are very heavy and expensive — reconstituted stone ones are much cheaper and are available in a wide assortment of sizes and finishes.

## PLASTIC
A variety of heavy-duty plastics (polypropylene, polystyrene etc) are used to make pots and troughs in all sizes. Very popular, lightweight, inexpensive. Wide range of surfaces and colours are available.

## TERRACOTTA
The familiar clay pot is the first choice of many garden designers, but they are brittle and lose water more rapidly than other types. Check that it is frost-proof. Glazed earthenware pots are less popular.

## GROWING BAG
The cheapest of all but also the least decorative. Use for bedding plant display only if you intend to cover the plastic surface with trailing plants.

# Plants

Pots and troughs are looked at more closely than ordinary beds, which means that you should plan and choose carefully. As a general rule it is wise to pick more compact varieties than are used in outdoor bedding and to set them more closely together than you would do in a garden bed.

Small containers may be used for growing a single variety but in large pots and troughs it is much more usual to house a collection of plants. Aim for a variety of flower colours, leaf shapes, growth habits and plant heights. The standard pattern is to have tall plants at the centre of free-standing containers or at the back of pots and troughs placed against a wall. Trailing plants are used at the front of the container in order to break up the edge and to add depth to the display.

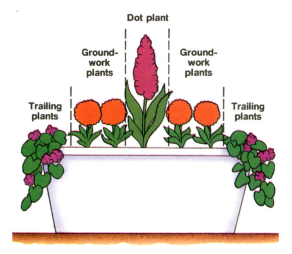

Dot plant

Ground-work plants

Ground-work plants

Trailing plants

Trailing plants

There are 2 basic ways of using bedding plants in containers:

● **ALL-OVER BEDDING** In this style the whole of the compost surface is used for growing bedding plants, although bulbs may be planted between them when creating a pot or trough for spring display.

The tallest plants are placed at the centre or along the back depending on the viewing direction. For large containers these tall bedding plants can be chosen from the dot plants described in the A-Z chapter, but in more modest pots and troughs it is often preferable to choose a tall groundwork plant such as Geranium, Bedding Dahlia, Aster or Antirrhinum 'Bright Butterflies'. At the front of the display set out edging plants (see page 85) and trailing plants (see page 97).

If the container is unusually shallow it is a good idea to grow plants requiring sandy soil and full sun — examples are Mesembryanthemum, Ursinia, Echium, Dimorphotheca and Gazania.

● **PART BEDDING** A large container can look uncomfortably bare from November to March unless it is used for winter bedding. A woody evergreen is sometimes planted in the centre of the pot or trough in order to get over the problem. Typical examples include:

| | | |
|---|---|---|
| Dwarf Conifers | Pieris | Box |
| Skimmia | Photinia | Yucca |

Groundwork, edging and trailing bedding plants are set out around this central permanent feature to provide a spring, summer or winter display.

## The 12 steps to success

**1** Make sure the inside is thoroughly clean if the container has been used before. Soak if material is porous. New wood must be treated with a water-based preservative. Half-barrels may be charred with a blowlamp for protection against rotting

**7** Plant firmly — see page 110

**8** A 1–3 in. watering space above the surface should be present after planting. Water the plants in immediately

**5** Add peat to reduce the cost of compost if the container is large — the compost layer above need be no more than 9 in. deep

**6** Add moist soil-based or peat-based potting compost or Multicompost

**4** Add a layer of rubble or gravel to help drainage and stability. Omit this step if weight is a problem

**3** Cover the drainage holes with crocks or a fine mesh screen

**2** Raise the container from the standing base if possible

**9** Do not let the plants dry out — watering every day may be necessary if the weather is hot and dry during the summer months. Water gently but thoroughly until water runs out of the drainage holes

**12** Always use a wheeled trolley if you have to move a filled and heavy container from one part of the garden to another

**10** Start to feed with a liquid fertilizer 6–8 weeks after planting. Repeat as instructed on the label

**11** Dead-head regularly to extend the flowering season of the specimens

# WINDOW BOXES

**Bedding plants used to cover the soil or compost in a container attached to the base of a window**

Countless flat dwellers rely on window boxes to provide their sole involvement with outdoor gardening. The garden owner has much wider scope for his or her activity, but window boxes do have a special place in exterior home decoration for everyone. They add colour and interest to dull walls and windows, but there are rules to follow to ensure success and safety. The construction material and its colour should not detract from the plants — you can buy plastic, wrought iron, terracotta, glass fibre ones etc but the preferred material is wood which is either painted or stained and may be varnished. The treatment of wood is up to you, but softwoods and plywood must be protected with some form of wood preservative.

Size is also important. A minimum depth and width of 8 in. is often quoted — less than this and your plants will dry out too quickly. Ideally the length of the box should be just a couple of inches less than the sill length. Secure fixing is essential, especially with boxes attached to upstairs windows, and frequent watering is vital. Positioning is important — sunny windows are perhaps the most satisfactory but with shade-loving plants such as Begonia and Impatiens you can create eye-catching displays against a north-facing wall. Think about watering — don't use window boxes in a location where daily watering will be a death-defying feat. Always attach the empty box to the wall before filling and planting — moving a filled box can be dangerous.

There is no reason why you cannot make your own box out of wood, and this is sometimes necessary if your windows are an odd size. Buy ¾ in. thick hardwood (teak, cedar or oak) if you can afford it — otherwise choose marine plywood or a softwood. Use water-resistant glue and brass screws, and drill ½–¾ in. drainage holes in the base at 4–6 in. intervals.

## Fixing

The preferred method of attachment will depend on the type of sill and window. You must choose one of the techniques illustrated below.

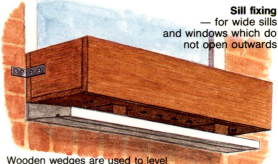

**Sill fixing** — for wide sills and windows which do not open outwards

Wooden wedges are used to level the box on the sloping sill and to allow water to drain away. Angle brackets secure the box to the wall

**Wall fixing** — for narrow sills or no sills and for windows which may open outwards

Strong steel brackets are used to support the box — make sure screws and wall fixings are large enough for the weight to be carried. Also screw the inside of the box to the wall

# Plants

The height of upright plants is, of course, a key factor. If the specimens are too small then one may be denied seeing them from inside the house, but if they are too large the light entering the room may be seriously reduced. This means that not all the plants in the A–Z guide can be used, but this is made up for by the fact that a number of house plants can flourish in the shelter of a south-facing window.

The best style to use is part bedding (see page 95). Window boxes cannot be taken down like hanging baskets when the display is over, so it is a good idea to have a year-round green skeleton which is enlivened with bedding plants. Popular subjects for this perennial background are young specimens of upright or spreading Conifers, variegated varieties of Ivy and the grey-leaved Glechoma.

Trailers at the front of the window box are highly desirable and climbers at the sides to clamber up trelliswork can be an attractive feature. Some plants (Nasturtium, Thunbergia, Ivy etc) can be used for both purposes.

Bulbs are widely used to enhance the spring display — use compact types such as Muscari, Crocus, Iris reticulata and Hyacinth rather than tall Tulips or Daffodils. Plant the bulbs after putting in bedding plants in autumn.

The schemes for summer displays vary widely from street to street and country to country. It is up to you, but a kaleidoscope of colour is generally not a good idea. The most successful schemes are usually simple ones in which the contrast is with the wall (bright flowers next to pale walls, pale ones next to dark walls) rather than between the plants themselves.

| Trailing Plants for the front of the window box | |
| --- | --- |
| Hedera | Pelargonium peltatum |
| Lobelia | Helichrysum petiolatum |
| Lysimachia (Creeping Jenny) | Helichrysum microphyllum |
| Plectranthus | Glechoma |
| Tradescantia | Thunbergia |
| Nasturtium | Campanula isophylla |
| Zebrina | Asparagus sprengeri |
| Begonia (pendant var.) | Verbena (trailing var.) |
| Impatiens (semi-trailing var.) | Petunia (pendant var.) |
| Fuchsia (trailing var.) | Mesembryanthemum |

*Lysimachia nummularia*

## The 8 steps to success

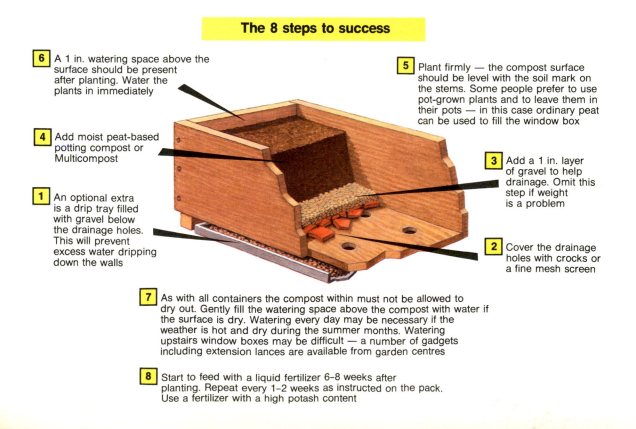

**6** A 1 in. watering space above the surface should be present after planting. Water the plants in immediately

**4** Add moist peat-based potting compost or Multicompost

**1** An optional extra is a drip tray filled with gravel below the drainage holes. This will prevent excess water dripping down the walls

**5** Plant firmly — the compost surface should be level with the soil mark on the stems. Some people prefer to use pot-grown plants and to leave them in their pots — in this case ordinary peat can be used to fill the window box

**3** Add a 1 in. layer of gravel to help drainage. Omit this step if weight is a problem

**2** Cover the drainage holes with crocks or a fine mesh screen

**7** As with all containers the compost within must not be allowed to dry out. Gently fill the watering space above the compost with water if the surface is dry. Watering every day may be necessary if the weather is hot and dry during the summer months. Watering upstairs window boxes may be difficult — a number of gadgets including extension lances are available from garden centres

**8** Start to feed with a liquid fertilizer 6–8 weeks after planting. Repeat every 1–2 weeks as instructed on the pack. Use a fertilizer with a high potash content

# HANGING BASKETS

Bedding plants used to cover
the soil or compost in a container
suspended from a hook or bracket

Hanging baskets share a number of features with window boxes — plants are grown well above ground level and trailing types are especially important. There are important differences, however — the planting area of a hanging basket is usually strictly limited and the object is generally to cover the sides as well as the top with leaves and flowers.

About 30 per cent of gardens have at least one hanging basket — a significant increase on the position just a few years ago. Most of these are bought ready-planted, but it is quite a simple job to buy an empty basket and plant your own.

There are a number of rules to follow. Firstly, choose the right type for the display you have in mind and the spare time available for watering — be guided by the virtues of the different types set out on the right. Next, choose a suitable site — the usual spot is either close to the front door or on the wall above the patio. For most plants the ideal place is a partly sunny location, which means avoiding north- and south-facing walls. Also keep clear of sites exposed to strong winds or where the basket can be bumped into by passing traffic.

It is vital to ensure that the hook or wall bracket is secure. A well-watered container may weigh 25 lb or more so fix the attachment properly. Remember that easy-watering brackets and baskets with spring loaded holders are available these days to make raising and lowering the container a simple job.

The attraction of a hanging basket is easy to understand. A living ball of beautiful plants can be created to transform a dull wall. However, you should realise before you start that a good deal of work is involved. Not with preparation and planting but with watering and trimming. A basket without a water-proof exterior will need watering daily or even more frequently in summer.

## Types

**OPEN BASKETS** More scope is offered, as sides as well as the top are available for planting. But without a waterproof liner the compost dries out quickly and drips after watering can spoil the surface below

**Wire baskets** are the most popular form — these days the wire is plastic-coated. Wrought iron versions are available

**Wooden boxes** are decorative in their own right. Usually available in kit form. More popular for indoor use than outdoors

**CLOSED BASKETS** Some are available with drip trays to prevent water dripping on to the ground. Filling and planting up is generally easier than with open baskets. But sides cannot be planted and living ball effect is harder to achieve

**Plastic baskets** usually have a drip tray which is built in or can be clipped on. Terracotta versions are available — preferable in old-world surroundings

**Fibre baskets** have a more natural look than plastic ones, but they are not as long-lasting and there is no drip tray attached to the base

*Plain basket — a single variety of Lobelia has been used, but the effect is still dramatic*

*Fancy basket — perhaps over the top. Petunia, Fuchsia, Nemesia, French Marigold, Lobelia, Glechoma, Geranium...*

*Vegetable basket — Tomato 'Tumbler' is ornamental as well as productive. A bedding plant/vegetable*

# Plants

The usual pattern is for the basket to be planted up with a variety of summer-flowering bedding plants and then placed outdoors in late May or early June. Open baskets have a central planting of compact upright types and trailing plants are set around the outer edge and into the sides. With closed baskets the planting of the sides is omitted.

In October or November the display is hit by frost and so the basket is emptied and brought indoors to wait for next year's summer display. This is indeed a shame as it is during the winter months that colour is most needed at the front of the house. For a November to March display the basic trio are Variegated Ivy, Universal Pansy and Winter Heather.

For summer display the big five are Geranium, Fuchsia, Lobelia, Petunia and Impatiens. But the range from which you can choose is much, much larger. Any of the trailing plants listed on page 97 for window boxes can be used — in addition you can try Helxine, Setcreasea, Nepeta, Tolmiea or Ficus pumila.

Plants for the top of the basket should be reasonably dwarf with an upright, bushy or spreading habit. There are lots to choose from — successful summer ones include:

| | |
|---|---|
| Bedding Begonia | French Marigold |
| Impatiens | Gazania |
| Petunia | Fuchsia |
| Chlorophytum | Geranium |
| Pansy & Viola | Coleus |
| Dwarf Sweet Pea | Cineraria |
| Calceolaria 'Sunshine' | Dianthus |
| Heliotrope | Brachycome |
| Alyssum | Felicia |
| Mimulus | Nemesia |

## The 10 steps to success

**7** Water in the plants thoroughly but gently. Let the plants settle before placing outdoors — ideally the basket should be kept in the greenhouse or near a sunny window for about 2 weeks before hardening off and placing outdoors

**6** Plant the centre of the basket with upright bedding plants — set trailing plants around the edge. Firm compost around the plants — there should be a 1 in. watering space between the compost surface and the top of the basket

**5** Add more compost to near the top of the basket. Press down gently to compact the growing medium — this will reduce the speed of drying

**4** Half fill the basket with moist peat-based potting compost or Multicompost. Press down and then make 3-5 slits in the polythene at the compost surface level. Through each slit push a trailing plant seedling so that the soil ball rests on the compost and the top of the plant is beyond the sphagnum layer

**3** Line the outside with a ½-1 in. layer of moist sphagnum moss. Place polythene sheeting over this layer and put a saucer at the bottom to hold it down

**2** A liner is required. This can be a pre-formed one (foam, cardboard or fibre) bought from your supplier. Many people prefer to use sphagnum moss which gives the basket a natural look, but rapid drying out and dripping can be problems. The sphagnum + polythene lining system is best — proceed to step 3

**1** Filling a plastic basket is a simple matter — just place a few crocks above any drainage holes which may be present and then add a peat-based potting compost or Multicompost. Firm, and then go on to step 6. With a wire basket the situation is more complex. Begin by standing the container in a large pot or bucket for support. Go on to step 2

**8** As with all containers the compost within the basket must not be allowed to dry out. Watering open baskets without a liner may be necessary every day or twice a day in summer — watering closed baskets with a drip tray will be required 2-3 times a week. Gently fill the watering space above the compost and allow to drain. Use steps to reach the basket for watering — if this is not possible use one of the gadgets described in the Watering section (page 111)

**9** Start to feed with a liquid fertilizer 6 weeks after planting. Repeat every 1-2 weeks as instructed on the pack. Use a fertilizer with a high potash content

**10** Trim regularly to keep the plants in check and to remove dead blooms. If necessary peg down shoots with hair pins pushed through the lining and into the compost

# Spring Bedding

The planting of spring bedding plants begins in October when the summer bedders are removed. The Marigolds and Alyssum may still be in flower, but the preparation of the ground for the new plants should not be delayed. Spring bedders need time to become established before the onset of winter which means the earlier you start in autumn the better. Soil preparation is easy — all you have to do is rake over the ground after removing weeds and surface rubbish, and then let it settle for a few days before you begin planting.

Only a small number of bedding plants can be employed to provide a spring display which will peak in April and May. The bedders used are hardy biennials, sown between May and July in a nursery bed before their transfer to bed, border or container in autumn.

They are used in various ways. Most popular of all is filling in gaps in the mixed bed or border which are left when the summer bedding plants like Geranium, Salvia, Lobelia, Impatiens and the rest are removed. Some of these vacated pockets are used solely for bedding plants like Wallflowers, Pansies etc. Others are used for spring-flowering bulbs, but the traditional pattern is to fill these planting pockets with a mixture of bulbs and spring bedders. Much less common is

the use of perennials as bedding plants, as described on page 101.

Sometimes whole beds or borders are devoted to spring bedding plants, with or without bulbs. This bedding out is more popular in public parks and grand gardens than in ordinary ones, but container planting with bulbs mixed with Daisies, Wallflowers, Myosotis etc is popular everywhere.

In most cases spring beds are less fussy than summer ones. Polyanthus is generally grown as a mixture of colours, but most other types are used as single colours. Close planting is recommended — not much growth takes place between planting and flowering. Water in after planting. Care is usually a simple matter with little need for watering or feeding. Root rot can be a problem in waterlogged soil.

It is time to clear the bed, border or container in mid May if the site is wanted for summer bedding. The biennials are dumped, but Polyanthus and Daisies can be moved to a spare patch of ground to grow on during summer in readiness for bedding out again in autumn. Divide large clumps at this May stage and not in autumn prior to bedding out. Perennials used for spring bedding (see page 101) are also moved to a spare patch of ground at this time.

## The Traditional Pattern

**Tall display plants** Usual ones are either tall Tulips or Wallflowers

**Underplanting of groundwork plants** Dwarf Wallflowers and all other spring bedders can be used. The height of the display plant governs which ones are suitable

**Edging plants** Pansies and Bellis are the favourite types

## The Big Five

**BELLIS**
Not as widely used as Wallflower, Pansy or Polyanthus but extremely useful for edging and containers. The 4 in. 'Pomponette' series is perhaps the best choice

**MYOSOTIS**
The standard way to bring blue into your bedding scheme. Choose your variety with care as heights vary from 'Blue Ball' (6 in.) to 'Bluebird' (1½ ft)

**PANSY/VIOLA**
The 'Universal' series is now a great favourite for edging and underplanting, providing winter as well as spring flowers. Summer-sown Violas provide April–May blooms

**POLYANTHUS**
The 'Pacific Giants' strain has been the favourite type for many years, but for winter hardiness and a prolonged flowering season it is better to choose the $F_1$ hybrid 'Crescendo'

**WALLFLOWER**
The most popular spring bedder — 9 in. to 2 ft tall depending on the variety. Red and yellow are the favourite colours — for succession plant the May-flowering Siberian Wallflower

## PERENNIALS FOR SPRING DISPLAY

*Doronicum plantagineum*

The usual spring bedding procedure is to plant biennials. When the blooms fade or when the site is needed for summer bedders, the plants are dug up and thrown away. Some, however, can be treated as perennials — Bellis, Polyanthus and Primroses can be lifted and then planted in an out-of-the-way spot in the garden. Divide, if necessary, at this stage and feed and water during the summer. In autumn lift once again and plant in the bed, border or container for a spring display. A number of spring-flowering perennials can be treated in this way — Doronicum, Dicentra eximia, Aubretia, Arabis and Auricula.

## MASSED BEDDING PLANTS FOR SPRING DISPLAY

*Polyanthus edged with Universal Pansies*

Spring bedding plants are usually grown with bulbs in the bed, border and container or they are planted in groups between shrubs, trees etc in the mixed border. In large gardens and public parks, however, you will sometimes see a blanket bed of a single spring bedding variety. This may be an impressive yellow drift of Wallflower 'Cloth of Gold' or a rainbow mixture of colours provided by Polyanthus 'Pacific Giants'. An edging is sometimes present — a line of Universal Pansies or a neatly trimmed hedge of dwarf Box. Regarded as too dull by most gardeners, it is still worth trying if you have a number of empty beds and containers to fill.

## THE TRADITIONAL BULB & BEDDING PLANT DISPLAY

*Tulip/Myosotis/Muscari display*

Ever since Victorian times the favourite spring bedding scheme has been a combination of bulbs with biennial bedding plants. It seems that it began with a professional gardener named John Fleming in the 1860s, and the basic scheme is still to be seen in flower between March and May in areas ranging from small tubs on balconies to vast beds in grand gardens.

Not all bulbs are equally suitable. Daffodils are best grown as drifts and left in the soil after flowering. Hyacinths are fine for containers, but are too expensive for filling a bed or border. Muscari and Anemone are also useful, but they do not provide height and are best for edging. May-flowering Tulips are by far the most popular and successful partners for spring bedding plants — tall Darwins as display plants or shorter Tulips for underplanting or growing in groups between other plants.

There are two basic approaches. The bulbs may be interplanted with the biennials — tall Tulips underplanted with yellow Wallflowers or blue Myosotis is the most popular of all combinations. To avoid disturbing the bulbs put the bedding plants in first in October and then plant the Tulips between them. Set the plants close together.

Another approach is to plant the bulbs and bedding plants in distinct groups to produce a formal or informal effect. Long succession is the advantage here — by careful selection the bed or container can be in flower from March to June.

The best selection depends on personal preference, but you have to think about height and soil conditions as well as colour. When interplanting do make sure that there is a minimum of 6 in. between the anticipated height of the display and groundwork plants. Also remember that Wallflowers, Arabis and Aubretia do best in sunny, free-draining locations whereas Myosotis, Pansy and Polyanthus thrive best in humus-rich, moist and semi-shady situations.

# Summer Bedding

For most people summer bedding is the *only* type of bedding that receives serious attention. The one exception is the planting of Wallflowers in lines or groups in autumn for spring flowering. Apart from these old favourites and perhaps the winter-flowering Universal Pansies (which are becoming increasingly popular) the bedding story in the average garden begins at the end of May or early June when the summer bedders are planted out. The general choice here is between half hardy annuals (e.g Salvia, Impatiens, Lobelia and Marigolds) and half hardy perennials such as Geranium and Fuchsia. Hardy annuals and perennials are less frequently used because the flowering season tends to be short, but there are exceptions such as Alyssum, Sweet Peas, Sunflower and Pot Marigold.

Bedding out a whole bed or border with a variety of summer bedders in a regimented way does of course take place, but these days it is only firmly entrenched in the small front garden and the municipal park or other public display planting. In other gardens summer bedding is much more likely to consist of putting in groups of bedding plants to cover bare areas between or around perennials and also to fill containers. In many gardens a formal/informal style is adopted. Summer bedders are planted in informal groups between other plants — at the front of the plot one or more straight lines of dwarf varieties are planted to provide a formal edging.

The first step, of course, is to choose what you want to grow. This is not too difficult with spring or winter bedding as there is only a limited choice, but with summer bedding the range seems limitless ... and bewildering for beginner and expert alike. It is not just a matter of looking through catalogues for blooms you like — some excellent plants don't bear flowers. These are the foliage plants used for summer bedding — in this book or in the catalogues you will find Coleus, Ricinus, Iresine, Hypoestes, Helichrysum petiolatum and microphyllum, Cineraria, Eucalyptus, Hedera, Pyrethrum, Hibiscus 'Coppertone', Kochia, Cordyline and Centaurea gymnocarpa. Next point — well-known variety or novelty? New varieties of Impatiens, Alyssum, Phlox, Begonia, Nicotiana, Nasturtium are all worthwhile advances, but do remember that most favourites have won their place at the top of the lists by being tolerant of a wide range of conditions. Then there are other considerations — height, colour, cost, length of flowering season, soil type, climatic conditions and so on. Not easy, but looking through catalogues to choose next season's bedding plants is one of the pleasures of midwinter for millions of gardeners.

In October or November it is all over, but don't be too quick to throw everything away. The perennials such as Fuchsia, Geranium, Heliotrope, Dahlia etc should be dug up and taken indoors to provide cuttings or for planting out again next year.

# CHOOSING SUMMER BEDDING PLANTS
## — by flower colour

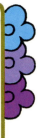

### YELLOW

| | | |
|---|---|---|
| Antirrhinum | Eschscholzia | Nicotiana |
| Arctotis | Gaillardia | Pansy |
| Aster | Gazania | Petunia |
| Begonia (Tuberous) | Helianthus | Phlox |
| Calceolaria | Helichrysum | Poppy |
| Calendula | Hibiscus | Portulaca |
| Canna | Limnanthes | Rudbeckia |
| Carnation | Limonium | Salpiglossis |
| Celosia | Lupin | Schizanthus |
| Centaurea | Marigold | Stock |
| Chrysanthemum | Matricaria | Tagetes |
| Coreopsis | Mesembryanthemum | Thunbergia |
| Cosmos | Mimulus | Ursinia |
| Dahlia | Nasturtium | Viola |
| Dimorphotheca | Nemesia | Zinnia |

### BLUE & PURPLE

| | | |
|---|---|---|
| Ageratum | Echium | Pansy |
| Alyssum | Eschscholzia | Pelargonium |
| Amaranthus | Felicia | Penstemon |
| Anchusa | Fuchsia | Petunia |
| Antirrhinum | Helichrysum | Phacelia |
| Arctotis | Heliotropium | Phlox |
| Aster | Iberis | Plumbago |
| Balsam | Impatiens | Poppy |
| Brachycome | Ipomoea | Portulaca |
| Campanula | Larkspur | Salpiglossis |
| Celosia | Limonium | Salvia |
| Centaurea | Lobelia | Scabiosa |
| Chrysanthemum | Lupin | Schizanthus |
| Clarkia | Nemesia | Stock |
| Cobaea | Nemophila | Sweet Pea |
| Convolvulus | Nicotiana | Viola |
| Dahlia | Nigella | Zinnia |

### PINK

| | | |
|---|---|---|
| Ageratum | Dimorphotheca | Nicotiana |
| Alyssum | Echium | Nigella |
| Antirrhinum | Eschscholzia | Pansy |
| Aster | Fuchsia | Pelargonium |
| Balsam | Gaillardia | Penstemon |
| Begonia (Bedding) | Gazania | Petunia |
| Begonia (Tuberous) | Godetia | Phlox |
| Brachycome | Gypsophila | Poppy |
| Campanula | Helichrysum | Portulaca |
| Canna | Hibiscus | Salpiglossis |
| Carnation | Iberis | Salvia |
| Celosia | Impatiens | Scabiosa |
| Centaurea | Ipomoea | Schizanthus |
| Chrysanthemum | Larkspur | Stock |
| Clarkia | Lavatera | Sweet Pea |
| Convolvulus | Limonium | Sweet William |
| Cosmos | Lobelia | Verbena |
| Dahlia | Mesembryanthemum | Viola |
| Dianthus | Nemesia | Zinnia |

### RED

| | | |
|---|---|---|
| Amaranthus | Eschscholzia | Nicotiana |
| Antirrhinum | Fuchsia | Pansy |
| Arctotis | Gaillardia | Pelargonium |
| Aster | Gazania | Penstemon |
| Balsam | Godetia | Petunia |
| Begonia (Bedding) | Gypsophila | Phlox |
| Begonia (Tuberous) | Helianthus | Poppy |
| Canna | Helichrysum | Portulaca |
| Carnation | Hibiscus | Rudbeckia |
| Celosia | Iberis | Salpiglossis |
| Centaurea | Impatiens | Salvia |
| Chrysanthemum | Ipomoea | Scabiosa |
| Clarkia | Larkspur | Schizanthus |
| Convolvulus | Lavatera | Stock |
| Coreopsis | Lobelia | Sweet Pea |
| Cosmos | Marigold | Sweet William |
| Dahlia | Mesembryanthemum | Tagetes |
| Dianthus | Mimulus | Verbena |
| Dimorphotheca | Nasturtium | Viola |
| Echium | Nemesia | Zinnia |

### ORANGE

| | | |
|---|---|---|
| Antirrhinum | Eschscholzia | Nemesia |
| Arctotis | Gaillardia | Nicotiana |
| Balsam | Gazania | Pansy |
| Begonia (Bedding) | Godetia | Pelargonium |
| Begonia (Tuberous) | Helianthus | Petunia |
| Calendula | Helichrysum | Poppy |
| Canna | Hibiscus | Rudbeckia |
| Carnation | Impatiens | Salpiglossis |
| Celosia | Limonium | Schizanthus |
| Chrysanthemum | Lupin | Tagetes |
| Clarkia | Marigold | Thunbergia |
| Cosmos | Mesembryanthemum | Ursinia |
| Dahlia | Mimulus | Viola |
| Dimorphotheca | Nasturtium | Zinnia |

### WHITE

| | | |
|---|---|---|
| Ageratum | Dimorphotheca | Nemesia |
| Alyssum | Echium | Nemophila |
| Antirrhinum | Eschscholzia | Nicotiana |
| Arctotis | Fuchsia | Nigella |
| Aster | Gazania | Pansy |
| Balsam | Godetia | Pelargonium |
| Begonia | Gypsophila | Penstemon |
| Brachycome | Helichrysum | Petunia |
| Calendula | Heliotropium | Phlox |
| Campanula | Hibiscus | Plumbago |
| Canna | Iberis | Poppy |
| Carnation | Impatiens | Portulaca |
| Centaurea | Ipomoea | Salpiglossis |
| Cerastium | Larkspur | Scabiosa |
| Chrysanthemum | Lavatera | Stock |
| Cineraria | Limonium | Sweet Pea |
| Clarkia | Lobelia | Sweet William |
| Convolvulus | Lupin | Thunbergia |
| Cosmos | Marigold | Verbena |
| Dahlia | Matricaria | Viola |
| Dianthus | Mesembryanthemum | Zinnia |

### GREEN

Amaranthus
Cobaea
Euphorbia
Grasses
Nicotiana
Reseda
Zinnia

# CHOOSING SUMMER BEDDING PLANTS
## — by resistance to difficult conditions

The average bedding plant thrives where the site has some protection from the prevailing wind but receives little or no shade during the day. The soil should be free-draining, reasonably rich in humus but not too rich in nitrogen which would produce lush leaves and few flowers. Unfortunately we can often do little or nothing to change the situation and it is therefore wise to select plants which are known to succeed under the conditions which will prevail in the bed, border or container. Some experts complain that the old favourites are over-used, but as noted earlier it must be remembered that these plants are popular because they are able to succeed under a wide range of conditions.

## SALT-AIR SITE

Bedding plants in seaside gardens are often outstandingly successful, but you must choose plants which can tolerate salt-laden air. Don't guess — Calendula is not affected but Marigolds are. The best guide is to look at local gardens and parks in midsummer to discover which bedding plants flourish. Popular ones which do particularly well at the coast include:

| | |
|---|---|
| Ageratum | Gazania |
| Alyssum | Lavatera |
| Antirrhinum | Lobelia |
| Calendula | Mesembryanthemum |
| Canna | Portulaca |
| Cineraria | Salvia |
| Eschscholzia | Stock |
| Fuchsia | Sweet Pea |

## SUNNY, DRY SITE

No plant can survive for too long in completely dry soil, which means that watering is always necessary during periods of prolonged drought in summer. However, there are sun-lovers which revel in sandy soil and do not require watering in the bed or border except under prolonged dry conditions. These dry soil plants include:

| | |
|---|---|
| Alyssum | Helichrysum |
| Arctotis | Kochia |
| Calandrinia | Mesembryanthemum |
| Calendula | Nasturtium |
| Celosia | Petunia |
| Cineraria | Phlox |
| Cordyline | Portulaca |
| Coreopsis | Salvia |
| Cosmos | Tagetes |
| Dimorphotheca | Ursinia |
| Eschscholzia | Vinca |
| Gazania | Zinnia |

## EXPOSED, WINDY SITE

As a general rule you can expect low-growing and compact plants such as Bedding Begonia, Impatiens and Pansies to do better than tall ones such as Cosmos or Gaillardia. Popular plants which are known to succeed in exposed sites include:

| | |
|---|---|
| Alyssum | Marigold |
| Antirrhinum | Matricaria |
| Balsam | Dwarf Nasturtium |
| Bedding Begonia | Nemesia |
| Calendula | Pansy |
| Cineraria | Pelargonium |
| Coleus | Petunia |
| Dahlia | Phlox |
| Dianthus | Stock |
| Felicia | Sweet William |
| Hedera | Tagetes |
| Iberis | Verbena |
| Impatiens | Viola |
| Lobelia | Zinnia |

## RAINY SITE

Persistent and heavy rain in summer can ruin the blooms of many varieties. Single flowers are usually more rain resistant than large double ones and $F_1$ hybrids are usually (but not always) more successful than open-pollinated varieties under such conditions. Popular plants with a good rain-resistance record include:

| | |
|---|---|
| Alyssum | Impatiens |
| Antirrhinum | Lobelia |
| Balsam | French Marigold |
| Bedding Begonia | Nasturtium |
| Calendula | Nemophila |
| Cineraria | Pansy |
| Coleus | Phlox |
| Dahlia | Salvia |
| Dianthus | Sweet William |
| Fuchsia | Tagetes |
| Gaillardia | Viola |

## SHADY SITE

Shade can be a problem, especially when it occurs for most of the day or is due to nearby trees. Undoubtedly the best two for a shady spot are Bedding Begonia and Impatiens, but all the following popular types will flourish despite some shade:

| | |
|---|---|
| Bedding Begonia | Impatiens |
| Tuberous Begonia | Kochia |
| Calceolaria | Lobelia |
| Calendula | Mimulus |
| Campanula | Nasturtium |
| Coleus | Nemophila |
| Conifers | Nicotiana |
| Euphorbia | Pansy |
| Fuchsia | Stock |
| Hedera | Viola |

## HOT SUMMER SITE

A prolonged spell of daytime temperatures in the 80°–90°F range can cause some bedding plants to stop flowering even when they are regularly watered. The hot summers of 1989 and 1990 proved the ability of some types to withstand months of above-average temperatures:

| | |
|---|---|
| Amaranthus | Kochia |
| Bedding Begonia | Pelargonium |
| Celosia | Petunia |
| Convolvulus | Portulaca |
| Coreopsis | Rudbeckia |
| Dahlia | Salvia |
| Euphorbia | Tagetes |
| Grasses | Verbena |
| Helianthus | Zinnia |

# Winter Bedding

After generations in the doldrums winter bedding is staging a comeback — an old idea brought up to date. It is strange indeed that winter bedding came into vogue before spring bedding — as early as the 1850s pots of woody evergreens with attractive foliage were being buried ('plunged') between the bulbs in beds during November and then lifted in the late spring to make way for summer bedding. Other hardy plants such as red-leaved Kale and Sedums were used.

After such an early start it is surprising that the idea died out and until recently we were willing to leave flower beds, tubs and window boxes quite bare from the time the summer bedders were taken out in late autumn until the early bulbs bloomed in February and March. Things began to change with the introduction of the Universal Pansy, now available in single colours as well as mixtures. Blooms appear throughout the winter prior to the main flush in spring, and an underplanting or an edging in a Wallflower/bulb bed or container will provide winter colour.

There are now enough winter bedding plants available to let you plant up a whole bed or border rather than having a mixed winter/spring scheme. You can certainly plant up window boxes, troughs and hanging baskets in a fairly wide variety of ways to provide colour from November to February.

Universal Pansies remain the bedrock but varieties of Erica (Winter Heather) provide an attractive feature as illustrated in the photograph below. Polyanthus 'Crescendo' produces blooms during the winter months and the Ornamental Brassicas can be used to carpet the whole surface of a bed with white, green and red foliage. Trailing subjects for window boxes and hanging baskets include Ivy, Glechoma, Lamium 'Gold' and Vinca minor variegata. Window boxes in mild districts offer further scope — these can be planted with hardened-off house plants such as Cyclamen, Cineraria and Solanum (Winter Cherry).

So after all these years winter bedding is returning — slowly at first but obviously a technique which will increase in popularity. Its style is quite different from the Victorian parent, but there is no reason why the old idea of plunge bedding of evergreens should not be used. To give the bed or container an air of permanence bury one or more pots at planting time in autumn. Conifers are favourite subjects (see page 32), but there are many others from which to make your choice. Even a partial list is quite extensive — Santolina, Holly, Skimmia, Osmanthus, Viburnum tinus, Laurel, Euonymus, Box, Mahonia, Aucuba, Hebe and Senecio greyi. The usual choice is a variegated or brightly coloured variety, but that is up to you. Pots are lifted in May when it is time to prepare for summer bedding and they are moved to an out-of-the-way spot for replanting in autumn. It is possible to plant these evergreens directly into the bed or border in autumn and then dig up for planting in the reserve bed for their spring to autumn holiday. The need for less frequent watering is one of the advantages here, but you must lift and plant carefully and make sure the specimens are moved from the display bed to the reserve bed no later than April.

A Winter Heather/Universal Pansy/Conifer
winter bed

A Polyanthus/Euonymus/Ivy
winter container

# CHAPTER 5

# COLOUR

The paramount purpose of bedding plants in the garden is to provide colour. As a rule it is not for their architectural shape, greenness nor air of permanence — they are grown for their colour.

For this reason an understanding of colour is important if you want to get the best out of them. This does not mean having to learn a list of rules on what goes with what and how to avoid colour clashes — "never put shocking pink next to orange or dark crimson" and so on. These purist rules are less important in the garden than is often supposed. The reason is quite simple — a solid sheet of colour placed directly next to another with which it clearly does not harmonise can clearly be distasteful and this does occur in interior decoration, dress etc. In a garden, however, the various hues, shades and tints are broken up by green foliage and earthen shades which dilute the so-called colour clashes.

The purpose of this chapter is to show you how to make colour work for you in the garden, and the basis of colour theory is the classic wheel shown below. As you can see there is a basic division into warm and cool colours. To make a plot look longer, plant warm-colour flowers as close as you can to the point from which you view the garden and put in cool-colour varieties right at the back. The weather has an effect on the appearance of flowers — pastel shades can look quite washed-out in brilliant sunshine but their colour is heightened on dull days.

Within this broad span of warm and cool colours you will find a number of individual hues. There are basically three ways of putting these hues together in an harmonious way — that is, a way in which they will 'go together'. The boldest way is to match contrasting colours, the most restful way is to match analogous colours which lie next to each other on the wheel and the most subtle way is to use the tints and shades of a single hue. Schemes based on these harmonies are described on pages 108–109.

## THE COLOUR WHEEL

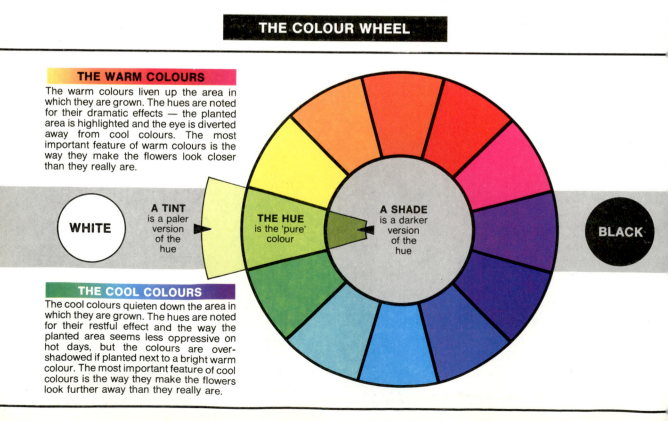

### THE WARM COLOURS

The warm colours liven up the area in which they are grown. The hues are noted for their dramatic effects — the planted area is highlighted and the eye is diverted away from cool colours. The most important feature of warm colours is the way they make the flowers look closer than they really are.

**WHITE**

**A TINT** is a paler version of the hue

**THE HUE** is the 'pure' colour

**A SHADE** is a darker version of the hue

**BLACK**

### THE COOL COLOURS

The cool colours quieten down the area in which they are grown. The hues are noted for their restful effect and the way the planted area seems less oppressive on hot days, but the colours are over-shadowed if planted next to a bright warm colour. The most important feature of cool colours is the way they make the flowers look further away than they really are.

# FLOWER COLOURS

**Primrose yellow**    **Mimosa**    **Canary yellow**    **Lemon yellow**    **Straw**    **Buff**

**Salmon**    **Apricot**    **Peach**    **Coral**    **Tangerine**    **Orange**

**Shell pink**    **Coral pink**    **Rose pink**    **Carmine rose**    **Nasturtium**    **Vermilion**

**Brick red**    **Scarlet**    **Blood red**    **Crimson**    **Magenta**    **Ruby**

**Mauve**    **Lilac**    **Cyclamen**    **Petunia**    **Violet**    **Heliotrope**

**Sea blue**    **Porcelain blue**    **Kingfisher blue**    **Delphinium blue**    **French blue**    **Gentian blue**

# COLOUR SCHEMES

## MONOCHROMATIC SCHEME

**In a monochromatic scheme the various tints and shades of a single hue are used.** The effect can be dramatic, as illustrated by the White Garden and Red Border at Sissinghurst Castle in Kent, but the effect can be distinctly monotonous if a large part of a small garden is devoted to such a concept. Monochromatic schemes still have a role to play in every garden. In an extensive property whole beds or borders can be treated in this way and all sorts of arrangements can be used — a typical example is an edging of pink Petunias or Impatiens with a groundwork of blood red Geraniums and maroon Antirrhinums. White and yellow are popular choices for monochromatic schemes, but blue is difficult as the range of available plants is limited. The blanket bed (page 89) is of course the ultimate example of the monochromatic scheme.

In the small garden this type of arrangement comes into its own as a way of planting troughs, hanging baskets and window boxes. The visual effect of a container can be heightened by the simplicity of such plantings. One final point — a truly monochromatic scheme in red, yellow, white etc is not really possible as there is the green of the foliage to take into account.

## ANALOGOUS SCHEME

**In an analogous (or related) scheme the two, three or four colours used are all neighbours on the wheel.** Such an arrangement has much of the subdued charm of a monochromatic scheme but there is of course a much larger range of plants from which to make a choice. The blues and violets of Ageratum, Canterbury Bells, Scabious and Stocks; the yellows, oranges and reds of Marigolds, Coreopsis and Helichrysum — pick your colour scheme first and then go through the seed catalogue or to your garden centre to make your selection.

Of course there is no need to keep to the hues — tints and shades are very important here and will add to the interest of the display. Analogous schemes based on cool colours (blues and violets) can look dull when seen from afar and often benefit from adding white-flowering plants to the scheme. Analogous arrangements really can be used anywhere, from a tiny container to a large border. They can be muted and restrained, working with just the greens, blues and mauves, or bright in the extreme with vivid reds and purples.

*Clumps of white flowers used to break up and brighten a polychromatic scheme*

### The role of whites and greys

Whites and greys have a special part to play in colour schemes in the garden. White on its own has a calming effect and it stands out on cloudy days or at dusk when purples and reds fade into dullness. The main purpose of whites and greys, however, is not to provide colour in their own right but to bring out the best in other colours. White flowers or grey-leaved plants will add interest to a monochromatic scheme or to a pastel analogous one — the whites and greys can either be scattered within the scheme or used as an edging. In this situation the colours of the scheme will look brighter whereas the whites and greys appear purer and more eye-catching.

When used in garish contrasting schemes whites and greys have a different role — they tend to remove the jarring effect of the contrast without in any way dimming the colours. In the same way grey-leaved foliage plants such as Cineraria and Pyrethrum are an excellent way of dividing brightly-coloured mixtures from each other.

## CONTRASTING SCHEME

**In a contrasting (or complementary) scheme the chosen colours are directly across from each other on the colour wheel** — orange and blue, yellow and violet, red and green. For maximum impact you should use the hues — yellow Marigolds and violet Verbenas; blue Lobelia surrounding orange Antirrhinums and so on. The effect is either dramatic or garish depending on your point of view, but in general such schemes are better in a park than in a home garden. The colours may be too brash in a small space, each contrasting colour heightens the visual effect of the other.

This does not mean that all contrasting schemes must be over-bright. The secret is to use tints of the colours involved to produce a pastel arrangement — pinks with powder blues, buffs alongside lilac-coloured blooms etc. Orange-pink Clarkias surrounded by sky blue Violas illustrate that contrasting schemes can be as subdued as analogous ones. Another approach is to use a tint of the warm colour and a shade of the cool contrasting one — cream and deep purple or pale green and maroon are examples.

## POLYCHROMATIC SCHEME

**In a polychromatic (or rainbow) scheme colours from all parts of the wheel are used** — a patchwork quilt of reds, violets, yellows, blues and oranges. Of course it can work, as any well-arranged cottage garden will reveal, but there are dangers.

First of all, the effect can be just too bright and it is usually wise to use tints of the various hues to ensure that a pastel effect is obtained. Next, a planting of a mixed variety of a bedding plant should not be right next to a mixture of another type of bedding plant — the effect here can be quite dreadful. The rule is to divide mixtures with either a single-coloured bedding plant or with a plain foliage variety.

There is a distinct movement away from polychromatic schemes these days and the appeal of simplicity is taking hold. The idea is to use single colours of bedding plants in analogous or contrasting arrangements with the incorporation of whites and greys rather than relying on an indiscriminate use of mixtures.

*Yellow and orange flowers highlighted by the dull grey wall in the background*

### The role of non-living objects

The appeal of your colour scheme is not controlled solely by the plants you choose to use — it is also influenced by the surroundings. The green of the lawn surrounding the bed or border is wonderfully accommodating, but a pink or yellow concrete patio can play havoc with the colour scheme used for the bedding arrangement in a container. The colour of the container itself is also important — a brightly-coloured window box bearing blooms in delicate shades of pink and lilac may really be an eyesore.

So the colour of both the paving and the container should be taken into consideration — you can save yourself a lot of trouble if you buy furniture, containers and paving in neutral shades. Of course personal preference is all-important but to make colour harmonisation easier you should consider plain wood or white furniture with cushions and covers in simple colours. Containers in white, stone, terracotta, black or natural wood should not clash with your colour scheme and a patio in dull grey or stone will not detract from the flower colours in pots and troughs.

There is usually little you can do to change the colour of the outside walls in order to improve the appearance of bedding plants, so you must adapt the planting scheme to the existing situation. This calls for using bright colours against white or pale-coloured walls and pastel or white flowers against dark-coloured stone, brick or wood.

**CHAPTER 6**

# PLANT CARE

Bedding plants are generally regarded as easy subjects — anyone can grow them. This gives great comfort to the beginner and a feeling of contempt amongst those experienced gardeners who demand a challenge. In fact this 'easy' reputation is only partly correct. The ever-popular varieties will succeed in all sorts of situations, but some of the more unusual types can be quite demanding. The basic secrets of success are to make sure you know the plants' needs before you start and then to carry out the straightforward tasks outlined in this chapter.

## GETTING THE SOIL READY

Forget the idea that bedding plants do best in poor, impoverished soil. A few do thrive in sandy infertile ground but the vast majority need something better if you want an impressive and prolonged display.

There are three basic requirements for the plants which need 'reasonable' soil in the A–Z section. The ground should be free draining as stagnant water standing around the roots is sure to lead to failure. Next, there must be adequate organic matter present to make sure that sufficient water is held around the roots in dry weather. Finally the soil must contain adequate plant nutrients, which means a proper balance of nitrogen, phosphate and potash together with the trace elements needed for healthy growth.

The standard way to prepare the bed or border is to dig or fork it over in autumn, at which time organic matter is incorporated if the soil is known to be low in humus. Use well-rotted manure, garden compost, leaf mould etc — peat is a poor substitute. For summer bedding rake over the soil in April or May, getting rid of weeds and mounding up beds to form a low dome . Make sure there is a shallow trench between the edge of the bed or border and the lawn. The final step is to rake Growmore into the surface about a week before planting.

## PLANTING

There are special rules for container growing — see pages 93–99. Planting outdoors calls for following 6 simple steps. Two basic elements are involved — proper timing and proper handling.

### The 6 steps to success

**1** **PICK THE RIGHT TIME** Hardy annuals raised indoors are planted in April or May — half hardy plants are put out between mid May (protected southern areas) and early June (northern areas and Scotland). Spring bedders are set out in September or October. Soil condition is as important as the calendar. Squeeze a handful of soil — it should be wet enough to form a ball and yet dry enough to shatter when dropped on to a hard surface

**2** **PLAN THE OPERATION** There is much disagreement here. Some people like to lay the seedlings on the ground where they are to be planted, and then put them in one by one. This is fine if the plants are in pots, but leaving bare roots laying on the soil on a dry day is not a good idea. A better plan is to remove each plant from the container just before planting. Again there are supporters of the idea of planting the edging first, but it is so easy to forget that they are there and then step on the seedlings as you move towards the centre. It is preferable to begin at the centre and work outwards. Water the plants 10–20 minutes before you begin digging the holes

**6** **COMPLETE THE PLANTING OPERATION** Return the soil removed from the hole and firm with your fingers. The edge of peat pots should be buried below the soil surface or break off if left above the surface. Gently water in each plant using a watering can without a rose

**5** **PLANT AT THE RIGHT DEPTH** Set bedding plants so that the top of the soil ball is just below ground level

**4** **PLANT PROPERLY** Lift out a plant from the tray by gently prising up with the trowel and place it into the hole in one operation. Tease the roots apart (don't cut them) when removing each plant. To extract a plant from a flimsy pot squeeze the bottom so that the soil ball pops out. Tease away any matted roots on the outside of the compost. Handle plants by the soil ball or leaves — never by the stems

**3** **DIG THE HOLE TO FIT THE ROOTS** Never push roots into a deep and narrow hole — the roots at the base and the sides should not have to be bent to fit into the hole

# WATERING

Plants cannot live without water — if the soil around the roots is allowed to dry out then a number of changes take place. The foliage starts to look dull. Leaves then begin to roll and wilt — flowers begin to fade and buds fail to open. The final stage is death. Some plants such as the South African Daisy family are able to cope remarkably well in dry weather, but most bedding plants are amongst the first to suffer from drought in the garden.

The reason is simple — the summer bedders are usually shallow rooted and have had only a matter of weeks to establish themselves. They cannot draw on the reservoir of water deep in the soil, and the plants most at risk are the newly-planted ones and those grown in containers. With these situations you must water regularly and not just during prolonged dry weather.

The battle against water shortage should begin well before the dry days of midsummer. Incorporate adequate organic matter into the soil before planting — the compost used in containers is already ideal in this respect. Make sure that the soil or compost is moist at planting time and mulch beds and borders (see page 112) after planting summer bedders.

Soil with an average cover of bedding plants loses about 2 gallons of water per sq.yd each week in summer, which is equivalent to ½ in. of rain or applied water. If there is no rain and you have not watered then this water must come from the soil or compost reserve and drying out occurs. If water is not applied then the plants start to suffer — to avoid problems read the 'steps to success' section.

## The 4 steps to success

💧 Don't wait until the plants have started to wilt. The time to begin watering is when the soil is dry to a depth of 2 in. or more and the foliage has a dullish tinge. When this occurs depends on the weather and the soil type. A sandy soil dries out much more rapidly than a heavy one, and low-humus soils hold less water than organic-rich earth.

💧 Once you decide to water then do the job thoroughly. Applying a small amount every few days may well do more harm than good as it encourages surface rooting and weed seed germination.

💧 The first job is to decide on the watering technique. **Point watering** is the simpler method — this calls for holding the spout of a watering can close to the base of each plant and then adding water gently to soak the ground around the root zone. Troughs, small beds, pots, window boxes and hanging baskets can be tackled in this way, but it is extremely time consuming if the area to be covered is extensive as you may need to apply 2–3 gallons per sq. yard. For large beds and borders with many plants of various sizes the obvious choice is **Overall watering**. This involves applying water to the whole area rather than treating each plant. You can try watering over the top of them with a watering can which is filled from a hose pipe but the usual procedure is to walk slowly along the border or around the bed with a hand-held hose and a suitable nozzle. This is a boring job and a common error is to move too quickly so that the plants receive too little water. A sprinkler which can be moved along the border at regular intervals is usually more satisfactory — always carry out this task in the evening and never in hot sunshine. Trickle irrigation through a perforated hose laid close to the plants is perhaps the best method of watering.

💧 Repeat the watering if rain does not fall but do not try to keep the land constantly soaked. There must be a period of drying-out between waterings. As a general rule you will need to water every 7 days if rain does not fall. The precise interval depends on many factors — to check if water is needed the best plan is to examine the soil 2 in. below the surface. Water immediately if it is dry.

## Watering overhead containers

The section on container growing (pages 93–99) stresses again and again the need to water containers frequently in hot and dry weather — watering every day may be necessary. This is a time-consuming but not difficult task in most cases, but it can be a problem with overhead containers such as window boxes and hanging baskets. It is possible to use steps and a watering can in some instances, but there are 3 alternatives which can make this task easier.

**HOSE LANCE**
Convenient with unlimited capacity — large areas can be covered. Difficult to direct accurately. Applying fertilizer with the water is not usually possible

**PUMP CAN**
Neat and simple to use — no hose pipe is needed. Suitable if you have one or two hanging baskets to water but not practical for large areas

**UP-DOWN MECHANISM**
Basket is brought down to easy reach. Two types available — a simple pulley on the bracket or a spring-loaded holder on the basket chain

# WEEDING & MULCHING

Weeds are plants growing in the wrong place — self-seeded Calendulas appearing amongst this year's Pansies are weeds in just the same way as ground elder and annual meadow-grass. Weeds of all types give the bed or border an untidy and neglected appearance but there are other problems. Vigorous types will compete for space, water, food etc and they can damage or even swamp low-growing bedding plants.

Obviously weeds must be kept at bay and there is no miracle cure. The way to tackle the problem is to use a number of interlinked tasks. At soil preparation time the roots of perennial weeds should be pulled out and destroyed — when getting the bed or border ready for planting it is necessary to remove all the weed seedlings which have appeared on the surface. Mulch around the newly-planted summer bedders in June. Hoeing may or may not be necessary — it certainly must stop when the bedding plants have grown and covered the ground between. This vigorous growth in midsummer should suppress nearly all weeds — any which come through should be hand pulled. All the techniques outlined above are centuries old — modern weedkillers have little or no part to play in the bedding plant story.

## Hoeing

The hoe has two important functions. Its main task is to keep weeds under control — hoeing must be carried out at regular intervals to keep annual weeds in check and to starve out the underground parts of perennial weeds. Weeds should be severed just below ground level rather than being dragged to the surface — to ensure success keep the blade sharp at all times. The second important function is to break up the surface pan which can be a problem in some soils after rain. Hoeing between bedding plants is a trickier task than working between shrubs — the plants are set more closely together and a touch of the blade on the stem can prove fatal. For this reason use a draw (swan-necked) hoe with a central shaft rather than the more usual Dutch hoe. Use with a downward chopping motion. Never dig deeply into the soil and stop hoeing once it starts to be difficult to get between the plants.

## Mulching

A mulch is a layer of bulky organic matter placed on the soil surface around the stems. Suitable materials include moist peat, well-rotted manure, leaf mould, shredded bark, Bio Humus, mushroom compost and well-made garden compost. A 2 in. layer spread on moist soil around bedding plants in June will keep annual weeds in check and there are additional benefits. The soil is kept moist in dry weather, soil structure is improved and some plant foods are provided. Fork the mulch into the soil when the plants are removed in late autumn.

| | | | | | |
|---|---|---|---|---|---|
| *Annual meadow-grass* Ⓐ | *Broad-leaved dock* Ⓟ | *Common chickweed* Ⓐ | *Common ragwort* Ⓟ | *Couch grass* Ⓟ | *Creeping thistle* Ⓟ |
| *Dandelion* Ⓟ | *Field bindweed* Ⓟ | *Field horsetail* Ⓟ | *Ground elder* Ⓟ | *Shepherd's purse* Ⓐ | *Slender speedwell* Ⓟ |

Ⓐ — Annual weed    Ⓟ — Perennial weed

## HARDENING OFF

Plants raised indoors or in a greenhouse have tender tissues — suddenly moving them outdoors in spring means a transition to colder conditions and drying winds for which they are not prepared. The result of this shock is either a severe check to growth or the death of the specimen, depending on the tenderness of the variety and the temperature of the air outdoors.

To avoid this problem there must be a gradual acclimatisation to the harsher conditions to be faced outdoors — a process known as hardening off. This task is the final stage in the steps to success for trouble-free seed raising described on page 12, and there are no short cuts. The ventilation is increased during the day in the greenhouse after which the plants are moved to a cold frame. The lights are kept closed for a week or two and the ventilation is steadily increased until the plants are continually exposed to the outside air for about 7 days before planting out. Watch the plants during hardening off — if the leaves turn blotchy or develop a bluish tinge and growth stops then you will have to slow down the process.

Of course most bedding plants are bought rather than being home-raised and that means you must take it on trust that they have been properly hardened off. This is one of the important reasons why you should always buy the more tender varieties from a supplier who you know is reliable and knowledgeable. If in doubt keep the plants in a sheltered and protected spot for a few days before planting out. Hanging baskets should be made up and kept in a greenhouse or a sunny room for about 2 weeks before placing outdoors.

## CUTTING FOR INDOORS

Cutting flowers and decorative leaves to take indoors for arranging is, of course, one of the pleasures of gardening. This will do no harm if it is not overdone but the full beauty of the flower bed or border is diminished.

If you have the space and are a keen flower arranger it is worthwhile having a separate bed where plants for cutting can be grown. Here you can cultivate varieties which are not particularly decorative as garden flowers but are much admired as dried flowers for indoor arrangements. Examples are Scabiosa stellata and Limonium sinuatum. Some other bedding plants are equally at home in the display bed and cutting garden — Sweet Pea, Aster, Helichrysum and Gypsophila belong here but there are many additional ones.

## FEEDING

Bedding plants, like all other living things, require food. The production of stems, leaves, roots and flowers is a drain on the soil's reserves of nitrogen, phosphate, potash and a number of trace elements. It is simply not true that bedding plants in general do best under starvation conditions. If one or more of the vital elements runs short, then hunger signs appear on the leaves or flowers and both vigour and display are affected.

The answer is to apply fertilizer at some stage or stages of the plant's life. There are two risks — the risk of applying too much and the risk of using an incorrectly balanced product. The advice set out below will guide you through the pitfalls.

For beds and borders work a powder or granular fertilizer into the soil surface during soil preparation prior to planting. Nitrogen, phosphate and potash contents should be approximately equal — the usual choice is Growmore but you can use a well-balanced organic mixture such as Bio Friendly Plant Food. This base feeding stage should be omitted if the A–Z guide makes it clear that the plant requires a poor soil — an example here is Nasturtium. This stage is also not necessary with composts used for containers as the fertilizer is already present.

The next stage is feeding the growing plants, and you do have to be careful here. With plants in the open garden it is helpful to apply a liquid feed in midsummer. If flowering is satisfactory you can use a balanced N:P:K product — if there is vigorous growth with a disappointing floral display then you must use a high potash/low nitrogen one. Repeat at approximately monthly intervals. A few rules. The soil should be moist before feeding — water first if the ground is dry. Keep solid fertilizers off leaves and flowers — water in after application. Finally, make sure that you use no more than the amount recommended on the package.

Magnesium deficiency

Feeding is more than applying nitrogen, phosphate and potash. The most usual starvation symptom is due to magnesium deficiency. This problem is associated with sandy soil and prolonged wet weather. The sign to look for is yellowing between the leaf veins on the older foliage — the remedy is to spray with MultiTonic and to apply a base fertilizer containing magnesium when preparing the bed or border next year.

As a general rule plants in the bed or border do not need a regular feeding programme, but the situation is quite different with plants growing in containers. The nutrients in soilless composts are designed to last for about 8 weeks, after which regular feeding with a liquid feed is essential — see pages 93–99 for details and suggested frequency.

Foliar feeding is an interesting technique which can be used when root feeding is ineffective. It is useful for all plants when the soil is shallow or where a pest attack has taken place. The response is rapid and root activity is restored — use a watering can or a Bio Hoser and apply Bio Plant Food or Fillip as directed.

## STAKING

Weak-stemmed plants, tall varieties on exposed sites, large-headed flowers and climbers all need some form of support, and care has to be taken to ensure that an attractive display is not ruined by ugly staking. The golden rule is to put the stake in position when the plant is quite small so that the stems can cover it. For many plants brushwood is the best idea — twiggy branches pushed into the soil when the stems are about 6 in. high.

This will not do for tall dot plants which often require staking at planting time. Stout bamboo canes are the usual answer, the stems being tied to the support as growth proceeds. This single-pole method is suitable for plants with a main stem such as a standard Fuchsia, but it should be avoided with bushy plants as an ugly 'drumstick' effect can be produced. A better plan is to insert 3 or 4 canes around the stems and enclose them with twine tied around the canes at 6–9 in. intervals.

Climbing plants are generally happier growing up netting, trellis etc rather than up a single pole, but there are exceptions. Whichever method you use it is essential to ensure that the framework is strong and well-anchored. It should be put in position at an early stage and new growth trained into it regularly.

## CUTTING BACK

Some cutting back usually takes place throughout the season in the well-tended bed, border or container filled with bedding plants. The operation starts at an early stage — either before or just after planting out. The growing point plus a small amount of stem is nipped out between finger and thumb — a procedure known as pinching out. Its purpose is to induce bushiness and it is used for Salvia, Antirrhinum, Lobelia, Petunia, Coleus etc. The removal of the tip stimulates buds lower down the stem and side shoots are thus produced.

Dead-heading is a form of cutting back, but in some cases more drastic action is needed during the growing season. Some plants such as Petunia have a straggly growth habit and cutting back the ends of the stems will encourage new shoots and flowers. In a container vigorous varieties can threaten to swamp more delicate types — Helichrysum petiolatum and Nasturtium are examples. The answer is to cut back these sprawling plants when their growth starts to get out of hand.

## DEAD-HEADING

The removal of dead flowers has several advantages — it helps to give the bed or border a well-maintained look, it prolongs the floral display and in a few cases it may induce a second flush of flowers late in the season. Use shears, secateurs, finger nails or a sharp knife — take care not to tear the stalk and do not remove too much stem and foliage.

Dead-heading is vital with many bedding plants. If flowers are left to go to seed then part of the plant's energy is wasted, but a much more important fact is that seed formation may produce a flower-blocking hormone within the plant. Despite these points dead-heading is not needed or not worth doing with some types. Sterile plants such as Afro-French Marigolds do not set seed so dead-heading here is merely a tidying-up operation — with tiny-flowered types like Lobelia it is not practical to cut off each dead bloom. Lobelia does have a longer flowering season if the tops are removed after the first flush of flowers, but some carpeting bedding plants such as Begonia semperflorens and Impatiens produce sheets of flowers all season long even though dead-heading is not carried out.

## WINTER CARE

For the annuals grown as summer bedding plants there is no winter care — their life span is over and their rebirth will be in the late winter or spring when the seeds are sown. The half hardy perennials must also leave the garden, but for them there is a stay indoors before being reintroduced into the garden with the return of frost-free weather in late spring.

The plants set out in autumn for winter or spring display are of course in a different situation. Such types have been selected for their hardiness and are not affected by snow or frost under normal winter conditions. However, a very heavy fall of snow can flatten Wallflowers, Forget-me-nots etc but this does not often happen. The real problem is waterlogging caused by prolonged heavy rain and poor drainage — many more spring bedding plants are killed as a result of drowned roots than frozen ones.

# CHAPTER 7

# TROUBLES

Bedding plants, like everything else in the garden, can be attacked by pests and diseases. Damping off is capable of wiping out whole trays of seedlings, and young plants can be shredded by slugs after planting out. Sweet Peas may be covered with mildew in August but it is fortunate that most bedding plants are not usually bothered by the various insects and fungi which can be such a problem on perennials, vegetables etc.

This does not mean that the cultivation of bedding plants is trouble-free. Things do go wrong, especially for the inexperienced, but this is more likely to be due to a cultural or environmental fault. Plants die, others stand still for weeks after planting out and in some cases the floral display is either disappointing or abnormally short-lived. In most cases it is the gardener and not some strange pest or disease which is to blame. The enemy may be poor soil preparation, careless handling of seedlings, lack of water, overfeeding, planting out too early or the wrong choice of plants. The golden rules are to try to prevent trouble before it starts and to deal with it quickly once it is seen.

## Prevent trouble before it starts

● **Choose wisely** Make sure each variety is suitable for your soil and location. Use the A–Z guide and avoid types which appear to be too tender for your situation. Never choose sun-lovers for growing under trees or in other shady areas. Don't sow home-grown seed — use seed bought from a reputable supplier.

● **Raise seedlings in the proper way** Do the right thing at the right time — read the A–Z guide for the plant in question and follow the rules on pages 11–13. Use thoroughly cleaned trays and fresh shop-bought compost for indoor propagation. Cover seeds if recommended and follow the light, temperature and watering instructions. Prick out before overcrowding occurs and remember to hold the seedlings by the leaves and not the stems. Check if the plant dislikes transplanting — if it does then prick out into pots, packs or cellular trays rather than into ordinary seed trays.

● **Buy good quality seedlings** Most bedding plants are bought as seedlings rather than being raised from seed by the gardener. Do buy good quality plants — study page 10. Avoid at all costs plants which are offered for sale well ahead of the recommended planting time.

● **Plant out at the right time and in the right way** This is perhaps the most important of all the rules for success. First of all, make sure the ground is ready — good drainage is vital for most bedding plants so add organic matter to improve the structure. Get rid of all perennial weed roots and add Bromophos or Chlorophos to the soil if pests have gnawed roots in previous years. The next point is to ensure that greenhouse-grown plants have been hardened off properly before they are put outdoors — failure to do so can lead to lack of growth or fatal disease attack. Equally important is the need to wait until the danger of frost has passed before planting half hardy subjects. The plants are ready and the time is right, so plant out on a suitable day following the rules on page 110.

● **Never leave rubbish lying about** Boxes, old flower pots etc are a breeding ground for slugs. Rotting plants can be a source of disease infection and may attract pests into the garden.

● **Feed and water the plants properly** Don't use fertilizer indiscriminately — remember that too much nitrogen will give you lots of leaves and very few flowers. Watering regularly in dry weather is essential, especially if the plants are growing in containers.

## Deal with trouble as soon as you can

● **Remove occasional problems by hand** Minor attacks by caterpillar or leaf miner can often be controlled by hand if the planted area is small. If a plant dies suddenly, dig it up and examine closely to see if you can find the cause. Search the earth and roots for soil pests — take remedial action if they are found.

● **Keep a few spare plants** It is a good idea to keep some spare plants after bedding out or filling containers so that gaps can be filled if early losses occur. This is especially important with formal bedding where empty spaces can spoil the display.

● **Keep a small plant-aid kit** A sudden attack by greenfly, caterpillars or slugs calls for immediate action, and serious diseases should be treated as soon as the first symptoms appear. It is therefore a good idea to keep a small selection of pesticides in the garden shed for emergency use. You will need a bottle of Long-last for all leaf pests or a Bio Friendly Pest Pistol if you prefer organics. In addition you should keep a carton of Slug Mini-Pellets and a carton of a general purpose fungicide. Don't buy more than you need — it is better to buy a new small container each year rather than keeping packs from one season to another.

● **Treat promptly and properly** Don't leap for a sprayer every time you see a stray insect, but there may be occasions when a serious disease or pest attack threatens the display — aphids, caterpillars etc can be crippling in some seasons. In such cases select the right product and read the label carefully — make sure you understand both the instructions and the precautions. Do not make the solution stronger than recommended and never use equipment which has contained a weedkiller. Pick a time when the weather is neither sunny nor windy and apply the spray in the evening when the bees have stopped working. Use a fine forceful spray and continue until the leaves are covered and the liquid has just started to run off. Wash out equipment and wash hands and face after spraying. Store packs in a safe place and do not keep unlabelled bottles or boxes.

● **Speed recovery with a foliar feed** Plants, like humans, can be invalids. The cause may have been a pest or disease attack or a period of cold or dry weather. The best way to get things moving again is to use a fertilizer which is recommended for spraying on to the leaves — Fillip is an example.

# Leaf & Stem Troubles

Holes and tears in leaves can sometimes be caused by severe weather, but the usual culprit is a pest. Seedlings and lower leaves are attacked by the night feeders which hide during the day — slugs, snails, woodlice, vine weevils etc. Above-ground pests attack leaves growing at all levels — included here are capsid bugs and caterpillars. Another group of pests do not make holes in the foliage but can be equally or even more debilitating — examples include aphid and eelworm. There are two serious general diseases — powdery mildew which attacks in dry weather and grey mould which is destructive when it is wet. Yellowing between the leaf veins is not a disease — it is usually a sign of magnesium deficiency. Abnormally thin and twisted foliage may be a symptom of lawn weedkiller drift.

## CATERPILLAR

Many different leaf-eating caterpillars attack bedding plants — look for rolled leaves and large irregular holes in the foliage. Some are uncommon but a few such as the angle shades moth can be serious pests. Pick off the caterpillars if this is practical — if damage is widespread spray with a persistent insecticide such as Long-last or Fenitrothion.

## WOODLICE

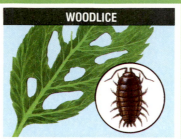

An abundant pest in shady town gardens, hiding under stones or leaves during the day and devouring young leaves of a wide range of flowering plants during the night. Woodlice favour plants which have already been damaged by a previous pest. Control is not easy — do not leave rubbish in the garden and scatter Slug Gard around the plants.

## SLUGS & SNAILS

Serious pests — the result of an attack on young plants can be devastating. Irregular holes are formed and tell-tale slime trails can be seen. Damage is worst on a shady, poorly drained site. These pests generally hide under garden rubbish during the day, so keeping the area clean and cultivated is the first control measure. Scatter Slug Gard or Slug Pellets around plants.

## CHRYSANTHEMUM EELWORM

The leaves develop brown areas between the veins; the plants may be killed if the infestation is severe. Aster, Calceolaria, Larkspur, Phlox and Zinnia as well as Chrysanthemum may be attacked. The closely-related leaf blotch eelworm produces similar symptoms on Begonia. Pick off and burn affected leaves; destroy severely infested plants.

## FLEA BEETLE

Tiny black or black and yellow beetles attack seedlings of the Crucifer family (Stock, Wallflower etc). Numerous, small round holes appear in the leaves. Growth is slowed down and seedlings may be killed. The beetles jump when disturbed. Spray with Long-last, Hexyl or Liquid Derris as soon as the first signs of damage are noticed.

## FROGHOPPER

The frothy white masses ('cuckoo spit') which occur on the stems of Phlox, Coreopsis, Campanula, Annual Chrysanthemum and many other bedding plants are familiar to everyone. Less well known is the cause — pinkish ⅛ in. froghoppers which suck the sap and distort young growth. Hose with water, then spray with Long-last or Hexyl.

## COLD DAMAGE

Frost will severely damage or kill half hardy annuals, and even a sudden cold but not frosty snap in spring can affect developing leaves by destroying chlorophyll. The affected leaf, when it expands, may be yellow-edged (Sweet Pea etc) or almost white (many bedding plants). Pick off badly affected leaves — spray with Fillip to speed recovery.

## FOOT ROT

The tell-tale sign is the blackening and rotting of the base of the stem. The name depends on the plant affected — geranium blackleg, pansy sickness, campanula crown rot etc. Use sterile compost in seed boxes or pots. Avoid waterlogging. Destroy infected plants and water remainder with Cheshunt Compound or Dithane.

## DAMPING OFF

The damping off fungi attack the roots and stem bases of seedlings. Shrinkage and rot occur at ground level and the plants topple over. The golden rules are to sow thinly and never overwater. Ensure adequate ventilation under glass. Remove collapsed seedlings immediately; water remainder with Cheshunt Compound.

## APHID

Several species of aphids infest bedding plants in warm, settled weather. The commonest are the black bean aphid and the peach-potato aphid. Young growth is distorted and weakened; leaves are covered with sticky honeydew which later becomes covered with sooty mould. Keep plants well-watered in dry weather. Spray with Long-last, Bio Sprayday or Bio Friendly Pest Pistol as soon as colonies start to appear.

Black bean aphid

Peach-potato aphid

## LEAF MINER

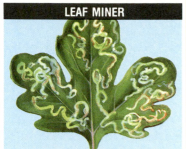

Long winding tunnels are eaten in the leaf tissue by small grubs. At first the tunnels appear white, later they turn brown. Chrysanthemum and Calendula leaves are commonly attacked in this way. The carnation fly behaves rather differently, producing blotches on the leaves and sometimes killing the plant. Pick and destroy mined leaves. Spray with Hexyl.

## WILT

Leaves and shoots sometimes wilt badly even though the soil is moist. If the plant is an Antirrhinum, Aster, Sweet Pea, Carnation, Chrysanthemum, Lupin or Poppy then the likely cause is a soil-borne fungus. Tissue inside stem will probably be stained brown. There is no cure. Remove diseased plants — do not grow susceptible plants on the same spot.

## RED SPIDER MITE

If leaves develop an unhealthy bronze colour, look for tiny spider-like mites on the underside of the leaves. The presence of fine silky webbing is a tell-tale sign. In hot settled weather spraying may be necessary — use Long-last or Liquid Derris.

## VIRUS

Viruses may be carried by insects, tools or fingers. There are many different symptoms of virus infection — leaves may be yellow, covered with yellow spots or patches ('mosaic'), crinkled and distorted or white-veined. Stems may be covered with brown stripes ('streak') or stunted and distorted. There is no cure, but fortunately annual bedding plants are rarely bothered. Buy healthy stock; keep aphids under control.

## GREY MOULD (Botrytis)

A destructive disease in wet seasons. Fluffy grey mould appears on the leaves; with many bedding plants (Godetia, Clarkia, Petunia, Zinnia etc) stems are attacked. Remove mouldy leaves and badly infected plants immediately. Spray with a systemic fungicide.

## RUST

Look for the tell-tale sign of coloured swellings on the leaves and stems. These raised spots may be yellow, orange or brown. It is a common disease of Antirrhinum, Hollyhock, Pelargonium, Carnation, Chrysanthemum and Sweet William. Pick off and burn diseased leaves; spray with Dithane every 2 weeks.

## LEAF SPOT

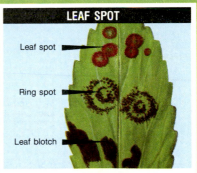

Leaf spot

Ring spot

Leaf blotch

Leaf spot is a family name for a wide group of diseases which appear on many types of flowering plants. Leaf spot (round or oval coloured spots) is an important disease of Pansy, Phlox, Polyanthus, Poppy and Sweet William. Ring spot (dark concentric rings of spores) is common on Carnation, and leaf blotch (irregular-shaped spots) affects Larkspur. Pick off diseased leaves. Spray with a Copper spray or Dithane, but control may be difficult.

## POWDERY MILDEW

The main symptom is a white mealy growth on the leaf surface. It is encouraged by overcrowding and lack of soil moisture. This is the disease commonly seen on Larkspur, Chrysanthemum, Nigella and Verbena. Plants may be crippled. Spray with a systemic fungicide at the first sign of disease and again 1 week later. Repeat if disease reappears.

## DOWNY MILDEW

Less likely to be troublesome than powdery mildew, although Antirrhinum, Sweet Pea, Poppy and Wallflower are often affected in damp weather. Upper leaf surface shows yellow or dull patches; greyish mould growth occurs below. Plants are crippled by a severe attack. Spray with Dithane at the first sign of disease; repeat at 14-day intervals.

# Root Troubles

The major problem with soil pests is that they work unseen. Most of the ones shown below eat away at roots and by the time the damage becomes obvious the plant may be beyond recovery. Rake Bromophos or Chlorophos into the soil before planting and sprinkle Slug Gard around the stems after planting if you know you have a soil pest problem or if the site was recently lawn or rough grassland.

## FUNGUS GNAT

The fungus gnat or sciarid is a tiny black fly which is often seen fluttering above the tiny plants in seed trays. It is harmless, but the eggs laid on the compost hatch into minute colourless maggots which eat young roots. In severe attacks the seedlings can be killed. Do not overwater — apply spray-strength malathion solution.

## WIREWORM

These hard, shiny insects are a problem in new gardens and in plots adjoining grassland. They are slow-moving — not active like the friendly centipede. They eat the roots of most flowering plants and may burrow up the stems of Chrysanthemums. Sprinkle Bromophos over the soil surface where they are a problem.

½–1 in. grub

## SWIFT MOTH

The favourite food of these soil-living caterpillars are bulbs, corms and rhizomes, but they will also attack Chrysanthemum, Larkspur, Dahlia and several other bedding plants. Unlike cutworms they move backwards when disturbed and stems are rarely attacked. Rake in Bromophos if it is known to be a problem — otherwise keep under control by regular hoeing.

## CUTWORM

These green, grey or brown soil-living caterpillars may be 2 in. long. They gnaw both roots and stems, but their tell-tale effect is to sever seedlings and young bedding plants at ground level. When this happens look for and destroy the cutworms near the attacked plants. Always remove the grubs exposed when digging the soil. Rake in Bromophos as a preventative.

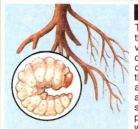

## VINE WEEVIL

These wrinkled white grubs are the larvae of the adult dark brown vine weevil. They are extremely destructive underground both outdoors and under glass, eating the roots of Polyanthus, Begonia and many other bedding plants. If a plant suddenly dies, look in the soil for this rolled-up grub. If present pick out and destroy — water with spray-strength Hexyl.

## CHAFER GRUB

The fat curved grubs of the chafer beetle feed throughout the year on the roots of garden plants. Bedding plants are occasionally attacked — badly affected plants are killed. If these grubs are found in the soil, or if you intend to plant into newly broken-up grassland, sprinkle Bromophos on to the soil and lightly rake in before planting.

## CLUB ROOT

This serious disease of the vegetable garden can affect Wallflowers and Stocks. Below ground the roots are swollen and distorted — above ground the plants are small and die off earlier than normal. The best precaution is to apply lime to the soil before planting and to avoid growing Wallflowers on the same site year after year.

## BLACK ROOT ROT

A common disease, affecting Antirrhinum, Begonia, Sweet Pea, Geranium etc. Above ground the leaves turn yellow and wilt. Below ground the roots are blackened. There is no cure, so avoid the causes — unsterilized compost indoors, uncomposted leaf mould outdoors and replanting the same type of plant in infected soil.

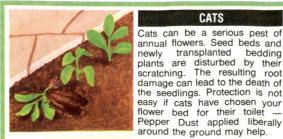

## CATS

Cats can be a serious pest of annual flowers. Seed beds and newly transplanted bedding plants are disturbed by their scratching. The resulting root damage can lead to the death of the seedlings. Protection is not easy if cats have chosen your flower bed for their toilet — Pepper Dust applied liberally around the ground may help.

## MOLES

An invasion by moles can cause havoc. The hills thrown up by their tunnelling are unsightly and cause severe root damage. Small plants may be uprooted. Eradication is not easy — smokes or sonic deterrents should be tried first. It may be necessary to set traps or to gas them; this work is best done by a professional exterminator.

# Flower Troubles

Blooms may be poor in size and quantity. They may also be damaged, distorted or spotted. In addition to the pests and diseases shown here there are other flower enemies which are illustrated and described on previous pages — slugs and caterpillars produce ragged holes in petals.

## BIRDS

Birds are extremely selective in their choice of flowers. Most blooms are ignored but Polyanthus is sometimes severely attacked in winter or spring — yellow varieties may be completely stripped of buds and flowers by sparrows and blackbirds. Sweet Peas are sometimes attacked later in the year. Surprisingly, plants in one garden may be ruined and similar plants next door may be spared. Control is difficult — netting is unsightly and repellants are rarely effective.

## BUD DROP

A common problem with Sweet Peas. Attack by sparrows or tits is sometimes the cause but the usual culprit is a sudden change in temperature or in the water content of the soil. Try to avoid stress conditions — add more organic matter to the soil when growing Sweet Peas next year.

## POOR DISPLAY

The two most frequent reasons for a disappointing show of flowers are too much shade and too much nitrogen. Some bedding plants will hardly bloom at all in dense shade — always choose carefully when you have such a situation. Too much nitrogen, due to overmanuring or use of the wrong fertilizer, is the cause of too much foliage and too little bloom — use a fertilizer which has more potash than nitrogen in order to redress the balance. There are many other possibilities — failure to pinch out the growing tips to induce bushiness, failure to water in dry weather, bud drop due to a sudden frost, pest and disease attack etc. Another cause of disappointment is a prolonged delay before the onset of flowering — the usual reason here is a failure to harden off the plants properly before planting out. A third reason for disappointment is a flowering period which is abnormally short. The two major culprits here are a failure to dead-head spent blooms regularly and an intolerance of the plant to prolonged hot weather — a problem with Mimulus, Nemesia and several other bedding plants.

## EARWIG

An important pest of Chrysanthemum and Dahlia which may also attack Pansies, Zinnia and Larkspur. At night the petals are eaten, making them ragged and unsightly. During the day the earwigs hide in the heart of the blooms or beneath leaves and in other debris on the ground. Clear away rubbish. Shake open blooms and if the attack is serious you should spray plants and soil thoroughly with Hexyl.

## CAPSID BUG

¼ in. greenish insect

These active, sap-sucking bugs are a serious pest of Dahlias, Chrysanthemums, Salvias and many other bedding plants. Small ragged holes with broad edges are formed in the leaves — the foliage becomes puckered and distorted. Buds may be killed — if they open the flowers are lop-sided. Begin spraying with Long-last when the first signs of damage appear on the leaves. Repeat 2 or 3 times at 14-day intervals.

## GREY MOULD (Botrytis)

Grey mould is a serious disease of bedding plants which strikes when the weather is humid. It can attack a wide variety of blooms — Chrysanthemum, Dahlia, Myosotis, Pelargonium, Zinnia, African Marigolds, Helianthus etc. Flowers may be spotted at first, but later rot and become covered with a fluffy mould. Badly diseased buds fail to open. Pick off mouldy leaves and flowers as soon as they are seen. Spray with a systemic fungicide.

## COLOUR BREAK

Normal

Virus infected

Petals sometimes possess streaks or patches of an abnormal colour. This colour break is caused by a virus and there is no cure. This effect may occur in Dahlia, Chrysanthemum, Viola and Wallflower. The effect is sometimes attractive but in a single-colour bed it is undesirable.

## APHID

Aphids, both greenfly and blackfly, can seriously reduce the quantity and quality of the floral display. When the weather is warm and dry, large colonies of these pests build up on the buds of many bedding plants, causing the flowers when they are open to be undersized. In a severe attack the buds may fail to open. Spray with Long-last, Bio Sprayday, Bio Friendly Pest Pistol or Liquid Derris when the pests are first seen.

# CHAPTER 8

# GLOSSARY

## A

**ACID SOIL** A soil which contains no free lime and has a *pH* of less than 6.5.

**AERATION** The loosening of soil by digging or other mechanical means to allow air to move freely.

**ALKALINE SOIL** A soil which has a *pH* of more than 7.3. Other terms are chalky and limy soil.

**ANALOGOUS SCHEME** A colour scheme in which the colours are neighbours on the *colour wheel*.

**ANNUAL** See page 4.

**ANTHER** The part of the flower which produces *pollen*. It is the upper part of the *stamen*.

**ASEXUAL** *Vegetative reproduction* — e.g cuttings and division.

## B

**BASAL SHOOT** A shoot arising from the neck or crown of the plant.

**BED** A planted area designed to be viewed from all sides.

**BEDDER** Alternative name for a *bedding plant.*

**BEDDING OUT** The covering of most or all of a bed or border with *bedding plants.*

**BEDDING PLANT** A plant which is moved at the leafy stage to its place in the garden or in a container where it provides a display for a limited period.

**BICOLOURED** A flower bearing two distinctly different colours.

**BIENNIAL** See page 4.

**BLANKET BEDDING** The use of a single variety to cover a whole bed or border.

**BLEND** A flower bearing two or more colours with one gradually merging into the other.

**BLOOM** Two meanings — either a fine powdery coating, or a flower.

**BLOTCHED** A flower with petals bearing distinctly coloured patches which are irregularly scattered.

**BORDER** A planted area designed to be viewed from one, two or three sides but not from all angles.

**BOSS** A ring of prominent and decorative *stamens.*

**BRACT** A modified leaf at the base of a flower. A cluster of small bracts is a bracteole.

**BUD** A flower bud is the unopened bloom. A growth bud or eye is a condensed shoot.

**BULB** Botanically an underground organ made up of fleshy or scale-like leaves arising from a basal plate. Popular meaning is any fleshy underground organ used for propagation.

## C

**CALYX** The ring of *sepals* which protect the unopened flower bud.

**CAMPANULATE** Bell-shaped flower.

**CARPET BEDDING** The *bedding out* of dwarf plants with coloured foliage into complex patterns.

**CHIMAERA** A *mutation* which produces two kinds of tissue — e.g one or more 'wild' coloured petals in a Dahlia.

**CHLOROPHYLL** The green pigment found in leaves which is capable of using light-energy to transform carbon dioxide and water into carbohydrates by the process known as photosynthesis.

**CHLOROSIS** An abnormal yellowing or blanching of the leaves due to lack of chlorophyll.

**CLIMBER** A plant which climbs by clinging to or twining round a support.

**CLONE** An identical plant produced by *vegetative reproduction* from a single parent plant.

**COLD FRAME** A rigid container for plants in which access is through the roof. This roof is made of one or more transparent and movable *lights* — the sides are brick, wood, metal, concrete, plastic or glass.

**COLLARETTE** A flower bearing large petals with an inner ring of small and narrow petals.

**COLOUR WHEEL** See page 106.

**COLOURED LEAF** A leaf with one or more distinct colours apart from green, white or cream. Compare *variegated leaf.*

**COMPOSITAE** The Daisy Family, in which each flower bears 'petals' which are really *florets.*

**COMPOST** Two meanings — either decomposed vegetable or animal matter for incorporation in the soil, or a potting/cutting/seed sowing mixture made from peat ('soilless compost') or sterilized soil ('loam compost') plus other materials such as sand, chalk and fertilizers.

**COMPOUND FLOWER** A flower composed of *florets.*

**CONE** A prominent and raised *disc* at the centre of a flower.

**CONTRASTING SCHEME** A colour scheme in which the chosen colours are directly across from each other on the *colour wheel.*

**CORDON** A plant which is pruned so that growth is restricted to one main stem.

**COROLLA** The ring of *petals* inside the *calyx* of the flower.

**COTYLEDON** A seed leaf which usually differs in shape from the true leaves which appear later.

**CROCK** A piece of broken flower pot used at the bottom of a container to improve drainage.

**CROWN** The bottom part of an *herbaceous* plant from which the roots grow downwards and the shoots arise.

**CULTIVAR** Short for 'cultivated variety' — it is a *variety* which originated in cultivation and not in the wild. Strictly speaking, virtually all modern varieties are cultivars, but the more familiar term 'variety' is used for them in this book.

**CUTTING** A part of a plant which is removed and used for *propagation*.

## D

**DEAD-HEADING** The removal of faded flowers.

**DECIDUOUS** A plant which loses its leaves at the end of the growing season.

**DISC (DISK)** The flat central part of a *compound flower*. It is made up of short, tubular *florets*.

**DORMANT PERIOD** The time when a plant has naturally stopped growing due to low temperatures and short day length.

**DOT PLANT** A bedding plant grown singly or in a small group at the centre of a bedding scheme where it is large enough and bold enough to act as a focal point.

**DOUBLE** A flower with many more than the normal number of petals. When the whole of the bloom appears to be composed of petals it is called 'fully double'.

**DRAWN** Term applied to pale and lanky seedlings which have been sown too thickly or grown in shady conditions.

**DRILL** A straight and shallow furrow in which seeds are sown.

## E

**EDGING PLANT** A low-growing bedding plant grown at the rim of the bed or border.

**EVERGREEN** A plant which retains its leaves in a living state during the winter.

**EVERLASTING** Flowers with papery petals which retain some or all of their colour when dried for indoor decoration.

**EXOTIC** Strictly any plant which is not native to the country, but popular meaning is any plant which is tender and has a 'tropical' appearance.

**EYE** Two meanings — a dormant growth bud, or the centre of a single or semi-double bloom where the colour of this area is distinctly different from the rest of the flower.

## F

**F₁ HYBRID** A first generation offspring of two pure-bred closely related plants. An $F_1$ hybrid is generally more vigorous and uniform than an ordinary *hybrid*. $F_1$ hybrids do not breed true.

**F₂ HYBRID** A plant produced by crossing $F_1$ *hybrids*. Usually less vigorous than $F_1$ hybrids and like them does not breed true.

**FAMILY** A group of related *genera*.

**FEATHERED** A flower with petals which have coloured edges and fine lines extending inwards.

**FERTILIZER** A material which provides appreciable quantities of one or more major plant nutrients without adding significantly to the *humus* content of the soil.

**FIBROUS-ROOTED** A root system which contains many thin roots rather than a single tap root.

**FILAMENT** The supporting column of the *anther*. It is the lower part of the *stamen*.

**FILLING IN** The covering of a small part of a bed or border with *bedding plants*.

**FLAKED** A flower with petals bearing broad stripes running inwards from the edges.

**FLORET** The individual flowers of a *compound flower* or dense flower head.

**FLOWER** The reproductive organ of the plant.

**FLUSH** The display of flowers when blooming is at its peak. Some *perennials* but not many *annuals* produce flowers in distinct flushes with a non-blooming gap between each one.

**FLUTED** A long and narrow petal which is loosely rolled. See *quilled*.

**FOLIAGE** A collective term for the leaves of a plant.

**FOLIAR FEED** A *fertilizer* capable of being sprayed on and absorbed by the leaves.

**FORMAL BEDDING** A bed or border in which the plants are arranged in a geometrical pattern.

**FRIABLE** Term applied to crumbly soil.

**FRILLED** A petal with a serrated or irregularly scalloped edge.

**FROST POCKET** An area where cold air is trapped during winter and in which *half hardy* plants are in much greater danger.

**FUNGICIDE** A substance used to control infectious diseases caused by fungi — e.g mildew, damping off and rust.

## G

**GENUS** (plural **GENERA**) A group of closely-related plants containing one or more *species*.

**GERMINATION** The emergence of the root and shoot from the seed.

**GROUND COLOUR** The main or background colour of a petal.

**GROUND COVER** An ornamental plant which requires little attention and is used to provide a low-growing carpet between other plants.

**GROUNDWORK PLANT** A medium-height bedding plant (8 in.–2 ft) used to fill most or all of a bedding scheme.

**GROWING ON** The process of transferring seedlings to larger containers and allowing them to increase in size before transferring outdoors.

**GROWING POINT** The tip of a stem which is responsible for extension growth.

## H

**HALF HARDY** A plant which will die outdoors in Britain when the temperature falls below freezing point.

**HARDENING OFF** The process of gradually acclimatising a plant raised under warm conditions to the environment it will have to withstand outdoors.

**HARDY** A plant which will withstand overwintering outdoors without frost protection.

**HEAVY LAND** Soil in which the clay content is high. Difficult to cultivate.

**HERBACEOUS** A plant which does not form permanent woody stems.

**HUE** The 'pure' version of a colour. See *shade* and *tint*.

**HUMUS** Term popularly (but not correctly) applied to partly decomposed organic matter in the soil. Actually humus is the jelly-like end-product which coats the soil particles.

**HYBRID** Plants with parents which are genetically distinct. The parent plants may be different *species*, *cultivars*, *varieties* or occasionally *genera*.

## I

**INFLORESCENCE** The part of the plant bearing the flowers — the flower head.

**INFORMAL BEDDING** A bed or border in which the plants are arranged in an irregular way without any attempt to create straight lines or geometrical patterns.

**INORGANIC** A chemical or fertilizer which is not obtained from a source which is or has been alive.

**INSECTICIDE** A substance used to control insects and other small pests.

**INTERNODE** The part of the stem between one *node* and another.

**ISLAND BED** A bed in which hardy perennials are dominant.

## J

**JOINT** See *node*.

## K

**KEEL** Boat-shaped structure formed by the two lower petals of many members of the Pea family.

## L

**LAYERING** A method of propagation in which the stem is pegged down into the soil.

**LEACHING** The loss of soluble chemicals from the soil due to the downward movement of water.

**LEGGY** Abnormally tall and spindly growth.

**LIGHT** The movable part of a *cold frame*.

**LIGHT LAND** Soil in which the sand content is high. Easy to cultivate.

**LOAM** Friable soil which is not obviously clayey or sandy.

**LOBE** Rounded segment which protrudes from the rest of the leaf, petal or other plant organ.

## M

**MEDIUM LAND** See *loam*.

**MONOCHROMATIC SCHEME** A colour scheme in which the various *tints* and *shades* of a single *hue* are used.

**MOUTH** The open end of a bell-shaped or tubular flower.

**MULCH** A layer of bulky organic matter placed around the stems — see page 112.

**MULTICOLOURED** A flower bearing at least three distinctly different colours.

**MULTI-PURPOSE COMPOST** A peat-based compost which can be used for seed sowing, potting up plants and for filling hanging baskets and other containers.

**MUTATION** A sudden change in the genetic make-up of a plant, leading to a new feature which can be inherited.

## N

**N : P : K** Shorthand for the nitrogen : phosphate : potash content of a fertilizer.

**NECTAR** Sweet substance secreted by some flowers to attract insects.

**NEUTRAL SOIL** A soil which is neither acid nor alkaline — *pH* 6.5–7.3.

**NODE** A point on the stem at which a leaf or bud arises.

**NURSERY BED** A plot of land on which seedlings are raised for transferring later to their permanent quarters.

## O

**ORGANIC** A chemical or fertilizer which is obtained from or is identical to a source which is or has been alive.

**OVAL** Egg-shaped, with the broadest part in the middle.

**OVARY** The part of the female organ of the flower which contains the *ovules*.

**OVULE** The part of the female organ of the flower which turns into a seed after fertilization.

## P

**PALMATE** Five or more lobes arising from one point — hand-like.

**PEAT** Plant matter in an arrested state of decay obtained from bogs or heathland.

**PERENNIAL** See page 4.

**PERGOLA** A series of arches forming a walkway.

**PERIANTH** The outer organs of a flower — the *petals* plus the *sepals*.

**PETAL** One of the divisions of the *corolla* — generally the showy part of the flower.

**pH** A measure of acidity and alkalinity. Below pH 6.5 is acid and above pH 7.3 is alkaline.

**PICOTEE** A flower with petals which bear a narrow band at the edge, the colour of the band being distinctly different from the *ground colour*.

**PICTURE BEDDING** A bed or border in which the plants are arranged to form an illustration such as a monogram, message or picture.

**PINCHING OUT** The removal between the finger and thumb of the growing tip of the stem to induce bushiness. Also known as pinching back.

**PISTIL** The female organ of a flower, consisting of the *stigma, style* and *ovary*.

**PLUG** A small but well-rooted seedling raised in a cellular tray and sold for *growing on*.

**PLUNGE** Term applied to the insertion of a plant in its pot up to the rim in soil, compost, sand or ashes.

**POLLEN** The yellow dust produced by the *anthers*. It is the male element which fertilizes the *ovule*.

**POLLINATION** The application of *pollen* to the *stigma* of the flower.

**POLYCHROMATIC SCHEME** A colour scheme in which a wide variety of *hues* are used — reds, violets, yellows, blues, oranges etc.

**POT-GROWN** A bedding plant which is offered for sale in an individual pot rather than in a communal container with other specimens.

**POTTING ON** The transfer of a plant from its pot into a larger one.

**POTTING UP** The first planting out of a rooted cutting into a container.

**PREVAILING WIND** The direction from which the wind usually blows — an important consideration on exposed sites.

**PRICKING OUT** The first planting out of a seedling into a container.

**PROPAGATION** The multiplication of plants.

**PROPAGATOR** A portable container with transparent top and sides for the germination of seeds and the striking of cuttings.

## Q

**QUILLED** A long and narrow petal which is tightly rolled. See *fluted*.

## R

**RAISED BED** A bed with its surface above ground level and enclosed by a retaining wall of stone, brick, wood etc.

**REVERSION** A *sport* which has gone back to the colour or growth habit of its parent.

**RHIZOME** A horizontally-creeping underground stem which produces shoots and roots.

**ROOTING HORMONE** A chemical in powder or liquid form which promotes the formation of roots at the base of a cutting.

**ROSETTE** Term applied to a *whorl* of leaves arising at the base of a plant.

## S

**SEED** The reproductive unit of a flowering plant.

**SEED LEAF** See *cotyledon*.

**SEEDLING** An immature plant raised from *seed* rather than by *vegetative reproduction*. There is no clear-cut point at which a 'seedling' becomes a 'young plant'.

**SELF-COLOURED** A flower bearing a single colour.

**SEMI-DOUBLE** A half-way point between a *single* bloom and a *double* one. In most cases there are two rows of petals.

**SEPAL** One of the divisions of the *calyx*.

**SERIES** A variety which is available in a number of different colours and/or a mixture of them.

**SERRATE** Saw-edged.

**SHADE** A darker version of a *hue* — see page 106.

**SINGLE** A flower with no more than the normal number of petals.

**SOILLESS COMPOST** A seed or potting compost with a peat rather than a soil base.

**SPECIES** Plants which are genetically similar and which breed true to type from seed.

**SPIKE** An unbranched *inflorescence* which bears stalkless flowers.

**SPLASHED** A flower with petals bearing broken stripes of various sizes.

**SPORT** A plant which shows a marked and inheritable change from its parent. A *mutation*.

**SPUR** A tube-like projection from a flower.

**STAMEN** The male organ of a flower, consisting of the *anther* and *filament*.

**STANDARD** Two meanings — either the large upper petal of Sweet Pea-like flowers, or a plant with a tall bare stem and a terminal head of leaves and flowers.

**STERILE** Two meanings — freedom from harmful pests and disease organisms, or flowers (e.g Afro-French Marigolds) which do not set seed.

**STIGMA** The part of the female organ of the flower which catches the *pollen*.

**STOPPING** See *pinching out*.

**STRAIN** A selection of a *variety*, *cultivar* or *species* which is raised from seed.

**STRIKE** The successful outcome of taking cuttings.

**STYLE** The part of the female organ of the flower which connects the *stigma* to the *ovary*.

**SUCCULENT** A plant with fleshy leaves and/or stems adapted to growing under dry conditions.

**SYSTEMIC** A pesticide which goes inside the plant and travels in the sap stream.

## T

**TENDRIL** A modified stem or leaf which can wind around a support.

**THROAT** The tube formed by the *corolla* of some flowers.

**TINT** A paler version of a *hue* — see page 106.

**TRACE ELEMENT** An element such as boron, manganese, magnesium and iron which is required in small quantity for healthy growth.

**TRAILING PLANT** A weak-stemmed plant with a postrate growth habit.

**TRANSPLANTING** The movement of a plant from one site to another.

**TUBER** A storage organ (a fleshy root or underground stem) used for propagation.

**TUBEROUS-ROOTED** A plant produced from a *tuber* — e.g Begonia multiflora.

## V

**VARIEGATED** Leaves which are spotted, blotched or edged with a colour which is different to the basic one.

**VARIETY** Strictly speaking, a naturally-occurring variation of a species — see *cultivar*.

**VEGETATIVE REPRODUCTION** Division, *cuttings* and *layering* as distinct from sexual reproduction by seeds.

**VERTICAL BEDDING** The use of bedding plants to cover the vertical face of a structure containing soil or compost.

**VIRUS** An organism which is too small to be seen through a microscope and which is capable of causing malformation or discolouration of a plant.

## W

**WEED** A plant growing in the wrong place.

**WHORL** Leaves, petals or branches arranged in a ring.

## Z

**ZONAL FOLIAGE** A leaf with a distinct horse-shoe shaped marking.

# CHAPTER 9

# PLANT INDEX

# The Experts

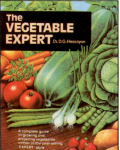

## Acknowledgements

The author wishes to acknowledge the painstaking work of Gill Jackson, Paul Norris, Linda Fensom, Angelina Gibbs and Constance Barry. Grateful acknowledgement is also made for the help or photographs received from Jane Ducarreaux, Joan Hessayon, Thompson & Morgan, Suttons Seeds Ltd, Samuel Dobie & Son Ltd, Harry Smith Horticultural Photographic Collection, Pat Brindley, Michael Warren, A–Z Photographic Collection, Barry Gould, Richard Mann, Carleton Photographic, Colegrave Seeds, The Iris Hardwick Library of Photographs, Springfields Gardens, The Gardeners' Royal Benevolent Society, Heather Angel, Brighton Borough Council – Parks & Recreation Dept, The Tidy Britain Group, Kernock Park Plants and Manchester City Council – Recreation Services.

John Woodbridge provided both artistry and design work. Deborah Mansfield prepared most of the paintings for this book. Other artists who contributed were Norman Barber, Derek Watson and Richard Bell (Bernard Thornton Artists).